The Interpreter's
R_x

a training program for Spanish/English medical interpreting

by
Holly Mikkelson

Printed in the USA.
Casey Printing, Inc.

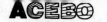

Acknowledgments

illustrations, editing & formatting, tape mastering
Jim Willis

simultaneous script development, consultation
Dr. V. E. Mikkelson, MD

Contents

Part I, Training
Sight Translation

Consecutive Interpretation

Simultaneous Interpretation

Part II, Reference

Terminology

Author's Introduction

The Interpreter's Rx is designed to teach English-Spanish and Spanish-English medical interpreting. This book and the tapes that accompany it assume that you are already fluent in both English and Spanish, but they do not assume that you have received any previous training in interpreting—*The Interpreter's Rx* can help you acquire the techniques of sight translation, consecutive interpretation, and simultaneous interpretation even if you've had no previous exposure to those techniques.

The Interpreter's Rx uses the same proven techniques as ACEBO's earlier interpreter training packages, *The Interpreter's Edge, The Interpreter's Edge Turbo Supplement*, and *The Interpreter's Edge*, Generic Edition. But whereas the various *Interpreter's Edge* packages are all designed to teach court-interpreting—and therefore concentrate on vocabulary and situations of particular interest to court interpreters—*The Interpreter's Rx* is designed specifically to train medical interpreters. The interpreting situations presented in these materials are designed to approximate as closely as possible those that medical interpreters actually face on a daily basis. The vocabulary used in the translating and interpreting lessons is chosen specifically for its relevance to medical interpreting. And the Terminology section of this book (Chapter 4) contains many hundreds of additional medical terms over and above those used in the lessons.

The Interpreter's Rx is a response to the increased demand for specialized training for medical interpreters. Medical professionals are finding that there are ever-growing numbers of non-English speakers in their patient loads, and they realize that they need the services of highly skilled interpreters to make sure they are communicating adequately with their patients. Some state governments, concerned about the serious problems that may arise when untrained interpreters are used in the medical setting, are looking at regulatory mechanisms to ensure quality interpreting. For example, California is now administering a certification exam to medical-legal interpreters, and a test for hospital interpreters may be in the offing. These training materials are designed to help you prepare for this challenging profession, whether or not you have to take an exam.

Medical interpreters work in a variety of settings: hospitals, clinics, doctor's offices, mental health and psychiatric facilities, and quasi-legal proceedings such as medical-legal evaluations for workers' compensation claims or personal injury lawsuits and hearings to determine mental competence or eligibility for benefits. A wide range of subject matter and terminology is covered in these different settings, and many interpreters choose to specialize in one field or another. It is difficult to predict what matters will arise in any given setting, however, and the interpreter needs to be prepared for anything and everything. The lessons in *The Interpreter's Rx* cover most of these possibilities, and if you are able to interpret all of these lessons accurately, you will be well prepared to interpret in any medical situation. The specialized word lists in Part II are included as an additional reference work to be used in preparing for specific interpreting assignments. You may even want to carry *The Interpreter's Rx* with you on interpreting assignments for quick reference. Don't think you have to memorize every term in the glossaries to become a medical interpreter.

If you are preparing for a certification exam as a medical interpreter, you may want to pay particular attention to certain lessons in this book. For example, if you intend to take an exam like the one required in the State of California for anyone who interprets in a medical evaluation to be used as evidence in a civil action (workers' compensation or personal injury lawsuits), the following lessons will be of greatest relevance: English Sight Translation Texts 5, 6, and 8; Spanish Sight Translation Texts 1, 2, 3, and 4; Consecutive Interpretation Lessons 1, 3, 7, 10, 11, 12, 14, and 16; and Simultaneous Interpretation Lessons 3, 4, 6, 7, and 9. If you are studying for a hospital interpreting exam, you may want to focus particularly on English Sight Translation Texts 1, 2, 3, 4, 7, 9, and 10; all of the Consecutive Interpretation lessons; and perhaps all of the Simultaneous Interpretation lessons (you should find out if that skill is to be tested in your exam).

This book is divided into four chapters:

■ Part I, Training

   ☐ Chapter 1, Sight Translation

   ☐ Chapter 2, Consecutive Interpretation

   ☐ Chapter 3, Simultaneous Interpretation

■ Part II, Reference

   ☐ Chapter 4, Terminology

The first three chapters cover the three modes of interpreting that medical interpreters are required to master. The fourth chapter, Terminology, is designed to serve both as an aid during training and as a reference work whose usefulness will last well beyond the training period.

How to Use This Book

How you should use this book and the accompanying tapes depends on whether you're studying on your own or studying as part of an organized class. If you're part of a class, your instructor will tell you how he or she wants you to use the materials. Therefore, this section concentrates on using these materials to study on your own.

For Self-Study

Use the first three chapters of this book together; that is, start with Sight Text 1, Consecutive Lesson 1, and Simultaneous Lesson 1 on the same day. The next time you use the book, go on to Sight Text 2, Consecutive Lesson 2, and Simultaneous Lesson 2. You may find that you need to repeat one of the lessons more often than the others, so you won't always be working on lessons with the same number in each chapter—since the chapters don't have the same number of lessons, you couldn't do that for long anyway. If you have more trouble picking up simultaneous interpretation than sight translation, you'll go through Chapter 1 faster than Chapter 3. That's perfectly OK; progress at a pace you feel comfortable with.

Interpreting isn't a skill you can develop overnight. Don't try to move through the lessons too quickly, or you won't acquire the mastery you'll need to be a professional medical interpreter. Because interpreting is so mentally taxing, you'll reach a point of diminishing returns after about 20 minutes spent on a given exercise. That's why you should work on each mode of interpreting for 20 minutes, for a total of one hour each practice session. You can practice twice a day if you want, as long as you allow a long enough interval between sessions.

Don't read along in the texts while you're playing the tapes; look at the texts afterwards.

When you're interpreting the consecutive lessons (the question-and-answer sessions between two people), have your finger on the pause button of your tape player so that you can stop the tape as soon as the question or answer ends. We've left a short gap on the tape between questions and answers to allow you to do this. The gap is just long enough to let you pause your machine, though—it isn't long enough for you to interpret what's been said. In the case of a long answer, stop the tape as soon as your short-term memory is saturated. Make sure you don't stop the tape in the middle of a thought, though. Learning to use the tapes in this way gives you valuable practice in determining where to intervene when you're actually interpreting for a client; if you interrupt a speaker before he's completed an idea, he'll lose his train of thought and won't be able to pick up where he left off. Try not to abuse your ability to stop the tape; push your memory to the limits to expand your retention capacity as much as possible.

You may find it useful to go back and repeat some of the earlier lessons after you've progressed well into the book, just to refresh some of the basic skills. Even after you've begun working as an interpreter, it's a good idea to come back to these exercises occasionally.

For Instructors

The Interpreter's Rx is designed to be used as a textbook in a course on medical interpreting. It provides all the materials necessary for the students to work on their interpreting skills. It should be supplemented, however, with materials on professional ethics (for example, an excellent code of ethics has been published by the University of Minnesota Refugee Assistance Program — Mental Health Technical Assistance Center) and perhaps guest speakers or field trips to hospitals, laboratories, and other settings where medical interpreters work. You may also want to give the students vocabulary drills or homework assignments to help them learn the terminology that you feel is most important for them to know.

When you are using *The Interpreter's Rx* in class, you can refer the students to the glossaries at the end of the book for proper terminology, but you may know of other terms that are also acceptable. It is always useful for the class to discuss alternative ways of translating terms so that students can develop the flexibility they need as interpreters. You may also be aware of regional variants that are of particular relevance to the area where your students will be working.

The sight translation texts can be used in a variety of ways. You may want to have one student stand up in front of the class and translate a text, and then have a class discussion about terminology and alternative translations. Another possibility is to divide the class into small groups and have the students sight translate the texts among themselves, followed by a general class discussion of problems that arose. Alternatively, you can assign some of the texts as written translations for the students to do at home and bring to class (this is especially appropriate for the more technical consent forms and reports).

The tapes that accompany this book can be used in a variety of ways, depending on the resources available to you and on your preferences.

For the consecutive lessons, you can play the tape in class and have the students interpret the questions and answers one at a time. You may find it more productive for them to play the roles of the different characters in the scripts, reading from the texts in the book (the student playing the role of interpreter would not read the script, obviously). Reading aloud in itself is an excellent way to develop the public speaking skills needed for interpreting. The lessons in this book can be supplemented with memory exercises to help the students develop better listening skills. Encourage the students to visualize the story being told by the patient and to expand their memory capacity by developing mnemonic techniques such as note-taking and association of ideas (see the introduction to Chapter 2, Consecutive Interpretation for a more detailed discussion of these techniques). Also emphasize the importance of accuracy in interpreting, and make it clear that students should ask for a repetition or clarification if there is anything they have forgotten or did not understand.

If you have access to a language lab for your simultaneous interpreting classes, you can use your simultaneous tapes as the master for the students to work from; their individual tapes will then be used for their practice sessions at home. If you do not have a language lab, you can play your tape for the entire class to interpret out loud in the classroom, or you can have the students bring tape players to class and play their own tapes individually. If you choose the latter option, you will have to work out a system whereby they all start and stop at the same time, so that you will all be working on the same passage at once. Obviously, it is preferable to have a language lab so that you can monitor the students individually, and to avoid the cacophony that inevitably results if all students are playing their tapes at once.

About the Tapes

The voices of the following people are heard on the tape set that accompanies this book:

- Javier Macías
- María Cecilia Marty
- Holly Mikkelson
- Jim Willis

The arrangement of material on the tapes is given below:

- Tape 1, Side A: Author's Introduction and Consecutive Lessons 1, 2, and 3.
- Tape 1, Side B: Consecutive Lessons 4 through 10.
- Tape 2, Side A: Consecutive Lessons 11 through 16.
- Tape 2, Side B: Simultaneous Lessons 1, 2, and 3.
- Tape 3, Side A: Simultaneous Lessons 4, 5, and 6.
- Tape 3, Side B: Simultaneous Lessons 7, 8, and 9.

Disclaimer

This product is intended to teach the skills of interpreting and translating in a medical context. It is **not** intended to teach medicine, first aid, or any skill other than interpreting and translating. While we have made every effort to make the texts presented in this book realistic and accurate, we make absolutely no representations as to the medical content of the texts. Medical advice, medical opinions, and apparent statements of medical fact presented in these materials are intended only to provide students with plausible material to interpret and translate. In no case should they be construed as the actual advice, opinion, or statements of medical professionals; they are not. **Do not use this book as a guide to medical action.**

All names used in the lessons in this book are fictitious. Any resemblance between the characters that appear in these materials and any actual people, living or dead, is entirely coincidental.

1 Sight Translation

Introduction

Sight translation is an oral translation of a written text. It is often given short shrift in interpreter training; because it appears to be such a simple task, not much attention is devoted to it. In fact, sight translation is just as difficult as simultaneous interpretation, and involves some of the same mental processes. In the case of sight translation, the input is visual (the written word) rather than oral (the spoken word), but the interpreter still has to process a thought in the source language and generate the target language version of that thought while simultaneously processing the next source language thought, and so on. Some interpreters find sight translation more difficult than the other modes of interpreting because they have more trouble focusing on meaning rather than words—the essence of proper interpretation—when the message is written in black and white on a piece of paper. Reading comprehension is an important element of sight translation, and the need to improve and maintain reading comprehension is one reason why medical interpreters (and prospective medical interpreters) should read as much and as widely as possible.

Another aspect of sight translation that should be emphasized is pacing. Often, in the medical setting, time is of the essence. The interpreter must translate the document quickly, but nothing should be omitted. Going too fast will result in translation errors or in sudden starts and stops and long pauses while the interpreter figures out a difficult translation problem. That sort of jerkiness can be very distracting to the listener. But going too slowly is disruptive for medical practitioners and patients alike. The interpreter should be familiar with the terminology and phrasing of medical documents so that he or she can render a speedy and accurate translation. Ideally, a sight translation should sound as if the interpreter were merely reading a document written in the target language.

The texts contained in this chapter are designed to help you develop the skills you need for sight translation. Most of them are typical of the texts you will be required to sight translate in medical situations. Different type faces and formats have been used so that you will become accustomed to dealing with different types of documents.

Try to sight translate the texts as smoothly as possible, solving problems as best you can. After you have completed the entire text, look up the terms you had trouble with. The technical medical terms that appear in the texts are included in the glossaries in Chapter 4. Any terms in the texts that are not medical terms but still pose translation problems are included in footnotes, with gender markers where appropriate.

When performing the exercises in this chapter, make sure you do them out loud, even if you have no audience. Record yourself on audio or video tape so that you know how you sound (and look, if you use video) to your audience.

English Sight Text 1

Valley Medical Clinic
Patient Information Form
Please Print

↑ Formulario / oja

Date: _____ - _____ - _____

Name: _____
Last   First   Middle Initial

Mailing Address: _____
Direccion postal / correo / envio   Street   City   State   Zip Code

Residential Address: _____
Domicilio   Street   City   State   Zip Code

Telephone: (_____) _____ - _____

Social Security Number: _____ - _____ - _____

Numero de licensia de conducir

Date of Birth: _____ - _____ - _____   Age: _____

Fecha de nacimiento

Driver's License Number: _____

Occupation: ← *Profección de oficio*

Employer: ← *Empleador / Compañia de trabajo*
Name   Address   Telephone Number

Marital Status[1]: ☐ married   ☐ single   ☐ divorced   ☐ widowed

Spouse's Name: ← *Pareja / esposo(a) / cónyuge*

Spouse's Employer: _____
Name   Address   Telephone Number

In case of emergency, call: _____

Telephone: (_____) _____ - _____

Person Responsible for Bill: ← *Factura*

Insurance Company: ← *Compañía de seguro medico*

Policy Number: ← *numero de polica*

Is this a work-related injury? ☐ yes   ☐ no

lesión relacionada del trabajo

Signature: _____

La Firma

You must also complete the other side of this form.

1. marital status: estado civil

Patient Information Form, Page 2   *✱ medico de familia*

Please answer the following questions: *✱ medico de atencion primaria*

✱ recientemente

1. Are you currently being treated by a physician? ☐ yes ☐ no If yes, give the name of the doctor and the condition for which you are being treated.

✱ Tiene algun impedimentos fisicos?

2. Do you have any physical handicaps? ☐ yes ☐ no If yes, specify. _____

3. Have you ever been hospitalized? ☐ yes ☐ no If yes, what for? Give date, name of hospital, and name of treating physician for each hospitalization. _____

4. Have you ever had surgery? ☐ yes ☐ no If yes, what procedure was performed? Give date, name of hospital, and name of treating physician for each surgery. _____

5. Have you ever been treated for psychological problems? ☐ yes ☐ no If yes, what was the nature of the problem? Give dates and name of treating psychologist. _____

6. Have you ever been in a mental hospital or undergone psychiatric treatment for other problems? ☐ yes ☐ no If yes, indicate date of hospitalization, name of hospital and treating physician, and diagnosis. _____

7. Have you ever had suicidal thoughts? ☐ yes ☐ no

8. Have you ever had any sexual dysfunction? ☐ yes ☐ no If yes, specify. _____

9. Have you ever been referred to or ordered to undergo counseling for substance abuse, marital problems, or other problem behaviors? ☐ yes ☐ no If yes, indicate date, problem, and name of counselor. _____

10. Do you smoke? ☐ yes ☐ no If yes, how many packs a day? ____

11. Do you drink alcohol? ☐ yes ☐ no If yes, how much per day or per week? _____

12. Do you take drugs? ☐ yes ☐ no If yes, specify what kind and how often. _____

13. For women only: Date of last visit to the gynecologist: ____ - ____ - ____

14. Have you or a member of your immediate family ever had any of the following diseases or conditions?

Condition	No	Yes*	If Yes: You/Family Member (specify relationship[2])
Abortion			
Abscesses			
Alcoholism			
Allergies			
Cancer (specify type)			
Cardiovascular Problems			
Circulatory Problems			
Dental Problems			
Diabetes			
Drug Abuse			
Epilepsy			
Hepatitis			
High Blood Pressure			
Jaundice			
Kidney Dialysis			
Migraine Headaches			
Miscarriage			
Nervous Disorders			
Organ Transplant			
Orthopedic Disorders			
Respiratory Problems			
Tuberculosis			
Ulcer			
Urinary Tract Disorders			
Venereal Disease			

* Provide an explanation below for each condition marked "yes." Include date, hospital, and treating physician.

_____

_____

Date: _____   Signature: _____

2. relationship: parentesco

English Sight Text 2

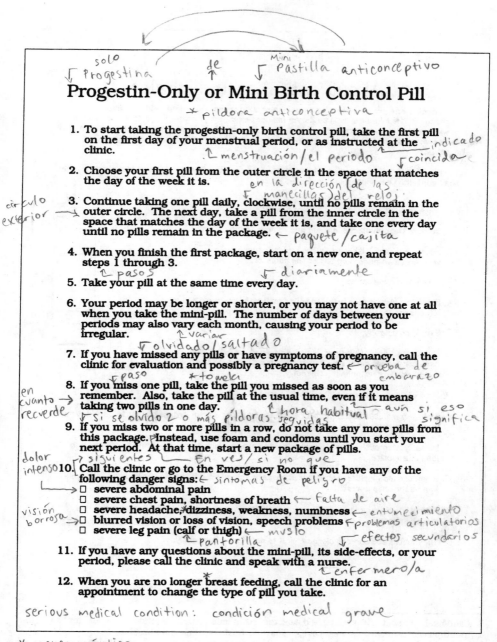

[handwritten annotations:] √ Progestina · solo · de · Mini √ Pastilla anticonceptivo

Progestin-Only or Mini Birth Control Pill

[handwritten: ✶ pildora anticonceptiva]

1. To start taking the progestin-only birth control pill, take the first pill on the first day of your menstrual period, or as instructed at the clinic. *[handwritten: indicado · menstruación/el periodo · coincida]*

2. Choose your first pill from the outer circle in the space that matches the day of the week it is. *[handwritten: en la dirección (de las manecillas) del reloj]*

3. Continue taking one pill daily, clockwise, until no pills remain in the outer circle. The next day, take a pill from the inner circle in the space that matches the day of the week it is, and take one every day until no pills remain in the package. *[handwritten: circulo exterior ; paquete/cajita]*

4. When you finish the first package, start on a new one, and repeat steps 1 through 3. *[handwritten: pasos]*

5. Take your pill at the same time every day. *[handwritten: diariamente]*

6. Your period may be longer or shorter, or you may not have one at all when you take the mini-pill. The number of days between your periods may also vary each month, causing your period to be irregular. *[handwritten: variar]*

7. If you have missed any pills or have symptoms of pregnancy, call the clinic for evaluation and possibly a pregnancy test. *[handwritten: olvidado/saltado ; prueba de embarazo]*

8. If you miss one pill, take the pill you missed as soon as you remember. Also, take the pill at the usual time, even if it means taking two pills in one day. *[handwritten: paso ✶ tomar ; en cuanto recuerde ; √ si se olvidó 2 o más pildoras seguidas ; hora habitual ; aun si eso significa]*

9. If you miss two or more pills in a row, do not take any more pills from this package. Instead, use foam and condoms until you start your next period. At that time, start a new package of pills. *[handwritten: siguientes ; En vez/si no que]*

10. Call the clinic or go to the Emergency Room if you have any of the following danger signs: *[handwritten: dolor intenso ; síntomas de peligro]*
    - [ ] severe abdominal pain
    - [ ] severe chest pain, shortness of breath *[handwritten: falta de aire]*
    - [ ] severe headache, dizziness, weakness, numbness *[handwritten: entumecimiento]*
    - [ ] blurred vision or loss of vision, speech problems *[handwritten: visión borrosa ; problemas articulatorios]*
    - [ ] severe leg pain (calf or thigh) *[handwritten: muslo ; pantorilla ; efectos secundarios]*

11. If you have any questions about the mini-pill, its side-effects, or your period, please call the clinic and speak with a nurse. *[handwritten: enfermero/a]*

12. When you are no longer breast feeding, call the clinic for an appointment to change the type of pill you take.

[handwritten: serious medical condition: condición medical grave]

[handwritten notes at bottom:]
✶ mareo, vértigo
✶ amamantar, dar el pecho
→ lactar/lactante: breastfeeding baby

English Sight Text 3

About Your Asthma Inhaler

Your doctor has prescribed an asthma inhaler, also known as a hand-held[1] nebulizer. The purposes of the inhaler are: 1) to deliver medication directly to your lungs, 2) to open your airways and help raise secretions, 3) to relieve the bronchial constriction and congestion that cause wheezing, and 4) to allow you to breathe more comfortably by increasing your lung function.

The medication is in a pressurized canister[2]. This canister fits upside down in a plastic holder[3] that contains the mouthpiece[4] and dust cover[5].

When operating the inhaler, follow these steps:

1. Be sure the canister is in place and remove the dust cover.

2. Hold the inhaler with your thumb under the mouthpiece and your first two fingers on top of the canister.

3. Shake the canister well.

4. Place the mouthpiece between your teeth with your mouth in an "O" shape.

5. Exhale completely.

6. Quickly and deeply inhale while pressing down (once) on the canister top. If mist[6] rolls out of your mouth around the edges, you are not inhaling correctly.

7. Hold your inhaled breath for 5 to 10 seconds.

8. Wait 2-3 minutes and repeat if necessary, or if the doctor orders two puffs[7]. Do not puff[8] more than twice at any one time.

9. Rinse[9] your mouth without swallowing; the medication can cause stomach cramps and loss of appetite.

10. Wash the mouthpiece with water after each use and wash the plastic housing with soap and water once a week.

Warning: If you do not rinse your mouth after using a steroid inhaler, you may get a mouth infection.

The mouthpiece can get clogged[10] if it is not rinsed frequently.

canister

dust cover

mouthpiece

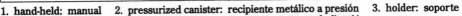

1. hand-held: manual   2. pressurized canister: recipiente metálico a presión   3. holder: soporte
4. mouthpiece: boquilla   5. dust cover: tapa   6. mist: espuma, nebulización
7. puffs: inhalaciones   8. to puff: inhalar   9. to rinse: enjuagarse   10. to get clogged: tapar

English Sight Text 4

Consent Form[1]

Consent for Testing Blood
to Detect Antibodies to the HIV Virus

I have been informed that my blood will be tested for[2] antibodies to the HIV Virus, the probable causative agent[3] of AIDS. I have been informed about the limitations and implications of the test. I have had a chance to ask questions, which were answered to my satisfaction. I understand that the test's accuracy[4] and reliability[5] are not 100% certain.

I have been informed that the test is performed by withdrawing blood[6] from my arm and testing that blood specimen. I consent to having my blood tested for antibodies to the HIV Virus.

By my signature below, I acknowledge[7] that I have been given all information concerning the benefits and risks and I have given consent for my blood to be tested for antibodies to the HIV Virus.

Date: _____

Signature: _____

Printed Name: _____

Authorization for Disclosure[8] of Results
of a Blood Test to Detect Antibodies to the HIV Virus

You are being asked to sign this authorization for use or disclosure of the results of a blood test to detect the antibodies to the HIV Virus to comply with the terms of the Confidentiality of Medical Information Act, Civil Code Section 56 *et seq.* and Health and Safety Code Section 199.21 (g).

Authorization

I hereby authorize _____ (name of physician, hospital or health care provider[9]) to furnish to _____ (name or title of person who is to receive the results) the results of blood tests to detect antibodies to the HIV Virus.

The requester may use the information for any purpose, subject only to the following limitations: _____

This authorization shall become effective immediately and shall remain in effect indefinitely or until _____.

I understand that the requester may not further use or disclose the medical information unless another authorization is obtained from me or unless such use or disclosure is specifically required or permitted by law.

I further understand that I have a right to receive a copy of this authorization upon my request.

Date: _____

Signature: _____

Printed Name: _____

1. consent form: hoja de consentimiento, formulario de autorización   2. to be tested for: someter a prueba para determinar la presencia de   3. causative agent: causante   4. accuracy: exactitud, precisión   5. reliability: confiabilidad   6. to withdraw blood: sacar sangre
7. to acknowledge: reconocer   8. disclosure: divulgación   9. health-care provider: prestador de atención médica

English Sight Text 5

Job Analysis

Claimant[1]: Eduardo Carrera Portillo
Employer: Mac's Restaurant
File No.: 892.cj/1200
Date of Injury: 12/9/92
Report Prepared by: Thomas Dodds

Job Title: Dishwasher
Industry designation: 318.687-010 Kitchen Helper - Dishwasher
Union Affiliation: None
Salary Range: $4.50 - $5.00 per hour
Date of On-Site Job Analysis: 1/15/94

Job Summary

A kitchen helper performs any combination of the following duties to maintain kitchen work areas and restaurant equipment and utensils in clean and orderly condition: Sweeps and mops floors, washes work tables, walls, refrigerators and meat blocks[2]. Segregates and removes trash and garbage and places it in designated containers. Steam cleans or hoses out garbage cans. Sorts bottles and breaks disposable ones in bottle-crushing machine. Washes pots, pans, and trays by hand. Scrapes food from dirty dishes and rinses them, then places them in racks or on a conveyor belt to dishwashing machine. Holds inverted glasses over revolving brushes to clean inside surfaces.

Description of Tasks

1. Using a plastic trash bag, the worker picks up trash in the parking lot.

2. Sets up dishwashing machine by placing the washer arms[3] in the machine and turning on the water.

3. Brings in trash cans with assistance, and sets them in appropriate areas in the kitchen.

4. Empties trash.

5. Washes dishes, which includes racking dishes[4], rinsing dishes, putting dishes in the dishwashing machine, and loading and stacking washed dishes.

6. Sweeps floor.

7. Mops floor.

At this particular work site, bus boys bring in the tubs of soiled dishes. The dishwasher is only required to sweep his immediate work area, which consists of a space measuring approximately 3 feet by 10 feet. The floor is cement covered with a rubber mat. The worker is required to do light mopping only, as the floor is hosed down by the night crew.

Physical Requirements

Walking: Employee must walk frequently, in the parking lot and in the kitchen area from one station to another.

Standing: Employee is required to stand while performing job duties in the kitchen area. The standing surface is a concrete floor covered by a rubber mat. The floor surface may be wet in the kitchen area, but the rubber mat provides appropriate protection.

Sitting: Infrequent sitting, only while employee is on break.

(over)

1. claimant: reclamante   2. meat blocks: tablas/mesas de picar   3. washer arms: molinillos
4. to rack dishes: colocar los trastes en el cesto/la parrilla

Job Analysis, Page 2

Stooping/Bending[5]: Occasionally, when picking up trash or items dropped in kitchen area.

Squatting[6]: Occasionally, when changing soap in the dishwashing machine.

Kneeling[7]/Crawling: None.

Climbing Ladders/Stairs: None.

Lifting: Employee is frequently required to lift dishes, trash, racks, and empty trash cans.

Pushing/Pulling: Employee is frequently required to put dishes into the dishwasher in a rack and pull them out of the dishwasher when the washing cycle is completed.

Reaching[8]: Employee must reach for dishes to rack or stack them, and to rinse them.

---

5. to stoop or bend: agacharse, doblarse, inclinarse   6. to squat: acuclillarse, sentarse en cuclillas
7. to kneel: hincarse, arrodillarse   8. to reach: estirar el brazo, alargar la mano, extender el brazo

English Sight Text 6

Accident Report

Mrs. Simon works at the Laguna Beach Hotel as a maid/housekeeper[1]. She has been employed there for the last three years, and prior to that she worked in the hospitality industry[2] at a variety of hotels, inns and motels for 16 years. At the present time, her duties are the following: vacuuming, sweeping, mopping, cleaning out the bath/shower unit and sinks and toilet in the bathroom, replacing items in the toiletry basket[3], changing bed linen, dusting, checking the honor bar[4] and replacing missing items. She works from 10:00 a.m. to 6:00 p.m. six days a week, with two 15-minute coffee breaks and a half-hour lunch break. Occasionally she is asked to fill in for a coworker on another shift, for which she is paid overtime. These additional duties may include working in the laundry room, working in the kitchen of the hotel restaurant, delivering room service, or doing landscaping and gardening[5] on the hotel grounds.

The accident occurred on January 5 of this year at approximately 3:15 p.m. Mrs. Simon was cleaning a room with another maid. The room was the honeymoon suite on the third floor, which is quite large and requires two maids. For reasons that are not clear at this time, Mrs. Simon and her coworker began to argue while they were pushing a large laundry cart. The coworker shoved the laundry cart at Mrs. Simon, propelling her backwards. Just outside the door of the honeymoon suite is a stairway, and Mrs. Simon fell backwards down that stairway. She landed on the second-floor landing[6] with the laundry cart on top of her.

Mrs. Simon sustained[7] a concussion when she hit her head on the stair landing, which is made of concrete covered with a 1/2" carpet. She also fractured her left arm and sprained her left ankle in the fall. Immediately after the accident, she complained of dizziness, blurred vision, and pain in the lower and upper back and the left upper and lower extremities. She was unable to walk without assistance, and was taken by ambulance to the emergency room of the hospital. At the hospital, x-rays were taken and a cast was placed on her left arm. She was kept under observation for several hours due to the blow to the head. Then she was given pain medication and released.

At present, Mrs. Simon reports that she has frequent headaches and back pain. She indicates that her arm and ankle are almost completely healed, although she still has pain in those areas when the weather is cold or damp. She also reports that she suffers from insomnia and stomach pains, possibly due to anxiety over her situation at work. Her employer fired both Mrs. Simon and her coworker. They contend that this is not an industrial injury because Mrs. Simon and her coworker were fighting on the job, a violation of the employee work rules. Mrs. Simon has hired an attorney to represent her, but the financial strain is taking its toll on her family, and she is under a great deal of emotional stress.

---

1. maid/housekeeper: camarera/ ama de llaves 2. hospitality industry: industria hotelera
3. toiletry basket: cesta de artículos de tocador 4. honor bar: heladora
5. landscaping and gardening: jardinería 6. landing: descanso, rellano 7. to sustain: sufrir

English Sight Text 7

Community Mental Health Services

Our Community Mental Health Services policy requires a written record of your consent to take psychiatric medications as a voluntary patient. To give "informed consent[1]," you must be informed clearly that you have the right to accept or refuse the medications. You must also be told:

1. The nature of your mental condition, why this medication is prescribed, the chances of improving or not improving without it, what other treatment is available, if any, and that you are not forced to take it.

2. Your medications are: _____

3. Dosage (how much you take) and frequency (how often you take it, including "as needed" doses), duration (how long you should take it), and form (tablets, capsules, shots, etc.).

4. Common side-effects that are seen with different types of medications (perhaps sedation or sleepiness, constipation, dry mouth, or indigestion) and possible interaction[2] with alcohol or other medicines.

5. Less common side-effects that are seen with some of these medications (muscle stiffness, tremor or shaking, blurred vision, weight gain, restlessness) and, in the case of minor tranquilizers like Librium and Xanax, a tendency toward overuse[3] and dependency. A 10- to 20-pound weight gain is seen in one-third of patients on lithium, and an itchy rash in one-fifth of those taking Tegretol (often in the first weeks). In the latter case, the medication must be discontinued[4].

6. Uncommon side-effects may occur if you take anti-psychotics (major tranquilizers) for more than three months. Specifically, the condition called "tardive dyskinesia" may occur. This neurologic syndrome usually consists of mouth, tongue, or hand twitching movements. Generally, it occurs in about one-third of patients after a few years of exposure to medications like Haldol, Prolixin, Navane, Trilafon, etc. These symptoms are potentially irreversible, and may appear after you stop taking the drug. Studies suggest that it is permanent in one-third of patients developing this syndrome; for another third, it gradually disappears over a period of several months; and for the rest, it clears[5] in a short period of time. Long-term lithium treatment has been associated with difficulty concentrating urine (with excessive urination as a symptom) in a very small percentage of cases. Yearly tests are advised to follow your kidney and thyroid-gland functioning, along with blood lithium levels. Tegretol (carbamazepine) can have a neurotoxic effect of confusion, double vision, or unsteady gait[6] (as can lithium) if too much is taken or if the dosage is increased too rapidly. There have been some reports of concerns about blood-cell counts with this drug. Therefore, periodic blood tests will be requested to monitor your level and response to the medications.

Your signature below means 1) that you have read and understand the above; 2) that the medication and treatment have been adequately explained and/or discussed with you by your attending physician or other support staff[7]; 3) that you have received all of the information you desire concerning such medications and treatment (brochures[8] are available upon request); and 4) that you authorize and consent to take these medicines and treatment.

Date: _____

Signature: _____

Witness: _____

1. informed consent: consentimiento prestado con conocimiento   2. interaction: interacción
3. overuse: use excesivo   4. to discontinue: suspender, suprimir, eliminar
5. to clear: resolverse, desaparacer   6. to walk with an unsteady gait: andar de manera inestable
7. support staff: personal *m* auxiliar   8. brochure: folleto

English Sight Text 8

Antonia Herrera, MD
A Professional Corporation

1066 Hastings Blvd., Suite 16
Miramar, KS 66949
(316) 555-1212

```
Re:  Samuel Cardozo
Employer:  Hansen Nurseries
File No.:  60116-695-DY
Date of Interview:  4/16/94
Date of Birth:  2/7/65
```

The undersigned was asked to prepare a medical-legal psychiatric report on Mr. Cardozo in an extended interview to determine if he suffers from a psychiatric illness, and if so, if it is industrially related.

Mr. Cardozo began experiencing anxiety attacks in childhood, manifested by stuttering throughout his life, which I saw evidence of during my interview. There is a genetic component in that his father and daughter also suffer from stuttering. There are records that indicate his brother also possibly suffers from anxiety attacks. Records from Valley Memorial Hospital indicate that the patient has suffered from anxiety attacks since 1986, when he first saw Dr. Harmon. He has been tried on Xanax and BuSpar. During my interview with Mr. Cardozo, he minimized his prior psychiatric history, although he did mention that he had had some family problems and needed counseling for parenting[1], which he has undergone at Valley Hospital for approximately three months. He did not mention the anxiety attacks he has suffered in the past. His wife was present during the interview and she prompted him to answer all the questions.

Mr. Cardozo denied any weight change, crying spells[2], or feeling depressed. He did admit experiencing family problems, with arguments and feeling out of control and desperate[3]. Actually, he has experienced these feelings for years, as documented in the medical records since 1987. I do not see any evidence of depression per se, either in the interview or in the medical records. I saw more evidence of anxiety, which was making him feel out of control. He also experienced psychosomatic problems, such as gastritis and epigastric pains. Records indicate that he has sought medical attention on several occasions for the epigastric pain and diarrhea.

Unfortunately, Mr. Cardozo has tried physical therapy, chiropractic therapy and orthopedic evaluation with little result. He has only improved about 25%. He still sleeps poorly due to the pain in the neck and back. Different doctors have diagnosed sprain, but nothing major. Psychological evaluations have noted that he suffers from a Somatoform Pain Disorder and Dependent Personality Disorder. This was diagnosed by Dr. Torres, who felt that he was blowing his physical discomfort completely out of proportion[4].

In conclusion, Mr. Cardozo is a 29-year-old male who has had problems with anxiety since childhood, which has been manifested in his stuttering. He was able to hold various jobs. He has lived with his wife and their two children, and his anxiety has become worse. He has felt stressed over marital problems, to the point that he feels dependent on her. She currently has assumed the role of breadwinner[5], working two jobs, and he performs the household duties. This has caused him to become more dependent, as noted by the various doctors who have examined him. During the interview, his wife was prompting him what to answer to many of my questions. Since I was able to observe this behavior between them during the interview, later on I asked questions of him directly and he began to

page 1 of 2

1. parenting: el cuidar de los hijos   2. crying spell: acceso de llanto   3. desperate: desesperado
4. to blow out of proportion: exagerar   5. breadwinner: mantenedora de la familia

stutter, and I was able to obtain more history about his prior psychiatric problems.

In my opinion, Mr. Cardozo suffers from a psychiatric illness, anxiety, which has been present for many years, as documented in the medical records, and is not a new condition. Of course, this is not industrially related and is not due to the injury of 3/9/92. I feel that his injury of 3/9/92 has caused him to become even more dependent on his wife, which in turn has created more somatic complaints and symptoms which causes him to be passive-dependent and histrionic. He tends to exaggerate some of the symptoms, which has been documented in the hospital records all the way back to 1987.

In this examiner's opinion, there are no issues of permanent and stationary status[4]. There are also no issues of apportionment[5]. From the psychiatric point of view, he is capable of returning to his prior job at Hansen Nurseries. However, I doubt he will return to that job because of his increased dependency on his wife and the Workers' Compensation[6] system. He has assumed this dependent role and does not have to assume any responsibilities.

If you have any further questions or concerns, please feel free to contact me.

Sincerely,

Antonia Herrera

Antonia Herrera, MD

page 2 of 2

---

4. permanent and stationary status: condición permanente y estable   5. apportionment: prorrateo
6. Workers' Compensation: indemnización por accidentes de trabajo

English Sight Text 9

Consent for Angiogram

Your doctor has referred you to the Department of Diagnostic Imaging for an angiogram. An angiogram is an x-ray examination that produces a picture of the arteries and veins supplying blood to specific areas of the body for diagnostic purposes. After reading this special consent form and after discussion of the procedure with the radiologist, it is hoped that you will understand the procedure and the risks involved.

Angiograms are performed in the Department of Diagnostic Imaging in a room especially designed for this purpose. Before the test, you may receive an injection or mild sedation. At the beginning of the procedure, you will receive an injection of local anesthesia (Xylocaine) in your groin over the area of the artery. The radiologist will then puncture a leg artery with a special needle. Using a special technique, the needle will then be removed and a thin soft tube will be passed into the leg artery. The radiologist will guide this tube, or catheter, under fluoroscopic control into the vessel to be examined. A special liquid contrast, which is visible on x-rays due to the iodine content, is then injected through the catheter into the artery, and x-ray pictures are made over the area of interest. During the injection of contrast, you may feel a warm or burning sensation in the portion of the body being examined. This usually lasts between 10 and 20 seconds. Several injections may be necessary. After the study is completed, the radiologist will remove the tube from the leg artery and apply pressure over this area for approximately 10 minutes or until the bleeding stops.

You will be awake throughout the entire procedure, not only to assist with the examination, but also to tell the radiologist if you are having any problems. At the conclusion of the procedure, you will be returned to your room for bed rest for approximately 4-6 hours.

The risks of this test are varied, depending on the examination. Bleeding at the puncture site, clotting at the puncture site, pain with catheter and needle placement are local problems that will be watched for carefully during the procedure. Allergy to the contrast can raise more significant problems, ranging from the mild reaction of hives to more serious reactions such as shortness of breath, low blood pressure, and even possibly death. These more serious reactions are rare, and only occur in approximately 1 in 30,000 cases. A significant risk also is that of developing small emboli (clots) during the procedure, which may block arteries. This can also happen if hardening of the arteries is present and plaques are dislodged[1] with catheter movement. Should this occur in the abdomen, local tissue death may occur (i.e., bowel, kidneys, etc.). If the head is being studied, there is a possibility of a stroke (temporary or permanent). This may result in a neurologic disability or even death. The possibility of stroke happening is less than 1 in 100.

Your physician and the radiologist both feel that this examination is the only way to assist in your medical or surgical management and that the information to be obtained outweighs the risk.

I, _____, have read and understand the information and risks involved and consent to have an angiogram.

Signature of Patient   Date   Signature of Witness   Date

---

1. to dislodge: separar, desplazar

English Sight Text 10

Arthroscopy

A joint, or articulation, is the junction of two or more parts of the skeleton that are attached in such a way that the two parts can move relative to each other in one or more directions. The bones of the joints are held together by tough, fibrous strands[1] called ligaments. The opposing surfaces of the bones that form a joint are molded to each other and are covered by a layer of cartilage, a dense, pad-like tissue. The space between bones in the joint is the joint cavity, and it is enclosed by the capsular sac, a durable, fibrous tissue fastened to the ends of the bones. This membrane is lined with a very sensitive lining, the synovial membrane, which secretes a lubricating substance that also furnishes nourishment for the joint cartilage. Tendons and muscles, which are attached to the bones in the joint, provide additional stability and the ability to control movement.

Disease and injuries can damage bones, cartilage, ligaments, muscles and tendons. They include torn[2] or abnormal cartilage, torn ligaments, loose fragments of bone or cartilage, damaged joint surfaces, inflammation of the joint lining, and misaligned[3] bones. When a patient comes to the doctor with a joint injury or disease, the doctor must reach a diagnosis by conducting a thorough medical history and physical examination, and sometimes x-rays. Further diagnosis may require what is known as arthroscopy to provide a better view of the affected bones and soft tissues (ligaments and cartilage).

Arthroscopy is a surgical procedure employed by orthopedic surgeons to view, diagnose and treat problems inside a joint. To perform an arthroscopic examination, the surgeon makes a small incision in the patient's skin and then inserts the arthroscope, a miniature lens[4] and lighting system about the size of a pencil that magnifies and illuminates the structures inside the joint. Since this technique was developed in the 1970s, hundreds of thousands of patients have chosen it over other types of surgery because the scar is smaller, the hospital stay shorter, and recovery faster.

The term "arthroscopy" is derived from two Greek words, "arthro" (joint) and "skopein" (to look). Thus, it literally means "to look within the joint." Light is transmitted through fiberoptic cables[5] to the end of the arthroscope, which is inserted into the joint. By using a miniature television camera and screen[6] combination, the surgeon can see inside the joint. The television camera attached to the arthroscope displays the image of the joint on a television screen. The surgeon can thus look directly at the joint shown in the large image on the screen, determine the extent of injury, and then perform whatever surgical procedure is necessary. The arthroscope enables the surgeon to see more of the joint than is possible even with a large incision made during an open operation. Moreover, areas that are sometimes difficult to see on an x-ray can be seen during arthroscopy. The knee is by far the most common joint to be examined using this technique. Other joints include the shoulder, elbow, ankle, hip, and wrist.

Diagnostic arthroscopy must be performed in a hospital operating room or outpatient surgical suite. The patient is given an anesthetic, either general, spinal, or local. After the surgery is over, the patient is moved to a recovery room where ice packs may be applied to the incision sites to reduce swelling, and medications may be administered to reduce pain. Before being discharged, the patient will be instructed on the proper care of the incision, what activities should be avoided, and what exercises should be done to speed recovery. An appointment is made for a followup visit so that the surgeon can inspect the incisions, remove sutures, and discuss the rehabilitation program.

Recovery time varies considerably from one patient to the next. Not all arthroscopies are the same. Some patients are able to return to work or school or resume daily activities within a few days. Athletes and others who are in good physical condition may, in some cases, return to athletic activities within a few weeks. Each case is unique, however, and recovery time depends on the nature of the joint problem and the individual's physical condition.

1. strand: filamento   2. torn: desgarrado   3. misaligned: mal alineado   4. lens: lente *f*
5. fiberoptic cable: cable de fibra óptica   6. screen: pantalla

Spanish Sight Text 1

Tijuana B.C. a 21 de febrero de 1993

A QUIEN CORRESPONDA:

La SRA. HIPOLITA MORALES CUEVAS de 40 años de edad, acudió a mi consultorio, por referir[1] dolor en regiones cervical, hombros y escapular bilateral de 5 años de evolución[2].
Tiene como antecedentes de importancia: trabajar en los últimos 10 años en una empacadora de alimentos, en donde permanecía con movimientos de flexión del cuello durante períodos prolongados de tiempo en el desempeño de sus labores; permanecía en lugares helados y húmedos (refrigeradores de alimentos). No refiere padecimientos cardiovasculares, diabéticos, etc.

Padecimiento actual: refiere haberlo iniciado hace 5 años aproximadamente al manifestar parestesias en región escapular derecha, dolor en misma región con irradiación[3] hacia el cuello y hombro del mismo lado y del lado contrario. El dolor se fijó en región cervical con sensación de ''tirantez'', exacerbado a los movimientos de rotación y de flexiones laterales. Hace 2 meses se agregó dolor y sensación de entumido en ambos brazos y antebrazos, con trastornos vasomotores difusos de predominio en manos. El dolor y parestesias distales aumentan al elevar los brazos o durante el sueño con los brazos en abducción y extensión. Ha notado disminución de la fuerza de prensión[4] de las manos de predominio

---

1 referir: to report, complain of
2 de 5 años de evolución: for the past 5 years, dating back 5 years
3 irradiación: radiating
4 fuerza de prensión: grip (strength)

en la derecha. Por lo anterior acude a este consultorio.

Previa[1] exploración neurológica y radiografías de columna cervical, se recomienda estudios de gabinete de resonancia magnética nuclear y mielotomografía de la misma región con miras a tomar una conducta terapéutica definitiva[2], la cual más probablemente será quirúrgica.

En caso de requerir mayor información, siéntanse en la confianza de solicitarla y con gusto se la enviaremos.

Atentamente,

Dr. Francisco Moreno Durán

---

1 previa: after [Note: The neurological examination and cervical x-rays **precede** the lab tests—hence the adjective *previa* describing them—but the way the English sentence will be constructed, *after* is the appropriate term.]
2 conducta terapéutica definitiva: definite/specific course of treatment

Spanish Sight Text 2

CENTRO DE SALUD RURAL SANTA MARIA

A QUIEN CORRESPONDA:

El pasado día 14 de junio del presente año, se presenta a mi consulta el Sr. Julio Rodríguez León, con el antecedente de haber sufrido caída de aproximadamente metro y medio al encontrarse cabalgando en un caballo. El paciente muestra datos de conmoción cerebral, además de probable fractura de quinto, sexto, noveno y onceavo arcos costales, por lo cual presenta datos de insuficiencia respiratoria de moderada a severa, motivo por el cual permanece internado[1] en esta unidad por espacio de cuatro días, siendo manejado con tratamiento antiedema cerebral, relajantes musculares y fisioterapia pulmonar para adecuar su ventilación.

Es dado de alta pero se recomienda reposo absoluto por espacio de diez días adicionales, después de los cuales podrá reincorporarse a sus actividades normalmente.

Se extiende la presente carta a petición del interesado y para los fines que a éste convengan.

Atentamente,

Norma Mejía Alvarado
Médico Cirujano

---

1 internado: hospitalized, admitted

Spanish Sight Text 3

DR. FIDEL HERRERA SORIA
ORTOPEDIA Y TRAUMATOLOGIA

A QUIEN CORRESPONDA:

El suscrito médico cirujano[1], legalmente autorizado para ejercer la profesión con cédula no. 88902 y reg. no. 43302, certifica que:

Examinó al paciente Alfonso Suárez Castro, quien presenta padecimiento localizado al tobillo izquierdo y rodilla derecha. Hay historia de una caída de superficie en el año 1988 cuando lavaba el piso con manguera, se resbaló, presentó dolor muy escaso que no le impidió continuar con sus labores. Posteriormente empezó con dolor y aumento de volumen en el tobillo sobre todo a la marcha. Tuvo que suspender sus actividades normales durante un mes durante el cual le daban analgésicos; reanudó su trabajo al desaparecer sus molestias, pero al reiniciar sus labores volvió nuevamente a presentar dolor[2], recibiendo tratamiento a base de analgésicos e inyecciones intraarticulares, posiblemente de corticoides. Regresó a sus labores durante dos meses y posteriormente ya no recibió tratamiento alguno.

El paciente continúa con dolor e inflamación del tobillo. El dolor es constante pero se hace más intenso durante la marcha. No puede correr, no puede saltar. A la exploración se encuentra limitación funcional intensa del tobillo izquierdo con dorsiflexión plantar, abducción y aducción prácticamente nulas, pie en ángulo recto. La exploración de la rodilla derecha nos muestra rodilla deformada por aumento de volumen,

---

1 médico cirujano: physician and surgeon
2 presentar dolor: feel pain

choque rotuliano[1], movilidad activa de 0 a 100
grados, flexión pasiva hasta 110 pero dolorosa.

Radiológicamente se encuentra anquilosis
parcial de la articulación del tobillo con
cambios avanzados de osteoartritis degenerativa.
Para el diagnóstico más certero del problema de
la rodilla derecha debe ser sujeto a
procedimiento artroscópico.

A petición del interesado y para los fines
legales a que haya lugar[2], se extiende el
presente certificado a los 15 días del mes de
abril de 1993.

El paciente se encuentra incapacitado para sus
labores ordinarias. Amerita artrodesis de
tobillo.

Atentamente,

Dr. Fidel Herrera Soria

---

1 choque rotuliano: patellar trauma
2 para los fines legales a que haya lugar: for the legal purposes deemed appropriate

---

Spanish Sight Text 4

Dr. Porfirio Huerta Díaz
Av. Hurtado 2302
Guadalajara, Jalisco, México

Enero 28 de 1994

Sra. Madeline Cook
Law Offices
289 Sacramento St.
San José, CA 95103

Asunto: Alberto Muñoz
Se trata de paciente masculino de 25 años de edad
aparentemente sano.

Antecedentes:
Inició su padecimiento el 27 de mayo de 1991 al
sufrir aplastamiento de ambas manos con una
máquina tortilladora. Fue atendido en un
hospital donde hicieron diagnóstico de
laceraciones y abrasiones múltiples en ambas
manos.

Mano izquierda:
Fracturas conminutas severas de las falanges
distal y media del quinto dedo.

Mano derecha:
Amputación del extremo distal del dedo índice y
fractura angulada de la quinta falange proximal.

Cirugía:
Debridación de las heridas de ambas manos,
revisión de la amputación de dedo índice y quinto
dedo derechos. Reducción de la luxación
interfalángica del dedo largo, reparación del

---

ligamento colateral, inserción de alambre de K,
en la articulación interfalángica distal del dedo
largo derecho y sutura de múltiples laceraciones.
En la mano izquierda reducción abierta de
fractura de las falanges distal y media del dedo
medio.

Quejas objetivas:
El paciente dice sentirse acomplejado cuando
personas observan su mano derecha.

Limitaciones físicas:
El paciente dice desempeñar cualquier tipo de
trabajo con sus manos sin tener dolor ni
limitaciones físicas.

La revisión clínica radiográfica de hoy muestra:

1. Heridas cicatrizadas.
2. Ausencia del quinto dedo conservando la
   primera falange de la mano derecha.
3. Subluxación y osteoartrosis de articulación
   interfalángica distal del dedo medio mano
   derecha.
4. Pérdida de tercio distal de la tercera falange
   dedo índice mano derecha.

Mano izquierda:
Clínica y radiológicamente normal.

Recomendaciones para tratamiento médico:
Artrodesis a mediano plazo de articulación
interfalángica distal del tercer dedo de la mano
derecha.

Atentamente,

Dr. Porfirio Huerta Díaz

Spanish Sight Text 5

Dormidol (Flunitrazepam)

Estimado Paciente:

Su médico le ha recetado Dormidol (flunitracepam) para ayudarle a dormir. El Dormidol es un hipnótico eficaz que posee un amplio margen de seguridad. Es particularmente adecuado para el tratamiento de pacientes que presentan grandes dificultades para permanecer dormidos y para los que, además, tienen dificultad en conciliar el sueño.

Se indica en casos de insomnio severo, crónico, rebelde, o psiquiátrico, y se caracteriza por rápida inducción al sueño (de 15 a 20 minutos), sueño tranquilo de duración normal (de 6 a 8 horas), y posología flexible. El paciente despierta lúcido, y no hay riesgo de acumulación. Un medicamento usado para ayudar a los pacientes a disfrutar de un sueño nocturno ininterrumpido debe tener una acción que esté limitada al período de sueño y que presente tan escasos efectos residuales como sea posible al día siguiente.

La duración de acción del Dormidol depende principalmente de la farmacocinética (fase de absorción y distribución) y la dosis. Puesto que los parámetros farmacocinéticos de Dormidol y la sensibilidad de las neuronas en el sistema nervioso varían de un individuo a otro, la duración deseada del efecto tiene que obtenerse por medio del ajuste de la posología. Esto es cierto tanto para la administración única como—y más particularmente—para el uso repetido.

Dependiendo de la severidad del insomnio y de la edad del paciente, peso corporal y estado general, el Dormidol debe administrarse en dosis de 0.5 a 2.0 mg (o más en algunos casos) al paciente con dificultad crónica para permanecer dormido. Para obtener la tolerancia óptima y evitar los efectos residuales, se recomienda la dosis mínima efectiva.

Precauciones: El Dormidol puede modificar la habilidad para la conducción de vehículos. Su administración durante el embarazo queda bajo responsabilidad médica. Si en el lapso de 6-8 horas, en que actúa el medicamento hubiera alguna interrupción del sueño, algunos pacientes pudieran no recordarlo.

Contraindicaciones: Hipersensibilidad al medicamento.

Reacciones secundarias: Puede provocar mareo y aturdimiento que generalmente desaparecen al ajustar la dosis.

Spanish Sight Text 6

Hiperton (metildopa, MSD)

Antihipertensivo

Hiperton (metildopa, MSD) es un agente antihipertensivo sumamente eficaz que reduce la presión arterial en todas las posiciones del paciente: acostado, sentado o de pie. No tiene efectos adversos sobre la función renal, por lo que puede ser empleado en tratamientos prolongados.

Rara vez provoca síntomas de hipotensión postural o de esfuerzo o variaciones de la presión arterial en el transcurso del día. Ajustando la dosificación, se puede evitar la hipotensión matutina sin menoscabo del control de la presión arterial vespertina.

Hiperton permite su empleo en pacientes ambulatorios con hipertensión mínima o moderada. En la mayoría de los enfermos con hipertensión arterial moderada, el Hiperton logra su control por un efecto progresivo y sostenido, que permite mantener las cifras tensionales dentro de los límites normales en forma estable.

La metildopa no ejerce efecto directo alguno sobre la función cardiaca, y por lo general no disminuye el flujo sanguíneo renal. En la mayoría de los casos, se mantiene el gasto cardiaco sin aceleración del corazón, y en algunos pacientes reduce la frecuencia cardiaca.

Puesto que la metildopa es excretada en gran parte por el riñón, está relativamente exenta de efectos nocivos sobre la función renal. Así, puede ser de beneficio en el control de la presión arterial elevada aún cuando exista daño renal, pero en tal caso puede ser necesario usar dosis menores. Puede ayudar a detener o a retardar el deterioro de la función renal y los daños causados por el aumento sostenido de la presión arterial.

Indicaciones:

Hipertensión arterial (leve o moderada)

Dosificación y administración:

La dosificación inicial usual de Hiperton es de 250 mg 2 ó 3 veces al día durante las primeras 48 horas. Después, se puede aumentar o disminuir la dosificación diaria, de preferencia a intervalos no menores de 2 días, hasta obtener una respuesta adecuada. La dosificación diaria máxima recomendada es de 3 g.

Contraindicaciones: Insuficiencia hepática grave. Hepatitis activa y durante el embarazo. Cirrosis activa. Hipersensibilidad al medicamento.

Efectos colaterales:

Al principio del tratamiento, puede observarse un efecto sedante que desaparece al continuarlo. En ocasiones, vértigo, cefalea, congestión nasal y molestias gastrointestinales.

2 Consecutive Interpretation

Introduction

Consecutive interpretation, in which the interpreter waits until a complete statement has been spoken and then begins interpreting (so only one person is speaking at a time), is the primary form of interpretation used in medical situations. Simultaneous interpretation is generally inappropriate in such situations.

A very high standard of accuracy prevails in consecutive interpretation. Not only must you convey the content of the source-language message, but you must also convey structural elements of that message that are not contained in the words: pauses, tone of voice, stress, etc. Many interpreters regard consecutive as the most difficult mode of interpreting because it is so hard to retain all of these aspects of the source-language message, particularly when a question or answer is very lengthy or is not entirely coherent (an unfortunate fact of life in all types of interpreting).

Consecutive Lessons

Consecutive Lessons 1-16 (Tapes 1A – 2A) are typical medical interpreting situations. When you play the tapes, pause the recorder at the end of each question, give your interpretation, resume playing the tape, pause at the end of the answer, give your interpretation, and so on. Do not read the script while you are interpreting; consult it afterwards to check for accuracy or to look up problem terms.

When you do the consecutive lessons, ideally you should have two tape recorders: one to play the tape, and one to record your own rendition. Pause the tape as described above. Then record your version of the passage on the second tape recorder. When you play back your own rendition, read along in the script as you are listening to it, to check for accuracy. If you do not have two tape recorders, you can switch cassettes in the same recorder. Alternatively, you can give your rendition without recording it, and simply read the script immediately afterwards to check for omissions.

As with the sight translation texts, terms that may pose translation problems are footnoted; the medical terms can be found in the glossaries in Chapter 4. Many of the Spanish terms can be found in

"Términos coloquiales relacionados con la medicina popular" in Chapter 4.

After the title of each lesson in this book, enclosed in parentheses, is the tape number and tape side on which the lesson is recorded (e.g., 1A, 1B, 2A, etc.).

Tips for Consecutive Interpreting

Many student interpreters are intimidated by consecutive interpreting because they think they don't have an adequate memory. In fact, the average person's memory is more than adequate for consecutive interpreting; the main problem is listening skills. If you are in a high-pressure situation (in class, with fellow students listening to your interpretation; in an exam, with the examiners grading you; in real life, with an impatient doctor anxious to move on to the next patient) you may not devote all of your energy to concentrating on what the speaker is saying. The first thing you need to do is learn to shut out distractions and focus all of your attention on the message that is to be interpreted.

If a friend tells you some juicy gossip in a 20-minute phone conversation, chances are you can recount the story almost verbatim to another friend immediately afterwards. You can apply the same mnemonic techiques to enhance your memory in medical interpreting. Most of the messages you will be interpreting in the medical setting are simply stories: a patient describing an accident or a series of symptoms; a doctor explaining a medical procedure or describing the effects of a medication. These stories tend to follow a logical sequence that is fairly easy to remember if you are listening carefully and have some background knowledge. You remember the gossip your friend tells you because you have background knowledge (i.e., you know the parties involved and the circumstances surrounding the story), and you are interested in retaining the content of the message (you want to be the first to break the news to your other friend). In the medical setting, you will be able to listen more attentively and retain more information if you develop an interest in the subject matter and learn background information to help you better understand what the patients and health professionals are talking about.

To help yourself remember a long, detailed statement, imagine that the person is a friend telling you a story. Visualize the story taking place, step by step, and when you interpret it into the target language, play it back like a movie. You may want to organize the words into meaningful groups, or "chunks," either mentally or by writing down a

list of key words, one for each idea. For example, consider the
following statement by a patient:

Estaba haciendo mis compras en el mercado y cuando estaba en el
departamento de verduras, el piso estaba mojado y me resbalé. Me caí
boca arriba con los pies estirados así, y sentí que me tronó algo en la
espalda. Me dolía mucho la cabeza, casi me desmayé. Me ayudaron a
levantarme y llamaron a la ambulancia para llevarme al hospital.

You can divide it up into these chunks, visualizing each step:

Estaba haciendo mis compras en el mercado

cuando estaba en el departamento de verduras

el piso estaba mojado

me resbalé

Me caí boca arriba con los pies estirados así

sentí que me tronó algo en la espalda

Me dolía mucho la cabeza

casi me desmayé

Me ayudaron a levantarme

llamaron a la ambulancia para llevarme al hospital

If you want to take down key words for each chunk, you might write or
abbreviate the following words:

compras

verduras

mojado

resbalé

boca arriba

tronó espalda

cabeza

desmayé

levantarme

ambulancia

Of course, these notes should be just a supplement to your memory; if
you did not listen carefully and understand the message fully, this list
of words would be almost meaningless to you. Some interpreters find
note-taking very helpful, others find it a hindrance. Some statements
are very easy to visualize, while others are more abstract or technical
in nature. If the message is something that does not lend itself to
visualization, like a list of symptoms or side-effects, you may rely more
on notes than on your visual memory. You should experiment with

different mnemonic techniques as you do the lessons in this book to help you understand how your memory works and develop the techniques that work best for you.

Consecutive Lesson 1: Medical History (1A)

Q   Good afternoon, Mrs. Bonilla. I'm going to ask you a few questions about your medical history before the doctor examines you, all right?

A   Sí, señorita, está bien.

Q   First of all, what is the reason for your visit today?

A   Pues, mi abogado me dijo que viniera con este doctor porque me accidenté en el trabajo y me mandó a que este doctor me examinara.

Q   How did you injure yourself?

A   Estaba sorteando zanahorias en la línea, trabajo en una canería, y cuando estiré la mano así, de repente sentí un tirón, ¡zas! y luego no podía usar la mano.

Q   Had you ever had this problem before?

A   No exactamente, no. Es que trabajábamos muchas horas en ese rato, hasta diez o doce horas en un solo turno, y estaba cansadísima.

Q   Do you work standing at a conveyor belt?

A   Sí.

Q   And do you have to do a lot of reaching?

A   Sí. Y no nos dejan descansar cuando deben hacerlo. Sólo nos dan un descanso a las doce del día, por 15 minutos, y creo que eso es ilegal.

Q   Now, I'm going to ask you some questions about your family. Does anyone in your family have heart disease?

A   No, que yo sepa, no.

Q   How about diabetes?

A   No, salvo mi abuelita, pero ya murió hace años.

Q   Has anyone in your family suffered from cancer?

A   No, gracias a Dios, no.

Q   Have you ever had any infectious disease such as typhoid, cholera, or diphtheria?

A   Que sepa yo, no. Siempre he gozado de buena salud.

Q   Have you been vaccinated against tetanus, measles, and smallpox?

A   Creo que sí, pero no estoy segura. Cuando era niña, vivíamos en un rancho, y era muy difícil conseguir atención médica, pero creo que me vacuné contra todas esas enfermedades. Mi papá insistía en eso.

Q   Did you have any common childhood illnesses, such as chicken pox or mumps?

A   Sí, recuerdo que tuve paperas, y también sarampión. Será que no me prendió la vacuna, o no sé.

Q   Have you ever had any operations?

A   Si, en el '85 me sacaron la matriz, y también el apéndice hace unos 10 años.

Q   I take it you were hospitalized for those operations?

A   Sí, estuve internada una semana por lo de la matriz, y no me acuerdo cuánto tiempo por el apéndice.

Q   Do you have any allergies to any food or drug?

A   No, que yo sepa, no.

Q   Do you suffer from headaches?

A   No, nada fuera de lo común, Ud. sabe, de vez en cuando cuando vuelvo del trabajo muy cansada, me duele la cabeza, pero no padezco de jaquecas ni nada de eso.

Q   Do you have any trouble with your throat, a persistent cough or sore throat?

A   No, nada de eso.

Q   When was the last time you had a chest X-ray?

A   El año pasado en el trabajo nos obligaron a someternos a un chequeo, y me sacaron radiografías.

Q   Have you had any heart palpitations, chest pain, shortness of breath?

A   No, nada de eso, por fortuna. Sólo el dolor de la mano, aquí en el codo y en la canilla, y me corre hasta los dedos.

Q   Okay, that's all the questions I have. Just slip on a gown and get up on the examining table. The doctor will be right with you.

Consecutive Lesson 2: Hospital Admissions (1A)

Q   Can I help you?

A   Sí, señora. Me dijo el doctor que me presentara aquí.

Q   Do you have some medical records for me?

A   Sí, aquí están.

Q   I see we've been treating you here as an outpatient, and now the doctor wants you admitted for tests, is that right?

A   Sí, así me dijo.

Q   First I'd like you to fill out these forms[1]. Here's a pen. Can you read English all right?

A   No, señora, prefiero que me interpreten los papeles, por favor.

Q   All right, the interpreter can help you with these. First, there's the medical history, then the insurance forms, and finally the consent form.

A   Pero ya di esa información a la recepcionista en la clínica. ¿Es necesario hacer todo de nuevo?

Q   I'm afraid so, Mr. García. Things may have changed since you last filled out the forms, and we don't want to take any chances.

A   Está bien. Perdone, señora, ¿no hay baño aquí?

Q   Yes, it's down the hall and to the left, just past the nursing station.

A   Gracias, muy amable.

. . .

Q   Let me just go through these forms and make sure everything's filled out all right. You didn't put down any next of kin[2] here.

A   Ah, sí, es que no sabía qué poner. Todos mis hermanos viven en Puerto Rico.

---

1 to fill out a form: llenar la hoja, rellenar el formulario
2 next of kin: familiar más cercano

Q   But don't you have someone here in the U.S. that can be notified in case of an emergency?

A   Sí, mi vecino me hace el favor de atender ciertos asuntos cuando yo no puedo. ¿Pongo el nombre de él?

Q   Yes, that'll be fine. And what is the name of the doctor who referred you here?

A   El doctor Salinas. Bueno, fue el último que vi por este problema del estómago. No es mi médico de cabecera.

Q   Who is your family physician?

A   La doctora Thomas.

Q   Thank you. All right, if you'll just take a seat in the waiting room, someone will come and take you to the ward where you'll be staying.

A   ¿Mi esposa me puede acompañar?

Q   No, I'm afraid she'll have to wait down here in the admissions area until you're all settled in. Then she can visit you during visiting hours. She may want to look around in the gift shop while she's waiting. It's over by the elevators.

          . . .

Q   Hello, Mr. García, I'm a volunteer here at the hospital. I'll take you up to your room now. Have a seat in the wheel chair.

A   ¿La silla de ruedas? ¡Pero mis pies están perfectamente bien! ¡Puedo andar muy bien!

Q   I know, Mr. García, it's just hospital regulations. We don't want anything to happen to you while you're on your way up to the ward.

A   Ah, bueno. Pero no soy tullido.

Q   I know. I see you're here for some tests. Have you ever been hospitalized before?

A   Sí, tuve una hernia que me operaron, en el '86.

Q   Okay, so you know the routine. You're probably only going to be here for a couple of days. Here we are.

A   ¿Habrá otro paciente en este cuarto?

Q   There isn't anyone here right now. There may be later. Now, I'd like you to disrobe[1] and slip on this gown, with the opening in the back.

A   Ah, sí, ya me estoy acordando de estas malditas batas de hospital.

Q   After you've put on the gown, hop into bed, and the nurse will be here shortly to take your temperature and get a urine sample.

A   ¿Me tengo que quitar todo?

Q   Yes, I'm afraid so. Here's the nurse's call button[2] in case you need anything. You can watch TV if you like. The bathroom's right here. I hope everything goes well for you.

1   to disrobe: desvestirse
2   call button: timbre, botón

Consecutive Lesson 3: Getting a Prescription (1A)

Q   Good morning, Mr. Velásquez. The nurse tells me you're still having some problems.

A   Sí, doctor, todavía me molesta donde me operó, y me siento mareado. Creo que se debe a la anestesia.

Q   Yes, that will pass soon. I tell you what, I'll write you a couple of prescriptions, one for the nausea and the other for the pain.

A   Gracias, doctor, muy amable.

Q   The trouble is, you won't be able to operate machinery or drive a car when you're on this stuff, because it produces some drowsiness.

A   Pues, no le hace porque no puedo trabajar de todos modos. Y no necesito arrear[1]. Si necesito ir a alguna parte, mi señora me puede llevar.

Q   Good. Now, there are certain things you should know about this medication.

A   Sí, doctor, a ver.

Q   First, the pain medication. It may cause a little stomach upset if you don't take it with food. Be sure to take it with a meal.

A   Andele, doctor.

Q   And the one for nausea should help you with that, anyway. But you should take this medicine on an empty stomach, you understand?

A   Sí, está bien.

Q   So take the aspirin with codeine twice a day, with breakfast and with dinner, and take the antacid in between meals.

A   Está bien, doctor. Y ¿dónde puedo surtir estas recetas? Tengo una tarjeta de la aseguranza. ¿La aceptan?

Q   Yes, any pharmacy will accept your insurance card. You can fill it anywhere.

A   Muy bien.

1   arrear: to drive

Q   Now, let's take a look at those sutures and see how you're doing.

A   Sí, cada vez que me agacho siento que me van a reventar las puntadas. ¿Es normal eso?

Q   Yes, that's normal for the first couple of weeks after surgery. You have to be sure to change the dressing frequently, though, so that it doesn't get infected.

A   Sí, mi esposa me puede ayudar con eso. Ella estudió enfermería.

Q   Good. So avoid heavy lifting[1] and exertion for the next few weeks, okay? No weight lifting[2] or soccer matches, now.

A   Vaya, sí, doctor, claro que no. Paso todo el día viendo la tele porque no hay otra cosa que pueda hacer.

Q   We'll schedule a follow-up visit for two weeks from today, and at that time I'll probably take out the sutures. Any questions?

A   Sí, una cosa. También tomo medicina para la presión alta. ¿Habrá algún problema por eso?

Q   No, there shouldn't be any interaction between those drugs. But sometimes the side-effects of the hypertension drug will compound those of the pain killer. If you have any problems, just give me a ring, okay?

A   Es que la etiqueta dice también que puede dar sueño, y no quiero que las dos medicinas me tengan dormido todo el tiempo, ¿verdad?

Q   No, I don't think you have to worry about that, but I'm glad you're reading the labels. With the dosage I'm giving you I don't think there'll be any problems.

A   Muy bien, doctor.

Q   So, we'll see you in a couple of weeks. In the meantime, get plenty of rest and don't put too much pressure on those stitches.

---

1 heavy lifting: levantar objetos pesados
2 weight lifting: levantar pesas

A   Está bien, doctor. Muchas gracias. Que le vaya bien.

Q   Sure. Take care, now.

Consecutive Lesson 4: Laboratory Tests (1B)

Q   Good morning, may I help you, Ma'am?

A   Sí, mi doctor me mandó a hacerme unos análisis.

Q   May I see the slip from the doctor? Okay, he wants some blood drawn, urine and stool specimens, and an X-ray.

A   Sí, así me dijo.

Q   Did he tell you to fast before coming in?

A   Sí, estoy en ayunas. No he comido nada desde anoche.

Q   Good. First we'll get the blood and urine, and then we'll take you into the X-ray lab. Take this cup into the bathroom.

A   ¿Nada más llenar el vasito?

Q   We need a midstream specimen. That means you start to urinate into the toilet, and after a few seconds, urinate directly into the cup. Clean your genitals with this napkin before urinating.

A   Está bien. ¿Y lo del excremento?

Q   Put it in this container, which I've labeled with your name. When you've finished, put both specimens in the little cabinet in the bathroom, and a technician will take them from there.

A   ¿Dónde está el baño?

Q   Down the hall, the second door on the left.

A   Gracias.

· · ·

Q   Now, for the blood sample. Have a seat right here, Mrs. Reyes.

A   ¿Me va a picar con esa aguja?

Q   Yes, I'm afraid so, Mrs. Reyes. First I need to prick your right index finger. It'll smart a little.

A   Pero no tanto como lo otro, ¿verdad?

Q	Right. Okay, roll up your sleeve[1], please, I'm going to draw blood from the vein.
A	Sí, señora.
Q	Stretch your arm out and open your hand, then make a fist[2] and leave it like that.
A	¿Así?
Q	That's fine. Now, I'm going to tie this tourniquet around your arm.
A	Está muy apretado.
Q	Yes it's supposed to be tight. Now, open your hand gradually, like that. Now the syringe is full, and we're all done. You can open your eyes.
A	¡Ay! Estos análisis me duelen más que el accidente que sufrí.
Q	I'm sorry, Mrs. Reyes. I'm just going to put this cotton ball and a band-aid on, and you're all set. Next we go to the X-ray lab.
A	Otra cámara de tortura, ¿eh?
Q	This won't hurt a bit. Stand here, and drink this liquid.
A	¡Ay, qué feo[3]! ¿Qué tiene?
Q	It's just something to help us see your stomach better on the X-rays. I know it doesn't taste very good.
A	¡Y bien que no! ¡Sabe a rayos[4]!
Q	Now, take a sip, and swallow now.
A	¿Lo tengo que tomar todo?
Q	Yes, but only when I tell you to. Take another sip, swallow now, don't swallow. Hold still.
A	¿Ya?
Q	One more, then we're done. Okay, you can go now.

1 to roll up one's sleeve: subirse la manga
2 to make a fist: cerrar la mano
3 feo: awful, terrible
4 sabe a rayos: it tastes awful/terrible

A   ¿Cuándo saldrán los resultados?

Q   We'll send a report of all the test results to your doctor. It
         should take a week or so. His office will notify you.

A   Me dijo también el doctor que tengo que hacerme un
         "marai" o algo así, en el hospital. ¿Qué es eso?

Q   Oh, you mean an MRI? That stands for Magnetic
         Resonance Imaging. We don't do those here. It's a special
         X-ray that allows the doctor to see more than conventional
         X-rays would show.

A   ¿Y duele?

Q   No, it doesn't hurt. They make you lie very still in this big
         tube for a long time. It's hard to stay still that long, but it
         doesn't hurt.

Consecutive Lesson 5: Pediatrician (1B)

Q   Hello, Luz, I'm Dr. Jensen. I understand you haven't been feeling too well.

A   No, no me siento bien.

Q   Have you had to stay home from school?

A   Sí.

Q   What grade are you in?

A   Primero.

Q   Oh, you're a big girl now. First we'll take your temperature. Keep your mouth closed around the thermometer, and don't bite on it.

A   Sí.

Q   You have a little fever, honey. Does your tummy ache?

A   Sí, un poquito.

Q   Have you been going to the bathroom normally?

A   Hago pipí, pero hace tiempo que no hago caca. Me duele.

Q   Now I'm going to look at your eyes and your ears. I'm going to shine this little flashlight, but try not to blink.

A   Me duelen los ojos también.

Q   How about your ears? Have you had any earaches?

A   Sí, eso también.

Q   Now I'm going to look at your throat. Open wide and say "Ahhh." Your throat looks a little red. Has it been bothering you?

A   Sí, cuando hablo mucho.

Q   Now I'm going to listen to your breathing. This is called a stethoscope. Have you ever seen one?

A   Sí, mi tía es enfermera y ella tiene uno de esos.

Q   Now I'm going to lift up your shirt and put this on your back. I hope it's not too cold, honey.

A   No, está bien.

Q   Now, I want you to breathe deeply, Luz, so I can listen to your lungs.

A   Mi tía me deja escuchar el corazón con esto.

Q   Yes, that's just what I'm going to do now. Can you show me where your heart is?

A   Aquí, ¿verdad?

Q   That's right. After I've listened to your heart, I'll let you have a turn.

A   Me gusta el ruido que hace.

Q   You have a very healthy heart. Now I want you to lie down on your back, Luz, so I can feel your tummy.

A   Eso es lo que hace mi abuelita, para quitarme el empacho.

Q   Well, everything seems to be fine there. Have you been throwing up at all?

A   No, nomás me duele el estómago, mi mamá dice que se llama agruras. Y no puedo hacer el número dos[1].

Q   I see you have a little rash here. Did you go near some poison oak?

A   Sí, fuimos al parque el domingo, y luego me salieron estos granitos. Me da mucha comezón.

Q   Yes, you should try not to scratch it, though.

A   ¿Me va a dar un "chat"? Mi hermano me dijo que me van a picar.

Q   No, I'm not going to give you any shots today. I'm going to give your mommy something for you to take so you won't be constipated.

A   No me gusta tomar medicina. Tiene un sabor muy feo.

Q   This one tastes pretty good. But make sure you don't take any medicine unless your mommy or daddy gives it to you.

A   Sí, lo sé.

---

1 hacer el número dos: to go number two

Q   I'm also going to give you a piece of paper called a prescription, so your mommy can go to the drug store and buy some medicine that will kill those germs that are making you feel bad.

A   ¿Son pastillas?

Q   No, it's a liquid medicine that you'll have to take three times a day with meals. You'll feel much better in a couple of days.

Consecutive Lesson 6: Dentist (1B)

Q Hello, Mrs. Rudín, have a seat in the chair.

A Buenas tardes, doctor.

Q The nurse says you have a toothache. Which tooth is bothering you?

A Es esta muela de aquí, doctor. No puedo masticar bien.

Q I see. Open a little wider, please. Is it this one?

A No, la de al lado. Sí, esa. ¡Ay!

Q Yes, I see you have quite a few caries here. When was the last time you saw a dentist?

A Pues, hace mucho. Es que no tengo seguro para cubrir visitas al dentista.

Q That's too bad. If you had the money to pay for it, I would recommend some orthodontic work. When your wisdom teeth came in they crowded[1] the rest of your teeth. It looks like one of them may be impacted.

A Sí.

Q Does your jaw ever bother you?

A Sí, doctor, tengo muchos dolores de cabeza, y tengo dificultad en abrir la boca. Además, no mastico muy bien. Evito comer cosas.

Q Sounds like TMJ.

A ¿Qué es eso?

Q Temporal mandibular joint. Problems with that joint can cause the symptoms you described. Does your jaw ever make a noise when you chew?

A Sí, me truena.

Q Getting back to this molar here, does it bother you more when you drink hot or cold liquids?

A Ah, sí, es como un toque eléctrico[2].

---

1 to crowd: apretar contra
2 toque eléctrico: electric shock

Q   It looks like the filling is cracked here, and the whole tooth is probably cracked. You may need a root canal and a crown.

A   ¡Ay, Dios mío! Sáquemela mejor. No tengo el dinero para todo eso.

Q   Well, we'll take a look at the X-rays and see what needs to be done. Your gums look a little swollen. Do they bleed when you brush your teeth?

A   Sí.

Q   You'd better be careful, because that's the first sign of gingivitis, or gum disease. You don't want to lose all your teeth, do you?

A   No, doctor.

Q   How often do you brush?

A   Pues, a diario me cepillo los dientes.

Q   You should brush three times a day, after every meal, and floss at least once a day.

A   Sí, doctor.

Q   What kind of toothpaste do you use?

A   Pues, lo que se venda más barato en la tienda, no me fijo en la marca.

Q   Make sure you use an anti-plaque toothpaste. You have a lot of plaque.

A   Sí, doctor.

Q   I'm going to give you a local anesthetic now, to deaden the nerve[1]. Then I'm going to drill[2] into that molar and see if we can't solve the problem with a filling.

A   Está bien.

Q   Raise your head, rinse your mouth[3] and spit[4] into the bowl.

A   Sí, doctor.

1 to deaden the nerve: adormecer el nervio
2 to drill: perforar, fresar
3 to rinse one's mouth: enjuagarse (la boca)
4 to spit: escupir

Q   I know it's expensive to get regular dental checkups, but it pays off[1] in the long run. First one tooth goes, and then the ones next to it have to be extracted.

A   Sí, doctor, lo sé, pero no tengo el dinero.

Q   You may end up having some expensive dental work here, a bridge or a partial plate.

A   Espero que no, doctor. Trataré de cepillarme con más regularidad.

Q   Okay. Let me know if you have any more problems with that tooth.

---

1 it pays off: vale la pena

Consecutive Lesson 7: Orthopedist (Back) (1B)

Q   Hello, I'm Dr. Swanson. What seems to be the problem today, Mrs. Rubio?

A   Buenos días, doctora. Tengo un dolor muy feo aquí en la cintura. Me duele tanto que no puedo ni dormir.

Q   When did this come on? I mean, when did you first notice this pain?

A   Hace una quincena, más o menos. Al principio pensé que se me iba a quitar, que era nada más por cansancio. Pero todavía me duele, hasta se ha empeorado.

Q   I see. Can you describe the pain in more detail? Is it a dull ache or a sharp, jabbing pain?

A   Es un dolor constante, y cuando me agacho para levantar algo, o cuando le abrazo[1] a mi hijo, me clava un dolor muy fuerte.

Q   Does the pain stay right there in your back, or does it travel[2] to another part of your body?

A   Me corre para abajo, hasta los pies, y para arriba, hasta la nuca. A veces me duele mucho el cerebro.

Q   How far down the leg does the pain go?

A   Hasta el tobillo, más por el lado derecho que el izquierdo. Y me duele mucho aquí, también, en el hueso de la rodilla derecha.

Q   Do you have any other symptoms besides pain?

A   Sí, doctora. Cuando estoy muy cansada, por ejemplo cuando salgo a hacer el mandado[3], ya cuando regreso a casa están completamente entumidos los pies. Se me desguanzan.

Q   When you feel this numbness in your legs, do you also feel tingling?

A   Sí, me hormiguean, y también me arden a veces.

---

1   abrazar: to pick up
2   to travel: correr
3   hacer el mandado: to buy groceries, to do the shopping

Q What about the pain you mentioned in your upper back and neck? What kind of pain is that?

A Pues, no sé decirle exactamente, es difícil de describir, pero yo diría más bien que me retacha. Es como un latido.

Q What brings on the pain?

A Pues, me duele mucho la cintura y toda esta parte de la espalda, y como le digo, los pies también a veces.

Q No, but what I'm trying to find out is, when do you feel this pain? With what activities or positions of the body?

A Oh, pues, cuando me agacho, cuando duro mucho rato sentada o parada. Y después de estar sentada, cuando me levanto no puedo enderezarme bien. Y cuando me ahinco o estoy en culequillas, también me duele.

Q Do you limp when you walk?

A Sí, rengueo bastante. Por eso empecé a usar este bastón.

Q I'm going to ask you to do some movements here so that we can identify the problems you're having. First, bend over and touch your toes, keeping your knees straight.

A ¡Ay, eso me duele muy fuerte!

Q I'm sorry to cause you pain, but I have to see the range of mobility. Now, twist to the right and the left.

A Eso me duele también, más por el lado izquierdo.

Q Sit up on the examining table, please.

A Me duele mucho cuando levanto el pie así. Necesito agarrarme de algo para apoyarme.

Q Now, straighten your legs and pull your toes back.

A Eso no me duele tanto, doctora.

Q Curl your toes down.

A Eso sí me duele. ¿Por qué será eso?

Q It may be a pinched nerve, I can't say for sure until I see your X-rays and test results. Now lie down on your back.

A No puedo acostarme así, tengo que estar de lado primero y luego voltearme. Así duermo, de lado, porque no puedo estar boca arriba mucho rato.

Q   Now sit up straight, as if you were doing sit-ups.

A   No puedo, doctora, disculpe, pero no tengo fuerzas para hacer eso.

Q   I'm going to prescribe a back brace for you to wear, and I'll take you off work[1] for another couple of weeks. Come back in for a follow-up examination in two weeks.

---

1   to take someone off work: descansar/parar del trabajo

Consecutive Lesson 8: Labor and Delivery (1B)

Q   Hello, Mrs. Ramírez, I'm Dr. Erickson. I know you're in some discomfort with the contractions, but since you haven't been in for prenatal care, I'm going to have to ask you some questions.

A   Sí, Doctora.

Q   Is this your first pregnancy?

A   No, tengo tres hijos.

Q   Have you ever had a miscarriage?

A   No, gracias a Dios, no.

Q   How about an induced abortion?

A   No, claro que no.

Q   Did you have any complications with your other pregnancies—high blood pressure, eclampsia, toxemia, diabetes?

A   No, todo fue perfectamente bien.

Q   Did you carry your other children to term?

A   ¿Que si nacieron temprano? No, todos nacieron a su tiempo.

Q   Were any of them born by cesarean section?

A   No, todos de la manera normal.

Q   How many months pregnant are you now?

A   No sé exactamente, pero hace más de ocho meses que no me baja la regla.

Q   I don't suppose you've had any ultrasound done, much less amniocentesis.

A   No, doctora. Es que no tenemos ni un cinco, mi esposo no está trabajando y no recibimos ayuda de ningún tipo.

Q   How much weight have you gained?

A   No sé, no me he pesado, pero yo diría que como ... diez o quince kilos, más o menos.

Q   When did you start having the contractions?

A   Esta tarde, como a las cuatro.

Q   How often are you feeling them right now?

A   Cada cinco, diez minutos. Es que varía. Pero duele muy feo, doctora.

Q   Yes, I know. Well, the nurse says you're three centimeters dilated, so it'll be a while yet. When was the last time you had a bowel movement?

A   Esta mañana, como a las diez.

Q   Has your bag of waters broken yet?

A   Sí, por eso vine al hospital.

Q   Okay, just try to relax. The nurse will be in in a moment to shave you and give you an enema.

A   Gracias, doctora.

         . . .

Q   Okay, the nurse says you're fully dilated now. Have you felt the urge to push[1]?

A   Sí, doctora, es insoportable el dolor. ¿No me puede dar algo para calmar el dolor?

Q   No, that might harm the baby. It won't be much longer now. Try to breathe normally. Don't push until you feel a contraction.

A   Ahí viene. ¿Pujo?

Q   Yes, push now. I'm going to give you a local anesthetic and an episiotomy so that the baby will come out more easily.

A   ¡Que venga pronto, no aguanto el dolor!

Q   The head is crowning now. The fetal monitor indicates that the baby's in some distress, so I'm going to use the forceps.

A   ¿No le lastima al bebé?

Q   No, it'll be fine, don't worry. One more push. Here he comes. You have a fine, healthy boy, Mrs. Ramírez!

A   ¡Ay, gracias a Dios! Y a Ud., doctora.

Q   Now we have to wait for the afterbirth. One more push and you're all done, Mrs. Ramírez.

---

1 urge to push: ganas de pujar

A   ¿Todo está bien? ¿Está sano?

Q   Yes, he's just fine. He weighs eight pounds, two ounces. Are you going to nurse or bottle feed?

A   Pienso darle de mamar. Dicen que es mejor.

Consecutive Lesson 9: Emergency Room (1B)

Q What seems to be the problem here?

A No sé, doctor, mi hijo estaba jugando en el patio trasero, y luego oí un grito, y cuando salí, estaba estirado en el suelo. Se había desmayado.

Q How long was he unconscious?

A Es que estaba medio dormido, medio despierto, y le decía, ¿qué te pasó, m'hijo, qué te pasó? pero no me contestaba. Estaba como delirando.

Q Did he appear to have fallen? Is there playground equipment in your backyard, or a wall or something he could have fallen from?

A No, es un patio muy chiquito, no hay nada.

Q Do you have any toxic substances in your backyard? Any garden chemicals, cleaning products, gasoline cans?

A No, no hay nada. Le digo que es un patio muy chiquito, y no hay sustancias químicas ni venenos en ninguna parte. Guardo los productos de limpieza en un lugar muy seguro, porque sé que son peligrosos.

Q Did he appear to be in pain? Was he holding himself anywhere?

A Sí, se agarraba el brazo, así, y me fijé que había una herida en el antebrazo que no había notado antes. ¿Ve? Aquí.

Q Yes, it looks like an insect bite. Have you ever noticed any black widow spiders around your house?

A No, pero no tenemos mucho de vivir aquí, doctor.

Q Is there a cellar or shed or anything like that where a spider might hide?

A Sí, hay un escondrijo bajo la escalera del pórtico. Puede haber arañas ahí.

Q Has he vomited?

A Sí, dos veces.

Q His skin is kind of clammy, and he appears to be going into shock. This looks like a black widow spider bite to me.

A   ¿Estará bien, doctor?

Q   Yes, it's a good thing you brought him in right away. I'm going to give him a shot of antihistamines and an antidote. We'll have to keep him under observation for the next several hours.

A   Sí, doctor.

Q   His blood pressure is low, his temperature is down, and you can see how pale he is. I'm going to put him on an IV.

A   ¿Está grave, doctor?

Q   Well, a black widow spider bite can be very serious; it causes the patient to go into what we call anaphylactic shock. But I think we've caught it in time.

A   ¡Dios quiera que sí!

Q   He appears to be having cramps, and his abdomen is rigid. He's having some trouble breathing. These are the classic symptoms.

A   ¿Qué contiene el suero, doctor?

Q   It's a glucose solution with adrenalin and some other drugs to bring him out of the shock, keep him hydrated, and so on. There's also an analgesic for the pain.

A   Sí, muy bien.

Q   I'm going to put him on a cardiac monitor, too, just in case.

A   ¿Cuánto tiempo tendrá que quedarse aquí?

Q   We'll check his vital signs every couple of hours to see how he's doing, and we'll keep adjusting the dosages as his condition progresses. I can't tell you for sure.

A   Es que dejé a mis otros hijos con la vecina, y tengo que avisarle.

Q   Well, I really can't tell you. We can't release him until his blood pressure is back to normal, he's breathing normally, and he doesn't have any more pain.

A   Sí, por supuesto.

Q   I'd say he'll probably have to be admitted and spend the night in the hospital, just so we can keep an eye on him. We don't want to take any chances.

A Claro que no.

Q We'll also want to do some blood work on him, to see what his blood count is, and get a urine specimen.

A Sí, cómo no.

Q And as soon as he's alert and can eat solid food, he can go home and he'll be as good as new.

A Gracias, doctor, que Dios le bendiga.

Consecutive Lesson 10: Neurologist – EMG (1B)

Q Hi, I'm Dr. Green. I'm going to be giving you an EMG today. Did the nurse explain to you what the test is all about?

A Bueno, me dijo que Ud. me va a picar con agujas, pero no le entendí bien. ¿Duele?

Q Okay, I'll explain it to you. Yes, it will prick you a little, just like when you prick your finger with a needle while sewing.

A Está bien.

Q I'm going to put these electrodes[1] at various points in your body, and the purpose of this test is to see whether your nerves are communicating properly with your muscles.

A ¿Y por qué es necesario?

Q Well, the other tests you've taken, the CAT scan and the MRI, suggest there may be some nerve damage because of the accident you had last year.

A Ya veo. Bueno, ni modo[2], pues.

Q Now your muscles are going to twitch a little when the electricity goes through these wires, but it shouldn't hurt too much.

A Está bien. ¿Vamos a ver la tele? ¿Telenovelas, o qué?

Q No, that's called an oscilloscope[3]. We'll be able to see the electrical activity on the screen, and we'll hear it through the loudspeaker[4].

A ¿Me va a dar un toque?

Q Well, it's not exactly a shock, but your muscle will respond to the stimulation by contracting. Don't worry, it won't do you any harm.

A ¿Y Ud. va a mandar un reporte a mi abogado y a la aseguranza?

---

1 electrode: electrodo
2 ni modo: I have no choice, so be it
3 oscilloscope: osciloscopio
4 loudspeaker: altavoz *m*, altoparlante *m*

Q   Yes, this machine will produce a print-out[1], and after studying that, I'll be able to report on the results to your lawyer and the insurance company.

A   Muy bien. Espero que se resuelva todo esto muy pronto, porque ya ando varios meses en esto, y lo que quiero es que me curen para poder volver a trabajar.

Q   Yes, that's what we all want. Okay, just relax now.

A   Oiga, doctor, ¿me puede firmar un papel para el estado? Dicen que hay que mandar este papel, llenado por un doctor, para que me paguen beneficios.

Q   Well, your attorney just asked me to evaluate you. You should take that form to your treating physician to have it signed.

A   Oh, está bien.

Q   Now, what I want you to do is keep your arm relaxed while I insert this needle. You're going to feel a little discomfort here.

A   ¡Ay! Sí, a mi cuñada le hicieron esta prueba también, y me dijo que le dolió bastante.

Q   Well, I'm gonna try not to hurt you any more than I have to. Now, I want you to make a muscle[2], like a bodybuilder[3], okay?

A   ¿Así? No tengo mucha fuerza en este brazo desde el accidente.

Q   Yeah, that's what we're examining you for. Okay, now we're going to do the same thing down here. Relax your muscle.

A   Sí. Mire, estas rayitas están subiendo y bajando. ¿Qué significa eso?

Q   They're measuring the electrical activity that's taking place in your muscles. Now tighten your muscle, flex it like this.

---

1   print-out: lectura, impresión, resultado
2   to make a muscle: flexionar el músculo
3   bodybuilder: culturista, fisioculturista

A   ¿Así que esa electricidad está corriendo dentro de mí todo el tiempo? No lo sabía. Si pudiera iluminar la casa con ella, no tendría que pagar el pichiní[1], ¿verdad?

Q   That would be nice, wouldn't it? But this is a different kind of electricity, I'm afraid.

A   Ah, bueno.

Q   Okay, we're almost done now. Just turn over on your side like this, and stretch out your leg.

A   Está bien. ¿Cuándo estará listo el reporte?

Q   I'll send the report to your attorney in a couple of weeks, and he'll notify you when it's ready.

A   Gracias, doctor.

---

1   pichiní: PG&E (stands for "Pacific Gas and Electric")

Consecutive Lesson 11: Orthopedist (Hand) (2A)

Q   Good afternoon, Mr. Juárez. Your attorney asked me to take a look at the hand you injured at work.

A   Sí, gracias. Es que me duele mucho, no puedo usarla para nada.

Q   Tell me first how the accident happened.

A   Bueno, es que trabajo en la construcción, y ese día estaba cortando unas tablas y me corté el dedo con la sierra circular.

Q   Which finger did you cut?

A   Este, el dedo índice de la mano izquierda. Y también me corté parte de este dedo, el dedo corazón.

Q   Are you right-handed or left-handed?

A   Bueno, por desgracia, soy zurdo. Uso esta mano para todo.

Q   How did you cut yourself with the saw?

A   Bueno, por desidia o idiotez, no sé cuál, metí un pedacito de madera en la cubierta de protección[1] para fijarla en posición abierta.

Q   Why did you do that?

A   Es que la cubierta está cargada con un resorte[2] y va bajando a medida que la hoja de cortar[3] pasa por la madera. Pero es un estorbo, y no se puede ver lo que se está cortando. Así que la fijé para evitar que bajara.

Q   So, you disabled[4] the safety mechanism and that exposed the blade?

A   Sí, para ver lo que estaba haciendo y para hacer el trabajo más rápido.

Q   And the blade[5] caught your finger?

---

1 cubierta de protección: blade guard
2 resorte: spring
3 hoja de cortar: cutting blade
4 to disable: estropear
5 blade: hoja

A   Sí, cargaba la sierra con la mano derecha, porque así está diseñada, con el mango por este lado y el interruptor[1] aquí así, y con la mano izquierda guiaba la madera.

Q   Did you cut the tip of your index finger off entirely?

A   No completamente, un pedacito estaba colgando así, pero el doctor en la sala de emergencia me lo cortó porque dijo que no se podía salvar.

Q   And the finger next to it was cut also?

A   Sí, me cosió este dedo y ahora está chueco.

Q   Let's see what you can do with your hand. First, I want you to grip this instrument as hard as you can.

A   Sí, eso me duele, y no tengo la fuerza que tenía antes.

Q   What else causes you to feel pain, besides gripping and squeezing?

A   Pues, cuando hace frío me duele bastante, y también cuando trato de levantar algo, como un galón de leche. Y me molesta cuando escribo mucho.

Q   Now I want you to take this little instrument between your thumb and forefinger and pinch as hard as you can.

A   No puedo, doctor. Este dedo no me ayuda para nada.

Q   Do you have any other symptoms, such as numbness or tingling?

A   Sí, este dedo está completamente dormido, pero me duele adentro, como en el hueso. Y cuando agarro algo muy fuerte, me hormiguea aquí.

Q   Is there any swelling?

A   Sí, se me hincha cuando lo uso bastante, como por ejemplo, cuando manejo el carro, porque mi carro es estándar, y tengo que agarrar la palanca de cambios con la mano derecha y el volante con la mano izquierda, y en un viaje largo me duele bastante.

Q   Do you have any pain anywhere else, in your wrist, forearm, elbow, upper arm, or shoulder?

1 interruptor: switch

A   Bueno, cuando hago mucha fuerza con esta mano, por la noche me duele todo el brazo hasta arriba.

Q   What do you do to relieve the pain? Do you take any medications or apply heat?

A   Sí, me tomo unas aspirinas y me pongo una toalla caliente o una almohada eléctrica.

Q   And does that help?

A   Sí, me calma el dolor. Pero más bien trato de evitar usar esta mano.

Consecutive Lesson 12: Internist (2A)

Q Hello, Mr. Zúñiga, I'm Dr. Suárez. How are you today?

A Bueno, no ando muy bien, doctora. Es que me duele mucho el estómago.

Q I see. And how long have you had this complaint?

A Oh, hace tiempo ya. Creo que primero lo noté el año pasado, como en el verano más o menos.

Q What are your symptoms, Mr. Zúñiga?

A Pues, después de comer tengo agruras, y mucho regüeldo también. Pero me duele el estómago todo el tiempo.

Q Does it hurt more on an empty stomach or a full stomach?

A Bueno, antes me dolía más después de comer, y creía que era un estómago sucio nomás, especialmente cuando comía mucho, quedaba bien entripado. Pero fíjese que ahora me duele más cuando está vacío el estómago.

Q Is there anything you do to relieve the pain?

A Sí, cuando tomo un vaso de leche se me calma un poco.

Q Do you ever take antacids?

A Sí, a veces los compro en la tienda, pero no sirven para nada, ¿para qué gastar el dinero, pues?

Q Do you ever vomit when you have this stomach pain?

A Sí, a veces.

Q Have you ever noticed blood in your vomit?

A No, doctora, fíjese que no, pero claro que no lo inspecciono, ¡me da asco!

Q How about your bowel movements? Are they normal? Any black stool, blood in the stool, constipation, diarrhea?

A Pues, a veces me pega un entablazón de todos los diablos. Pero aparte de eso, cuando hago del cuerpo, todo está normal, que sepa. No inspecciono eso, tampoco.

Q Do you ever have stomach cramps or fever?

A No, nada de eso. Sólo el dolor. Es un dolor quelante, como algo acídico, no como un calambre o retorcijón.

Q   Now let's talk about things in your life that might be causing you this stomach discomfort. Have you been under any stress lately?

A   Pues, sí, doctora, en el trabajo, el nuevo mayordomo[1] nos da mucha carrilla[2]. Nos exige que trabajemos cada vez más recio[3].

Q   How long have you been working under this foreman, Mr. Zúñiga?

A   Desde el año pasado, entró al principio de la temporada. El otro mayordomo que estuvo ahí antes era muy buena gente, pero este tipo es insoportable.

Q   Have you gone through channels at the company, talked to your supervisor?

A   Pues, el supervisor habla puro inglés, y el único que nos pueda interpretar es el mismo mayordomo.

Q   I see. So does the onset of these stomach problems you've been describing coincide more or less with the arrival of the new foreman?

A   Pues, yo diría que sí, doctora, así es.

Q   Well, I think you have an ulcer, Mr. Zúñiga, but to be sure of that and to rule out[4] other possibilities, I'm going to run some tests.

A   Sí, doctora.

Q   First, we'll have some X-rays taken. I'm going to order complete blood work too, and a urinalysis, just to be sure. It's been a while since you had a complete physical.

A   Sí, doctora, está bien.

Q   And I'm going to order a barium enema, too, and some upper GI studies.

A   ¿Qué es eso, doctora?

Q   It's a chemical that helps us see your intestines better on the X-rays. Don't worry, it doesn't hurt.

---

1   mayordomo: foreman
2   dar carrilla: to push, hurry, harass
3   recio: fast
4   to rule out: excluir, descartar

A   Ojalá que no.

Q   In the meantime, stick to a bland diet. Don't eat spicy foods, and stay away from caffeine and alcohol. And don't smoke, of course.

A   Está bien, doctora.

Consecutive Lesson 13: Hospital Care (2A)

Q   Good morning, Mrs. Arias, are you feeling better today?

A   Todavía me duele la operación, señorita.

Q   You mean you have tenderness around the sutures?

A   Sí, me duele y me pica también.

Q   I'll just check your dressing here. The doctor says you can have solid food today, Mrs. Arias. I know they removed your dentures for the surgery, but you can put them back in now.

A   Gracias, pero no tengo hambre. Tengo el estómago un poco revuelto.

Q   Yes, that's because of the anesthesia. You'll get your appetite back soon. In the meantime, make sure you take plenty of liquids.

A   Oiga, señorita, el doctor me sacó la matriz, ¿verdad?

Q   Yes, do you remember when they explained it to you before the surgery and you signed the consent form? First he was going to do a biopsy, and if he found any cancerous tissue he was going to do the hysterectomy immediately.

A   Sí, me acuerdo. Y estos moretones, ¿de dónde vienen?

Q   That's from the IV during surgery. It's nothing to worry about.

A   ¿Me dieron sangre durante la operación?

Q   No, it wasn't necessary to give you a transfusion. Are you having pain right now?

A   No mucho, sólo lo que le dije, que me da picazón y hormigueo. ¿Qué es este aparatito?

Q   That's a TENS unit. It stands for "transcutaneous electric nerve stimulation."

A   Oh, ¿por qué le pusieron un nombre tan complicado? ¿Qué hace?

Q   It is supposed to alleviate pain through electrical stimuli to the nerve. That way we don't have to give you sedatives that will make you drowsy. We want you up and about as soon as possible.

A   ¿No me hace ningún daño? ¿No es radiactivo?

Q   No, there's nothing radioactive. It's perfectly harmless. But if you begin to feel more discomfort, just let me know.

A   Sí, señorita.

Q   Have you eliminated yet?

A   ¿Cómo?

Q   Have you urinated or had a bowel movement?

A   No, pero tengo ganas de orinar ahorita. ¿Me puede ayudar a ir al baño, señorita?

Q   The doctor doesn't want you getting out of bed just yet, Mrs. Arias. I'll bring the bedpan.

A   Gracias, muy amable.

Q   Raise your buttocks just a bit. There. Now I'm going to change the sheets, so just turn over on your right side. Now your left side.

A   Ay, me duele el vientre.

Q   I know you're a little uncomfortable now, but it won't last long. I'll give you a sponge bath now, and you'll feel better.

A   Gracias, señorita.

Q   Now I'll brush your hair and plump up your pillows and you can watch some TV. Do you want me to raise the head of the bed a little?

A   Sí, por favor. ¿Cuáles son las horas de visita?

Q   From 7:00 to 9:00 this evening. Are you expecting visitors?

A   Sí, tengo mucha familia.

Q   That's nice. Are you comfortable now, Mrs. Arias? Do you need another pillow, or another blanket?

A   No, gracias, estoy bien. Oiga, señorita, ¿qué me va a pasar ahora?

Q   What do you mean?

A   Pues, me sacaron la matriz por ser cancerosa. ¿Es todo lo que me van a hacer, o es necesario otro tratamiento?

Q   Well, the doctor is going to keep monitoring you to see how you're doing. You may need some chemotherapy.

A   ¿Cuánto durará eso?

Q   I really can't tell you, Mrs. Arias. The doctor will be
        making rounds this morning, and he'll be able to answer
        your questions.

Consecutive Lesson 14: Cardiologist (2A)

Q   Good morning, Mrs. Offerman, I'm Dr. Gómez. Your doctor has referred you to me to see whether you have a heart condition.

A   Sí, me dijo que mi iba a mandar con un cardiólogo porque cree que sufro del corazón.

Q   As I understand it, you've been having palpitations and angina pectoris, better known as chest pains.

A   Sí, así es, me preocupa mucho.

Q   Tell me about these chest pains. Where do they occur, and what brings them on?

A   Pues, el dolor empieza aquí, en medio, y me corre por acá, y por todo el brazo así. Es un dolor muy agudo.

Q   What are you doing when you have these pains?

A   Me pegan muy a menudo cuando subo escaleras, cuando hago mucha fuerza, por ejemplo en el trabajo cuando tengo que levantar a un paciente.

Q   Do you ever have episodes of tachycardia, that is, your heart suddenly speeds up?

A   No, eso no lo he notado, doctor.

Q   Do you ever have difficulty breathing?

A   Sí, cuando vienen los dolores, me siento ahogada, y tengo que sentarme para descansar, o si no, me desmayo.

Q   Do you sweat when this happens?

A   Sí, me pega un sudor frío, y también tengo calambres en las piernas.

Q   Do you have varicose veins?

A   Sí, en las dos piernas, aquí en la corva, y he notado que me han salido más últimamente.

Q   Now, let's talk a little bit about your medical history, and your family history. Have you ever had rheumatic fever?

A   No, que yo sepa, no, doctor.

Q   I see on the chart that you have high blood pressure, and you've had a weight problem for some time, is that right?

A   Pues sí, doctor, mi doctor me ha dicho que baje de peso, y me ha puesto a régimen, pero por mucho que me esfuerce, no puedo bajar.

Q   Has anyone in your family had heart problems, for example, a heart attack, a heart murmur, anything like that?

A   Sí, mi papá, que en paz descanse, murió hace cuatro años de un ataque al corazón. Le operaron dos veces, pero fue voluntad de Dios que muriera.

Q   I'm sorry, Mrs. Offerman. Does anyone else in your family have heart trouble, or circulatory problems, strokes, anything of that nature?

A   No, gracias a Dios, los demás estamos bien.

Q   Have you ever had an EKG, an electrocardiogram?

A   Creo que sí, es cuando le ponen esos alambres a uno, y sale un papelito con rayitas, mostrando los latidos del corazón, ¿verdad?

Q   Yes.

A   Sí, me hicieron eso en una clínica al lado del hospital.

Q   Now, your attorney has filed a claim alleging that your working conditions have contributed to and aggravated your heart condition, so I need to ask you some questions about that.

A   Sí, doctor, ándele.

Q   What aspects of your job as a nurse's aid do you think have contributed to your heart problems, Mrs. Offerman?

A   Pues, es un trabajo muy duro. Tengo que estar caminando todo el día, empujando sillas de ruedas, trayendo sábanas y toallas a la lavandería, y hay muchas escaleras en ese lugar.

Q   Do you have to lift heavy objects?

A   Oh, sí, hay que levantar a los pacientes para ayudarles a sentarse en la silla, para bañarlos, para cambiar la cama. Y algunos de ellos pesan bastante.

Q   Did you have any of these symptoms, the chest pains and shortness of breath, before you started working at the convalescent hospital?

A   No, doctor, estaba completamente sana, sin problemas.

Consecutive Lesson 15: AIDS Clinic (2A)

A   Hello, can I help you?

Q   Sí, necesito información acerca del SIDA.

A   Well, I think I can answer most of your questions. What would you like to know?

Q   Pues, ¿cómo se transmite? ¿Es cierto que nomás los homosexuales se enferman del SIDA?

A   No, anyone who comes into contact with the bodily fluids of someone carrying the AIDS virus can get the disease. That includes intravenous drug users who share needles, their sex partners[1], and even the babies of women who have the AIDS virus.

Q   ¿Cómo sabe uno si lo tiene?

A   Well, the surest way to find out is to take a blood test to see if you have the antibodies of the AIDS virus, which is called the human immunodeficiency virus, or HIV.

Q   Bueno, y ¿qué quiere decir todo eso? Ni siquiera sé lo que es el SIDA.

A   Let's start at the beginning. AIDS stands for "acquired immune deficiency syndrome." It affects the body's ability to fight infection.

Q   ¿Cuál es la causa de la enfermedad?

A   Researchers have discovered that it is caused by the virus they call HIV, but there's no cure for it yet.

Q   ¿Y qué es eso de "anticuerpos"?

A   That's what the body produces to fight off bacteria, viruses, and other organisms that invade it. So if you have the antibodies in your blood, we know you've been exposed to the virus.

Q   ¿Y todos los que se exponen al virus se enferman?

A   People can carry the virus around for months or years and show no signs of illness. That's why it's so important to take the test if you suspect you may have the virus.

---

1   sex partner: pareja (sexual)

Q   ¿Y cuáles son los signos del SIDA?

A   At first it's a lot like the flu: fever, night sweats, weight loss. They often get swollen lymph glands and diarrhea, and they feel tired all the time.

Q   ¿Pero estos síntomas pueden indicar otra enfermedad, también?

A   Yes.

Q   ¿Hay algún cobro por la prueba?

A   No, it's free here at the clinic.

Q   Mire, si me someto a este examen y salgo positivo, ¿lo sabrá todo el mundo?

A   Well, we'll give you a code name[1] if you like, and the test will be anonymous. If you need to have your name on the results, they will still be kept confidential.

Q   Bueno, este, yo he tenido algunos de los síntomas que Ud. mencionó, y, pues, creo que necesito hacerme la prueba.

A   Are you in one of the risk groups I mentioned?

Q   Sí, es que a veces me inyecto drogas, y a veces uso la aguja de un compa[2]. Uno de ellos murió la semana pasada, y dicen que padecía SIDA.

A   All right, I'll make an appointment for you to come in and have a test.

Q   En caso de que salga positivo, ¿qué debo hacer?

A   As I said, you may not feel sick right away. You should have regular medical checkups, and under no circumstances should you donate blood. If you do get sick, there are treatments available.

Q   ¿Y debo dejar el vicio[3]?

A   Yes, if at all possible. If you can't get into a drug treatment program and stop shooting up[4], you should at least avoid sharing needles.

---

1   code name: nombre en clave
2   compa: pal, buddy
3   dejar el vicio: to kick the habit
4   to shoot up: inyectarse, clavarse, picarse

Q   ¿Tengo que abstenerme del sexo?

A   No, but you should always practice safe sex.

Q   O sea, ¿usar hules?

A   Yes, and there are some other precautions you can take. Here's a pamphlet[1] that explains everything in Spanish.

Q   Gracias. ¿Y si salgo negativo?

A   A negative result doesn't mean you're immune. You should still follow the guidelines in the pamphlet. Try to kick your drug habit, and if you can't, always use clean needles.

Q   ¿Y el sexo?

A   Avoid having sex with people in high risk groups[2], and always wear protection. Avoid the unsafe sex acts[3] described in the pamphlet.

Q   Muy bien. Gracias.

---

1 pamphlet: folleto
2 high risk groups: grupos de alto riesgo
3 unsafe sex acts: actividades sexuales arriesgadas

Consecutive Lesson 16: Psychiatrist (2A)

Q Hello, Mr. Móntez, how are you today?

A Bien, gracias.

Q As you know, the insurance company that covers your employer for workers' compensation has asked me to examine you.

A Sí, eso me dijo mi abogado.

Q How do you feel about being here today, Mr. Móntez?

A Bueno, Ud. toma partido de la aseguranza, ¿verdad? Eso no me conviene. Ya me han molestado mucho, con sus espías y todo.

Q Spies?

A Sí, andan merodeando[1] por todo el barrio, haciéndoles preguntas a los vecinos y tomándome fotografías y videos.

Q Well, yes, I'm aware that they've taken some video footage of you, Mr. Móntez, but you don't need to worry about my taking sides. I'm a professional.

A Pues, estoy aquí porque mi abogado me dijo que era obligatorio, pero le advierto que no me siento cómodo con esto.

Q I'll make a note of that, Mr. Móntez. Now, what I'd like to talk to you about today is the injury you suffered at work and the effect it's had on your life.

A Sí. Pues, me duele por todas partes, constantemente.

Q Yes. First of all, tell me in your own words exactly how the accident happened, Mr. Móntez.

A Bueno, estaba pintando una casa de dos pisos, y me caí de la escalera.

Q How did you land[2] when you fell?

A Pues, no supe, porque perdí el conocimiento. Cuando volví en mí, estaba tirado boca arriba en el suelo. Me imagino que caí así.

---

1 merodear: to hang around
2 How did you land?: ¿Cómo quedó?

Q   Did you go to a doctor right away?

A   Pues, imagínese, doctor, el jefe no quiso hacer nada por mí. Ahí empezaron los problemas. Quería que volviera a trabajar, ¡fíjese!

Q   And how did you feel about that?

A   Pues, me encabroné[1]. Eso fue el colmo[2], después de todos los problemas que había tenido con él. Es que yo no le caía bien, por alguna razón.

Q   And what happened next?

A   Pues, insistí en que me llevaran al hospital, y puesto que no quisieron llamar a la ambulancia, mi compañero me llevó. Y por eso lo despidieron.

Q   When did this accident happen, Mr. Móntez?

A   Fue en mayo, hará tres años en mayo.

Q   Have you gone back to work since then?

A   No, no he podido encontrar un trabajo que pueda hacer.

Q   What kind of work have you been looking for?

A   Bueno, algo que no me lastime. No puedo levantar cosas pesadas, no puedo estar parado mucho rato ni sentado mucho rato, no puedo caminar.

Q   That rules out a lot of jobs, doesn't it?

A   Sí, claro, por eso no estoy trabajando.

Q   What effect has that had on you, Mr. Móntez?

A   Pues, me mortifico[3], porque no puedo mantener a mis hijos. Vivimos de lo que gane mi esposa, y como hombre, eso me da vergüenza.

Q   Do you ever have suicidal thoughts?

A   No, nada de eso, no puedo quebrantar las leyes de Dios. Pero sí me tiene muy deprimido. No puedo comer, ni dormir, ni nada.

Q   Do you ever feel anxious or worried?

---

1 encabronarse: to get mad, to get riled
2 el colmo: the last straw
3 mortificarse: to be ashamed, to feel humiliated

A Claro que sí. Me siento desesperado, muy nervioso. Y la aseguranza me ha cortado los beneficios, no me ha dado ni un cinco desde el año pasado.

Q Do you ever drink or take drugs as a result of these feelings?

A No, no tomo, ni fumo, ni uso drogas. No quiero meter esas cochinadas[1] en mi cuerpo.

Q What do you do when you feel anxious or nervous?

A Pues, salgo a caminar, pero luego luego[2] me canso. ¡Es que no hay remedio!

Q I sense your frustration, Mr. Móntez.

A Sí, me siento tan frustrado, a veces pienso que voy a estallar como una bomba. Y no quiero que mis hijos me vean así.

Q I'm going to say a few words, Mr. Móntez, and I want you to tell me the first thing that comes to mind when you hear each word.

A A ver.

Q Mother.

A Santa.

Q Work.

A Obligación.

Q How about the phrase, "like father, like son[3]"? What does that mean to you?

A Pues, que el hijo sigue los pasos del papá, que debe tratar de estar a la altura de la honra de su papá.

Q What about the proverb, "Heaven helps those who help themselves[4]"?

A Quiere decir que uno debe responsabilizarse por su propio destino, que nadie le va a regalar nada.

---

1 cochinadas: junk
2 luego luego: right away
3 like father, like son: tal padre, tal hijo; de tal palo, tal astilla
4 Heaven helps those who help themselves: ayúdate, que Dios te ayudará; el que madruga, Dios lo ayuda

---

Q   Finally: "There's many a slip twixt the cup and the lip[1]."

A   Sí, quiere decir que, aunque uno piensa que todo está bien y que no le va a pasar nada, de repente le mueven la silla para que se caiga. Eso me pasó a mí.

Q   Tell me about your fantasies, Mr. Móntez.

A   ¿Fantasías? No me doy el lujo de fantasear. Tengo demasiadas responsabilidades como para estar soñando.

Q   Well, what about your dreams? What was the most recent dream you had?

A   Soñé que estaba bien, que había regresado a mi trabajo y que estaba cumpliendo con mi familia, manteniéndoles bien. ¡Qué desilusión[2] sentí cuando desperté!

---

1 There's many a slip twixt the cup and the lip: Del dicho al hecho, hay un buen trecho; de la mano a la boca, se pierde la sopa
2 desilusión: disappointment

3 Simultaneous Interpretation

Introduction

Simultaneous interpretation, in which the interpreter speaks at the same time as the speaker, is seldom used in medical interpreting. We have nevertheless included this section on simultaneous both because some real-world medical interpreting situations may require simultaneous interpretation and because some medical interpreting exams include it.

Simultaneous interpretation is actually a misnomer, in that the word *simultaneous* suggests that the interpreter is interpreting a message as she hears it. In fact, there is a delay between the moment the interpreter hears a thought and the moment she renders that thought into the target language, because it takes time to understand the original message and generate a target-language rendition of it. Meanwhile, the speaker goes on to the next thought, so the interpreter must generate the target-language version of the first thought while processing the speaker's second thought, and so on. This delay is known as *décalage*, from the French word for *time lag*. The longer the interpreter is able to wait before beginning the target-language version, the more information she will have and the more accurate her target-language version will be.

Note that we have been speaking in terms of **thoughts** rather than **words**. It is the interpreter's task to convey the **meaning** of the original message. Every language organizes meaning differently, and trying to find direct equivalents in two languages often leads to absurd results.

Each simultaneous interpreting lesson in this chapter is preceded by a shadowing exercise on the same subject matter as the lesson. The purpose of shadowing—which means repeating what the speaker says, word for word, in the same language—is to help you later retrieve from memory words and phrases associated with the subject matter and in the language into which you will be interpreting. Shadowing practice helps your interpretation sound smooth and natural in the target language. When you shadow, try to lag a full thought behind the speaker. This allows you to become accustomed to speaking and listening at the same time. It is also particularly helpful in your second language, as it improves your pronunciation, enunciation, and speed. Moreover, repeating phrases constantly helps you retrieve them quickly when you are interpreting. Repeat the exercise as many times as necessary, until you can shadow everything the speaker says without omitting any words. Begin all of your simultaneous practice sessions with five or ten minutes of shadowing as a way of warming up.

The approximate speed at which each lesson is recorded is indicated in the script at the beginning of the lesson (e.g., 120 wpm). People speaking at normal conversational speeds may speak at anything from 140 WPM to 200 WPM or more. These exercises are designed for novice interpreters, however, and it is unrealistic to expect to be able to interpret at 200 words per minute at this stage. Additional speed will come with practice and experience.

Note that you may repeat the interpreting exercises as many times as you need; even if you have gotten to the point that you have memorized the tapes, you are still benefiting from the exercises. The lessons will develop the individual components of simultaneous interpretation (concentration, analysis, speed, etc.), and repeating them many times can only enhance those skills. Do not read the script while you are interpreting the tape; consult it afterwards to check for accuracy and to look up problem terms. The medical terms that appear in these lessons can be found in the glossaries in Chapter 4. Some of the Spanish terms used by patients in these lessons are included in "Términos coloquiales relacionados con la medicina popular" in Chapter 4. Non-medical terms that may not be found in an ordinary bilingual dictionary are footnoted.

Be sure to record yourself on a second tape recorder when you practice these simultaneous exercises. Afterwards, listen to yourself critically. It is important to hear how you sound to the listener when you interpret. Make sure you enunciate clearly and use correct grammar (subject-verb and gender agreement, for example) and style (word order and phrasing) in your target language.

After the title of each lesson in this book, enclosed in parentheses, is the tape number and tape side on which the lesson is recorded (e.g., 2B, 3A, 3B, etc.).

Simultaneous Lesson 1 (2B)

Directions: Shadow.

(110 WPM)

La inmunidad

La inmunidad es la capacidad de un organismo para defenderse contra las infecciones. La infección, a su vez, resulta cuando un microorganismo logra implantarse y desarrollarse en el cuerpo y éste reacciona de manera defensiva. El cuerpo humano se encuentra constantemente expuesto a la acción de estos microorganismos, comúnmente conocidos como gérmenes. En muchos casos, los gérmenes invasores causarían la muerte casi instantánea si el cuerpo no poseyera resistencia o inmunidad contra ellos.

Generalmente se divide la inmunidad en dos clases: natural y adquirida. La inmunidad natural es la resistencia a la infección que poseen los individuos o las especies en condiciones naturales normales. Los perros, por ejemplo, son inmunes a la tifoidea, los cerdos al veneno de las serpientes y las ratas a la toxina diftérica; de la misma manera, los seres humanos son resistentes a muchas enfermedades que atacan a otras especies. Dentro de la especie humana algunos grupos son más resistentes a las enfermedades que otros. Una persona debilitada será más susceptible al ataque de infecciones que un individuo que goza de buena salud.

La inmunidad adquirida es una forma de resistencia a la infección provocada por la actividad del propio cuerpo o de los tejidos de la persona. El organismo viviente posee la capacidad de responder a muchas infecciones con la producción en la sangre y en los tejidos de unas sustancias invisibles llamadas anticuerpos. Por ejemplo, cuando una persona contrae paperas, genera anticuerpos que permiten al organismo rechazar ataques futuros de paperas. La inmunidad o resistencia adquirida puede producirse artificialmente con la administración de vacunas que estimulen la formación de anticuerpos en los tejidos. Las vacunas, por lo general, son gérmenes extintos o debilitados, pero que poseen poder suficiente para estimular la formación de anticuerpos al ser inoculados. Otra forma de adquirir inmunidad es mediante la inyección de anticuerpos producidos en otra persona o en un animal, mediante sueros.

Sin embargo, a veces el organismo desarrolla anticuerpos para combatir las sustancias producidas por él mismo, en un trastorno denominado enfermedad autoinmune. Las alergias son un ejemplo de esta clase de enfermedad. Otro ejemplo de un trastorno del sistema

inmunológico es el SIDA, o Síndrome de Inmunodeficiencia Adquirida.
Este síndrome afecta ciertas células sanguíneas que forman parte de
las defensas naturales del cuerpo, causando que las membranas
interiores, al ser atacadas, comiencen a multiplicarse de forma
defectuosa y a disminuir sus funciones hasta que terminan por
desaparecer.

Directions: Interpret into Spanish.

(115 WPM)

The Immune System

Before we talk about the problems associated with a compromised immune system, I think it would be helpful if I gave you some background on the nature of the immune system itself.

The immune system is what enables the human body to defend itself against a large number of dangerous organisms and substances. These include germs, viruses, and other microscopic organisms such as parasitic larvae, various fungi, and toxic substances and proteins that originate within our own bodies.

The immune system is located primarily in the lymphatic system, which consists of the lymph nodes, the tonsils, the spleen, and the thymus. The immune system's effectiveness depends on its ability to recognize a threat and to develop antibodies that are designed to attack that specific threat (germ, virus, protein, etc.).

The potential number of antibodies is in the millions, and their effectiveness in attacking invading organisms is astonishing. Most antibodies are developed in response to infection by diseases such as chicken pox (varicella) or influenza. Antibodies against specific diseases can also be deliberately induced by a process called *immunization*. Immunization allows people to be protected against such diseases as polio, measles, mumps, and diphtheria. Unfortunately, there are many diseases, particularly viral diseases, for which no immunization yet exists.

We encounter countless pathogenic organisms beginning early in life, and our bodies develop specific antibodies to these organisms without any conscious effort on our part. We are often only mildly ill, or not recognizably ill at all, but our immune systems develop antibodies against these organisms anyway. The immune system is enormously versatile in the number and variety of antibodies it can produce.

There are times when this very versatility seems to be inappropriate though, causing some people to develop antibodies against substances produced by their own bodies. These antibodies cause a class of disorders known as *auto-immune diseases*. Rheumatoid arthritis is one of these, for example. *Allergies* are also auto-immune disorders. Why our bodies attack harmless substances like rose pollen[1] or cat

---

1 pollen: polen *m*

hair isn't well understood, but the immune system is definitely the culprit[1].

AIDS also involves the immune system. AIDS (A-I-D-S) stands for Acquired Immuno-Deficiency Syndrome. We don't know exactly how this disease causes such disastrous results, but we do know that victims' immune systems lose the capacity to effectively counteract[2] invading organisms. Victims then fall prey to[3] unusual infections, and are quite susceptible to infections that healthy people routinely withstand[4].

---

1 culprit: la causa, el elemento responsable
2 counteract: contrarrestar
3 fall prey to: sucumbir a
4 to withstand: aguantar, resistir

Simultaneous Lesson 2 (2B)

Directions: Shadow.

(110 WPM)

Las enfermedades infecciosas

Toda enfermedad originada por bacterias o por cualquier otro tipo de microorganismo se considera infecciosa. A diferencia de enfermedades como la diabetes o el cáncer, los agentes que causan las enfermedades infecciosas o contagiosas pueden transmitirse de la persona enferma a la sana. Frecuentemente la enfermedad se transmite de una persona a otra por contacto directo. En otros casos, se vale de distintos medios, tales como los mosquitos o algún material infectado. En este último caso el contagio puede ocurrir a través de heridas de la piel o de las membranas mucosas que entran en contacto con el vector infectante. La fiebre escarlatina, la tuberculosis y la fiebre amarilla son ejemplos de enfermedades infecciosas.

Cuando una persona contrae una enfermedad transmisible, se presupone dos premisas: uno, el germen debe entrar en contacto con el cuerpo; y dos, el cuerpo debe hallarse en tales condiciones que permita la invasión del microorganismo y la producción de sus lesiones o toxinas características. Si el microorganismo logra penetrar en un sujeto sensible, se desencadena una verdadera lucha entre invasor e invadido; el individuo responde con mecanismos diversos para destruir al microorganismo invasor y sus toxinas.

La inflamación es uno de los medios de defensa natural del organismo contra las infecciones y otras lesiones. En torno a la zona afectada se produce dolor, calor, rubor e hinchazón. Ello se debe a un mayor aflujo de sangre al punto lesionado; la circulación se hace más lenta, por lo que la sangre se estanca alrededor de la lesión. A consecuencia de esto, se produce una exudación de plasma y un escape de células sanguíneas de los pequeños vasos a los tejidos circundantes, dando lugar a la hinchazón.

Los agentes causales de las enfermedades contagiosas incluyen las bacterias, los virus, los parásitos animales, y los hongos. Las bacterias existen por todas partes. En un ambiente favorable a su desarrollo, una sola bacteria es capaz de multiplicarse en cientos de millones en un periodo de 24 horas. Los desinfectantes y la esterilización son métodos muy eficaces en el control de las bacterias. Los virus son los más pequeños y misteriosos de todos los microorganismos patógenos. Sólo pueden reproducirse en el interior de la célula, y generalmente la afectan adversamente de dos formas: o estimulan un crecimiento

anormal, o desintegran la célula misma. Los hongos son plantas de estructura simple, algunos de los cuales pueden parasitar al hombre y originar enfermedades. En general atacan la piel, el cabello, y las uñas, produciendo lesiones superficiales. Con menor frecuencia los hongos producen infecciones profundas o generales.

Directions: Interpret into Spanish

(110 WPM)

Infectious Diseases

We'll need to do some lab work before we can be certain, but I'm reasonably sure your symptoms are due to an infectious disease of some sort.

Infectious diseases are, by definition, caused by the invasion of the body by micro-organisms that become established and reproduce themselves in the body. The symptoms of such diseases are the result both of toxic materials produced by those micro-organisms and of the immune system's response to the infection. The classical symptoms of infection are: *Tumor* (swelling), *Rubor* (redness), *Calor* (heat), and *Dolor* (pain). These four characteristic signs are collectively referred to as *inflammation*. Drugs used to combat inflammation—*anti-inflammatories*—may thus interfere with the body's defense mechanisms, and must be used with caution. That's why I don't want to prescribe anything for your inflammation until I know just what we're dealing with.

When invaded by almost any noxious organism, one of the body's most common reactions is to develop a temperature higher than the "normal" one of 98.6 degrees Fahrenheit (37 degrees Celsius). The victim is then said to have a fever; the body is demonstrating the *calor* I talked about earlier. The body may also demonstrate *dolor* in the form of muscle or head aches like the ones you've been experiencing. *Rubor* may manifest itself as a flushing of the skin. *Tumor* is often too diffuse to notice unless the infection is on or just under the skin. Your condition, for instance, does not include any readily apparent *tumor*.

It isn't always a good idea to interfere with the body's natural defenses by taking drugs that tend to suppress either fever or pain. We may inadvertently interfere with our body's ability to counteract the infection. Such powerful anti-inflammatory drugs as cortisone, for example, may allow certain infections to increase in severity. Tuberculosis is one such infection. I'm quite certain, by the way, that you do **not** have tuberculosis, but until we know exactly what you **do** have, I want to stay away from anti-inflammatories.

In the mean time, I wouldn't worry too much about the slight fever you're running. Fever itself is an effective tool in fighting infection. You might be interested in an experiment done with lizards to

---

demonstrate that point. Lizards are cold-blooded animals[1] that take on the temperature of their surroundings. A cage full of lizards was deliberately infected with a common germ. Then the cage was divided by a barrier, and the population of lizards was divided into two separate groups, one in each half of the cage. An infrared lamp[2] and some shades were put over the cage in such a way that the lizards in one group could choose to bask[3] in the warmth of the lamp or to stay in the shade, while the lizards in the other group had no choice but to remain in the shade. The lizards in the first group stayed in the heated part of their enclosure and increased their body temperature. Almost all of those lizards survived. The lizards in the second group, who were unable to heat themselves, were much more susceptible to the infection, and most of them died. Although there are many important differences between humans and reptiles, most doctors agree that the lizard experiment has significance in human medicine.

Although I believe your condition to be infectious, I doubt—based on the continuing good health of the rest of your family—that it is highly *contagious*. You see, all contagious diseases are also infectious, but not all infectious diseases are contagious. The difference is in how the disease is transmitted. If the disease can easily be transmitted from one person to another, like the "Black Death" (bubonic plague) of the middle ages, the disease is contagious. If the disease does not transmit easily to another person, then it is simply infectious. Tetanus is an example of an infectious disease that is not contagious. But don't worry, I'm sure you don't have tetanus either.

One of the things we need to find out through lab tests is whether your infection is viral or bacterial. The difference between viruses and germs is primarily the capacity for germs to live freely and reproduce on their own, whereas viruses require a living cell for their replication. The virus particle (much smaller than any germ) has to invade a living cell, capture the cell's genetic equipment, and force the cell to propagate the virus. Only antibodies can penetrate the cell and destroy the virus without also destroying the cell. That's why viral infections are so much harder to treat than bacterial infections.

Take this form to the lab next door, and we'll get started on the necessary testing.

---

1 cold-blooded animal: animal de sangre fría
2 infrared lamp: lámpara infrarroja
3 to bask: disfrutar

Simultaneous Lesson 3 (2B)

Directions: Shadow.

(110 WPM)

Trastornos ortopédicos

La ortopedia es la especialidad médica que trata de la corrección quirúrgica y mecánica de las deformidades corporales, especialmente del esqueleto: la columna vertebral, las coyunturas, y las extremidades. Estas deformidades pueden originarse en problemas congénitos, traumatismo o degeneración cumulativa. Sea cual fuere la causa del trastorno, puede provocar grandes estragos en la vida del paciente, especialmente cuando se trata de un problema de la espina dorsal.

La columna vertebral se compone de las vértebras cervicales, dorsales y lumbares, así como el sacro y el cóccix. Una vértebra típicamente consta de un cuerpo sólido ventral y un arco dorsal neural, que, con dicho cuerpo, forma el foramen o agujero vertebral. La sucesión de forámenes sirve de acomodo y protección a la médula espinal, importantísimo centro nervioso del cual parten, a través de salidas en las vértebras, los pares de nervios que se distribuyen por todo el cuerpo. Entre las vértebras, separando una de otra, existen unos cartílagos fibrosos llamados discos intervertebrales, cuya misión consiste en servir de almohadilla y facilitar los movimientos vertebrales.

Desde que el hombre se irguió de la posición encorvada de sus antepasados, ha padecido dolor de espalda, particularmente en la región lumbar baja. La frecuencia del trastorno aumenta con la edad, acabando por afectar al 50% de las personas mayores de 60 años. En individuos de la tercera edad, el dolor de espalda crónico muchas veces es resultado de la artritis. Otras causas del dolor en la región lumbar baja incluyen la rotura de un disco intervertebral; una fractura, infección o tumor de la espalda o de la pelvis; la rotura traumática o desgarro de los músculos en la región dorsal; los defectos congénitos ligeros de la columna lumbar baja y sacra alta; el deslizamiento hacia adelante de una vértebra; y la tensión de la espalda por estiramiento de los músculos abdominales a consecuencia de obesidad o embarazo.

Ahora bien, el dolor de espalda no siempre surge de un trastorno musculoesquelético; también puede ser provocado por tuberculosis, una infección de las vías urinarias, o mal de la vesícula. Otros síntomas que comúnmente se atribuyen a los huesos y a las coyunturas pueden en realidad ser producto de un problema de los

nervios. Por ejemplo, si el paciente se queja de dolor, entumecimiento y hormigueo de la mano, es posible que padezca síndrome del túnel carpiano. Este síndrome resulta de la compresión del nervio mediano en la superficie palmar de la muñeca, entre los tendones longitudinales de los músculos del antebrazo que flexionan la mano y el ligamento transverso superficial del carpo. Para estar seguro, siempre es recomendable consultar con un profesional médico para obtener un diagnóstico confiable.

Directions: Interpret into Spanish

(130 WPM)

Carpal Tunnel Syndrome

What you have, Mrs. Madrugada, is a fairly mild case of carpal tunnel syndrome. The carpal tunnel is the space in the wrist that lies on the volar (that is, toward the palm) side between the ends of the radius and the ulna, the two bones inside your forearm. All the nerves and blood vessels, and many of the tendons entering the hand pass through this space. The carpal tunnel is always a tight fit[1] for all its contents, but it is especially tight in certain people, of whom, I'm afraid, you are one. When these people have occupations that require their wrists to flex frequently, as happens in many office jobs like yours, irritation to the contents of the carpal tunnel results. The most common source of this irritation is the median nerve, one of the three nerves entering the hand. The other two are the ulnar and the radial nerves, but they are rarely affected.

I'm going to give you a prescription for something to reduce the inflammation of your carpal tunnel. Try not to do any typing at all for the next couple of days, and after that, keep the wrist flexing to a minimum.

Slipped or Herniated Intervertebral Disks

(110 WPM)

Let me describe for you in general terms what having a "slipped disk" really means. The intervertebral disks are made of cartilage, the tough but flexible stuff you call *gristle*[2] when you run into it in meat. These disks are found between each pair of vertebrae in the normal human spine. There are seven cervical vertebrae (those in the neck), twelve thoracic vertebrae (those in the upper back), and five lumbar vertebrae (those in the lower back). (Interestingly, even the giraffe, with its enormously long neck, has only seven cervical vertebrae. Each vertebra is about a foot long, though.)

Each disk has a rim[3] of thick, tough cartilage, with a much softer liquid center. The primary function of the disk is to cushion[4] the impact of your feet hitting the ground. If it weren't for that cushioning effect, each step would make you feel like a hammer had struck the

1 a tight fit: viene muy estrecho
2 gristle: ternilla
3 rim: borde *m*
4 to cushion: amortiguar

base of your skull. Under certain circumstances, and perhaps with some predisposing anatomic conditions, the disk splits, or *herniates*, and the liquid center is squeezed out[1] like tooth paste being squeezed out of a tube. This herniation usually causes the center or *nucleus pulposis* to move backward into the spinal canal and to put pressure on a spinal nerve, or on the spinal cord itself, depending on which level of the spine is involved.

The herniation of a disk usually happens in the lumbar area, or, less frequently, in the cervical area. It rarely happens in the thoracic area, both because the ribs tend to splint the spine, and because both the cervical and the lumbar spinal segments are inherently more mobile. The herniation is usually caused by a violent flexing, or rotational movement of the spine. The problem is more common in men like yourself in their forties and fifties, though there are exceptions to this.

Treatment for a herniated disk can often be conservative, with postural restrictions imposed by a brace, or belt, together with selective muscle strengthening. This allows the squeezed-out material to return to its original location, and alleviates the nerve pressure, which is the source of most of the pain and weakness. If this method fails, or if the injury is obviously too severe for conservative techniques, surgery may be required. I'm afraid, in your case, that surgery will, in fact, be required.

The surgery usually performed—the surgery I'm going to recommend to you—is called a *laminectomy*. The lamina is the portion of the spinal bone that forms most of the bony protection of the spinal canal on the back side of the spine. This bone is chiseled[2] away on the side where MRI or CAT scans indicate the herniation to be, and the protruding disk material is snipped[3] out.

If your injury were substantially more serious, a more drastic procedure called a *fusion* would be required. A fusion entails gouging out a trench[4] along two or three spinal bones, filling the trench with bone chips (usually obtained from the patient's hip), and then placing the patient in a body cast for many weeks. This is not a procedure to be lightly undertaken—you should thank your lucky stars[5] you won't have to undergo it.

---

1 to squeeze out: exprimir
2 to chisel: escoplear, cincelar
3 to snip: tijeretear
4 trench: trinchera, foso
5 thank your lucky stars: dar gracias a Dios

Simultaneous Lesson 4 (3A)

Directions: Shadow.

(100 WPM)

La artritis

La artritis es, sencillamente, la inflamación de las articulaciones. Lo que no es tan sencillo es la tipificación de las distintas enfermedades articulares, las cuales tienen etiologías y tratamientos bastante diferenciados. El dolor de las coyunturas es un problema crónico en los seres humanos al cual se ha buscado remedio desde tiempos inmemoriales. Con la evolución de la ciencia moderna de la medicina, se ha mejorado nuestra comprensión de este trastorno y, por tanto, los métodos disponibles para aliviarlo.

Hace tan solo cuarenta años, la ciencia médica admitía dos categorías principales para los tipos más comunes de artritis: artritis inflamatoria (ahora llamada artritis reumatoide) y artritis hipertrófica o enfermedad articular degenerativa (hoy en día denominada osteoartritis), además de unos cuantos procesos de medicina general como la gota y la artritis bacteriana. No obstante, en la actualidad se reconocen más de cien procesos específicamente identificables. Un mismo paciente puede sufrir distintas clases de artritis en articulaciones distintas, y una misma articulación puede comenzar con una de ellas y adquirir posteriormente la otra.

Normalmente, los extremos de los huesos de las articulaciones están recubiertos por una capa dura y lisa de cartílago denominada cartílago articular. Uniendo los dos huesos y llenando la cavidad comprendida entre ellos existe un tejido recio y fibroso llamado cápsula, tapizada por una membrana, la membrana sinovial, que segrega el líquido lubrificante de la articulación. En la artritis se afectan alguna o todas estas estructuras, lo que limita la libre movilidad articular. Una radiografía de una articulación con artritis reumatoidea revela que el cartílago está ulcerado, la cavidad articular reducida, y la membrana sinovial inflamada. Por otro lado, en la articulación osteoartrítica se ve que la terminación de los huesos está deformada y el cartílago desgastado, y hay evidencia de derrame del líquido sinovial.

El tratamiento de las enfermedades articulares, sea cual fuere el diagnóstico, suele incluir medicamentos específicos o inespecíficos y, al mismo tiempo, diversas técnicas medicoquirúrgicas que contribuyen en grado variable a aliviar las molestias de articulaciones, tendones y músculos. Incluyen medidas como reposo, calor, inmovilización, ejercicio, movimientos activos o pasivos, soportes elásticos, masaje, tracción, hidroterapia, bastones, muletas, andaderas, ultrasonido, psicoterapia, acupuntura y cirugía ortopédica reconstructora.

Nos queda todavía mucho por aprender, y debemos desarrollar tratamientos aún mejores, pero los adelantos logrados durante los últimos cuarenta años resultan impresionantes y justifican un cierto optimismo.

Directions: Interpret into Spanish

(110 WPM)

Arthritis

I think you already know, Mr. Jaramillo, that you're suffering from arthritis. Unfortunately, that in itself doesn't give you much useful information.

Arthritis is one of the most abused, misused, and misunderstood terms in medicine. Its literal meaning is simply "inflamed joint." An acceptable collective term for the various conditions commonly identified as arthritis is the *arthritides*. The corresponding medical specialty is *rheumatology*. Arthritis is actually a very complex problem; there are many different diseases that include inflamed joints among their symptoms. Most medical texts include complicated charts to help doctors distinguish among the many forms of arthritis.

The most common form, one suffered by nearly all mature human beings, including you, Mr. Jaramillo, is *degenerative arthritis*, also known as *hypertrophic*, or *wear-and-tear*[1] arthritis. This is the type of arthritis that causes lumpy[2] finger joints and joint pain after heavy use. Very few people live to any considerable age without suffering from at least some degree of this disorder. A close relative is *traumatic arthritis*, which occurs when a joint is severely injured and is unable to heal completely. This is common among former athletes.

Perhaps the most serious form of arthritis, one that, thankfully, you do not suffer from, is *rheumatoid arthritis*, which is a member of a class of diseases referred to as *collagen diseases*. Collagen is the "glue" that holds our bodies together. Collagen is found between the cells of many organs and structures. It is the major component of ligaments, tendons, and joint structures, and contributes heavily to the structure of bone. For reasons that are not well understood, all the collagen in the body can be affected by inflammatory changes that are believed to represent inappropriate immune responses. A wide variety of body structures other than joints can be involved. Rheumatoid arthritis itself can be seriously disabling because of the severe joint damage it can inflict. Whenever you see a wheel-chair-bound person with swollen and deformed joints, you can be reasonably sure that that person is a victim of rheumatoid arthritis.

1 wear and tear: desgaste
2 lumpy: abultado

When cortisone was discovered in 1948, many people believed that a cure for rheumatoid arthritis had been found. Unfortunately, that turned out not to be the case. While cortisone is an extremely useful substance in the treatment of all the collagen disorders, it doesn't cure any of them.

Many different germs can invade joints and produce severe inflammation that can be painful and, occasionally, even lead to permanent joint damage. This is called *infectious*, or *bacterial* arthritis. The germ that causes gonorrhea is particularly prone to cause this condition. Another common cause of bacterial arthritis is the germ that causes tuberculosis.

Simultaneous Lesson 5 (3A)

Directions: Shadow.

(115 WPM)

La hipertensión

La tensión arterial (TA) es la presión ejercida por la sangre sobre las paredes de los vasos por los cuales circula. La presión sanguínea en las arterias ha de mantenerse a un nivel suficientemente alto para que la sangre circule por ellas, pase después por los capilares y regrese al corazón por las venas. No obstante, también debe fluctuar para atender a las diferentes necesidades de sangre de los tejidos cuando aumenta la actividad. La tensión arterial es la resultante de dos fuerzas opuestas: una que impulsa la sangre hacia adelante en los vasos y otra que resiste esta corriente.

Hoy en día, la mayoría de los reconocimientos médicos incluyen la medición de la tensión arterial. Para ello se emplea un aparato llamado esfigmomanómetro. La tensión se mide generalmente en la arteria humeral, la más grande del brazo. Se toma la tensión envolviendo el brazo con el manguito e inflando el saco hermético de goma que lleva dentro hasta que cese el latido de la arteria. Luego se coloca el estetoscopio sobre la arteria radial, debajo de la línea de flexión del codo, y se deja salir el aire lentamente del saco de goma, lo que permite a la sangre circular nuevamente a través de la arteria humeral. En ese momento se oye un latido bien claro con el estetoscopio. La altura de la presión a la cual se percibe, leída en la escala que hay junto a la columna de mercurio, se conoce con el nombre de presión sistólica, porque corresponde a la sístole cardiaca o contracción ventricular. Mientras el observador continúa desinflando lentamente el aire contenido en la bolsa de goma, sigue oyendo el mismo sonido a cada contracción cardiaca. Al ir recobrando la arteria su calibre normal, el sonido se desvanece hasta extinguirse y el nivel de la columna de mercurio en ese momento se denomina presión diastólica, por corresponder a la fase diastólica o relajada del trabajo del corazón.

La alta presión sanguínea o hipertensión arterial es un proceso que en la mayoría de los casos cursa en silencio. Si la condición sigue sin tratamiento, puede dar lugar a la aparición de una variedad de trastornos cardiacos. Es un hecho conocido que la incidencia de infarto de miocardio es hasta tres veces mayor en la población hipertensa que en la que tiene cifras de TA normales.

Existen evidencias que parecen indicar que la posibilidad de desarrollar hipertensión es mayor en aquellas profesiones en las que el trabajador se ve sometido a un mayor estrés, y también en los estratos sociales de bajos ingresos y bajos niveles de escolaridad. La dieta también facilita una elevación de las cifras tensionales, fundamentalmente a través de su contenido en calorías, sal y grasas.

Directions: Interpret into Spanish.

(100 WPM)

Hypertension

Hypertension may well be the most significant health problem in the industrialized world. Its causes are not completely understood, but they certainly include genetic predisposition, diet, obesity, general health habits, and severe social pressures. Blood pressure is commonly expressed as a ratio of the *systolic* pressure to the *diastolic* pressure—for example, 135 over 80. In this case, 135 is the systolic pressure, and 80 is the diastolic pressure. The terms *systolic* and *diastolic* describe the heart's condition as it contracts in *systole* and relaxes in *diastole*.

The instrument used to determine blood pressure is the *sphygmomanometer*. It consists of an inflatable cuff[1] attached to either a glass column filled with mercury or to a dial barometer[2]. The cuff is inflated with sufficient pressure to block the major artery in the arm. The pressure within the cuff is slowly released as the operator listens with a stethoscope placed where the artery passes close to the surface on the inside of the elbow. The first heart beat able to squeeze blood past the obstruction of the cuff produces an audible "thump[3]" The reading on the barometer is noted: that value is the systolic pressure. As long as the cuff deforms the artery, the operator continues to hear a thump with each heart beat. When the thump disappears, the value on the barometer is again noted: that value is the diastolic pressure. To measure the precise pressure within the brachial artery, the artery would have to be pierced with a needle, and the blood itself would have to be forced into a pressure measuring device of some kind. Because this would be both painful and dangerous, the present method was devised. Its measurements are directly and constantly related to the actual pressure within the artery.

To deliver blood to the body's tissues, the heart has to pump it through the arteries. The walls of the arteries are elastic and keep the blood within them under sufficient pressure to move it along to the tissues. When these arterial walls lose their elasticity through age or through thickening due to the deposition of fatty material[4] called *atheromatous*

1 cuff: manguito, abrazadera
2 dial barometer: barómetro en forma de reloj, barómetro de cuadrante
3 thump: golpe *m*, zas *m*
4 fatty material: material grasoso

plaque, the heart has to work harder to deliver the blood. This is the underlying physics behind hardening of the arteries, and the resulting elevation of blood pressure.

Many problems are associated with high blood pressure. They include damage to the heart, damage to the brain, damage to the kidneys, and damage to other organs such as muscles, eyes, and almost any other organ you can think of. All of these problems combine to become a major cause of disability and death.

There is no single ideal blood pressure. In general though, the lower your blood pressure the better, provided you are otherwise healthy and able to function normally.

In general, men's blood pressure is higher than women's, and everyone's blood pressure tends to increase with age. What blood pressure reading a doctor will consider indicative of a problem requiring treatment therefore depends to some extent on the patient's sex and age and on other factors. Under some circumstances, some doctors might consider a blood pressure reading[1] as low as 140/90 to be hypertensive. Other authorities might, under other circumstances, consider the lower threshold[2] of hypertension to be as high as 200/110.

Often, hypertension can be successfully treated by lifestyle changes alone. Losing weight, lowering salt intake[3], instituting a program of regular aerobic exercise[4], reducing or eliminating smoking, reducing excessive alcohol consumption—these are all steps that tend to lower blood pressure.

If a patient's elevated blood pressure does not respond to lifestyle changes alone, or if the patient is unable or unwilling to make the recommended changes, treatment with antihypertensive drugs may be necessary.

1 reading: lectura, indicación
2 threshold: umbral
3 salt intake: consumo de sal
4 aerobic exercise: ejercicio aeróbico

Simultaneous Lesson 6 (3A)

Directions: Shadow.

(110 WPM)

Fármacos antidepresivos

La depresión es una enfermedad muy común en la sociedad moderna. Este trastorno se caracteriza por la disminución del tono afectivo, la tristeza y la melancolía. Casi uno de cada cuatro individuos sufre alguna forma de alteración afectiva durante su vida. Los adolescentes frecuentemente sufren cambios del estado de ánimo, pero la reciente ola de suicidios en este sector de la población ha provocado gran preocupación. La tensión premenstrual es una causa común de depresión, y entre las mujeres de edad madura, la misma puede ser un síntoma de la menopausia. Entre los hombres, la depresión puede acompañar el proceso de envejecimiento, a medida que disminuyen la potencia sexual y la capacidad física.

Cualquier persona puede experimentar un episodio de melancolía temporal como reacción al duelo, la separación marital, la desilución amorosa o los reveses financieros. Las alteraciones del ánimo son parte de la vida diaria, pero generalmente son transitorias, así que no hay necesidad de intervenir con tratamientos farmacológicos. Solamente cuando la depresión persiste mucho más allá del impacto esperado de un acontecimiento vital difícil o impide que el paciente lleve una vida normal, es menester acudir a soluciones más drásticas como lo son los fármacos, la hospitalización y la terapia electroconvulsiva.

La mayor parte de los pacientes que sufren depresión reciben tratamiento como pacientes externos. En un principio, el paciente acude al consultorio una o dos veces a la semana para recibir apoyo moral y para que el médico vigile su progreso. Muchos pacientes están confundidos y desmoralizados por las implicaciones de sufrir un trastorno mental, particularmente cuando afecta su capacidad para el trabajo, por lo que es muy importante explicar al enfermo, a sus familiares, y quizá a su patrón que la depresión es una enfermedad médica que desaparece espontáneamente y que generalmente tiene buen pronóstico.

Hoy en día los médicos disponen de una amplia gama de medicamentos antidepresivos aptos para el tratamiento de cualquier tipo de depresión. Uno de ellos es el clorhidrato de fluoxetina, vendido bajo el nombre comercial de Prozac, que ha recibido mucha atención periodística en tiempos recientes. Está indicado para el tratamiento

de pacientes que padecen varios de los siguientes síntomas: cambios en el apetito, cambios en el sueño, agitación o retardo psicomotor, falta de interés en las actividades habituales o disminución en la respuesta sexual, cansancio, sentimiento de culpa o de autodesvalorización, lentitud en el pensamiento o trastornos de la concentración, intento o ideas suicidas.

Es indispensable que el médico le explique al paciente los efectos secundarios del fármaco antidepresivo. Los efectos más comunes del Prozac, por ejemplo, son: síntomas asociados con el sistema nervioso, incluyendo ansiedad, nerviosismo e insomnio; somnolencia y fatiga o astenia; temblores; transpiración; molestias gastrointestinales, incluyendo anorexia, náuseas y diarrea; y mareos o inestabilidad, sedación y disminución de la libido.

Directions: Interpret into Spanish.

(125 WPM)

Prozac Discussion

I'd like to talk to you today, Mr. Guillermos, a little bit about your general condition and then, specifically, about the depression you've been feeling.

First of all, Mr. Guillermos, your general condition is really quite good, all things considered. The laminectomy Dr. Elsworth performed on you in March to alleviate some of your back problems went very well, as has your recovery from that procedure. There's no physical reason why you shouldn't be able to go back to work in another six to eight weeks.

It's perfectly understandable and even expected, though, that you're feeling a little depressed, a little "down in the dumps[1]," as they say. You haven't been able to work since last year, you've suffered a consequent loss of income, actual pain from your injury, occasional inability to perform your, shall we say, marital duties[2], enforced idleness. All these things can lead to a lowered sense of self esteem[3] and to what we call clinical depression.

This depression is normal, and there's every reason to believe it will pass when you're back at work and feeling a little better about yourself. Nevertheless, this depression represents a real problem for you right now, and it is, I'm happy to tell you, treatable.

What I want to do, Mr. Guillermos, is prescribe an antidepressant drug for you called Prozac. *Prozac* is actually a trade name for the drug fluoxetine hydrochloride, but, unless you become a doctor or a medical interpreter, I'm sure you'll never need to know that. There are some important things you do need to know about Prozac before I start you on it, though.

As I said, Prozac is an antidepressant. That means that its purpose is to fight off your depression, to make you feel better and make you better able to function on a day-to-day basis. Prozac is indicated for patients like yourself who suffer a major depressive episode. A major depressive episode is a strong sense of depression that occurs daily or

---

1 to be down in the dumps: tener murria
2 to perform one's marital duties: cumplir con la mujer, cumplir sus obligaciones matrimoniales
3 self esteem: autoestima, amor propio

almost daily for a period of two weeks or longer and is characterized by at least four of the following eight symptoms:

1. a change in appetite

2. a change in sleep patterns

3. psychomotor agitation or retardation

4. a loss of interest in usual activities or a decrease in sex drive

5. increased fatigue

6. feelings of guilt or worthlessness

7. slowed thinking or impaired concentration, or

8. a suicide attempt or suicidal ideation

Now I believe you've described at least five or six of those symptoms to me in our recent meetings, Mr. Guillermos, so I think you are definitely a candidate to be helped by Prozac.

I'm going to start you out on a relatively modest dosage, 20 mg. a day, taken every morning. It doesn't matter whether you take your capsule before or after breakfast, or even whether or not you have breakfast—your body's ability to metabolize Prozac is largely unaffected by food.

I want to caution you, Mr. Guillermos, that you're not going to feel any dramatic change in your mood right away. You may not feel any change at all immediately. Given a steady dosage, fluoxetine, Prozac that is, continues to build up in your blood stream for four to five weeks. That means that we won't actually have achieved the concentration of the drug in your body that we're looking for until you've been taking it for that long. You should therefore expect to experience a very gradual decrease in your feelings of depression and the symptoms associated with that depression. If we haven't achieved significant results within five weeks, we may then want to increase your dosage a little, but please be patient.

Although Prozac is generally quite safe, there are a few things you need to look out for and report to me if they occur.

A few Prozac patients—about 4%—experience a skin rash. While the rash itself is not terribly troubling, and can often be treated without discontinuing Prozac, there is a small but real chance that such a rash can be accompanied by serious lung, liver, or kidney problems. Therefore, if you break out in any sort of skin rash after you start on the drug, contact me immediately.

Five to 10% of Prozac patients report some degree of anxiety, nervousness, or insomnia. Some experience an alteration in their appetite that may result either in weight loss or weight gain. A very small number—0.2%—experience seizures.

For the first week or so after you start on Prozac, don't drive your car or operate any kind of heavy or dangerous equipment. Most people find that Prozac does not impair their ability to perform such tasks, but in a few cases judgment and motor skills may be affected. Wait until you're used to the drug and reasonably sure your judgment and motor skills are not impaired.

Other rare but possible side effects include drowsiness, fatigue, sweating, nausea, diarrhea, dizziness, lightheadedness, and abnormal dreams. If you experience any of these, contact this office right away.

Here's your prescription, Mr. Guillermos. Good luck.

Simultaneous Lesson 7 (3B)

Directions: Shadow

(120 WPM)

Mechanized Harvesting in the Fields of California

Farmers of 100 years ago would not believe their eyes if they witnessed the harvesting of vegetables in the fields of California today. Rather than painstakingly cultivating small patches by hand with primitive implements such as hoes and horse-drawn plows, modern farmers raise crops on vast tracts of land using the latest technology. Machines have not replaced people in agriculture, but the role of people has changed dramatically. No longer do we see the farmer and his family toiling in the fields, accompanied by a few hired hands. The "farmer" of today is likely to be a corporation consisting of men and women in business suits, while out in the fields, working alongside the machines, are highly skilled crews of employees, most of them Mexican immigrants.

Take the harvesting of cauliflower, for example. A huge field covering several acres is prepared and planted using sleek tractors pulling a variety of specialized implements that till the soil, shape it into furrows and raised beds, and drop in seeds at perfect intervals. The seedlings are watered by modern irrigation equipment at times specified by trained experts. Fertilizers and pesticides are applied using the latest scientific methods, and crews come through periodically to weed the crop. When the company expert decides it's time to harvest, large machines are hauled to the field. The harvesting crews are bused in to work in teams, cutting the cauliflowers, wrapping them in plastic, and packing them in boxes on a veritable assembly line right out in the field. As the boxes are packed, they are loaded onto a truck moving along with the machine. When the truck is full, it takes the boxes to the warehouse, where they will be kept in coolers until they are shipped to market.

All this mechanization has not, unfortunately, eliminated the occupational injuries that have always plagued farmworkers: cut fingers, aching backs, and broken bones due to a variety of accidents. Farming corporations generally provide medical insurance for their employees, and by law they must have workers' compensation insurance. But even with all the amenities of modern medicine, working in the fields is still an arduous and sometimes hazardous job.

Directions: Interpret into English.

(140 WPM)

Informe de Accidente

Sufrí un accidente de trabajo el día 23 de abril de este año. Trabajo para la compañía Fresh Pak, cortando y empacando coliflor. Ese día estaba lloviendo cuando llegamos al campo, como a las seis de la mañana. Había mucho lodo por todas partes, y aunque llevábamos botas y pantalones de hule, pronto nos mojamos. Era muy difícil andar, porque el lodo se pegaba a las botas y al levantar el pie para dar un paso, parecía que pesaba varios kilos.

Yo iba siguiendo la máquina de empaque, cortando coliflor y aventándola a la máquina para ser empacada. Al agacharme y levantarme tan seguido, se me desguanzó la cintura y empezó a dolerme. Además, las piernas se cansaron porque era tan trabajoso caminar en el lodo y mantener el paso de la máquina. Ya para las nueve y media, cuando tomamos el primer descanso, estaba cansadísimo, y sentía un ardor en la cintura. Pero, pues, ni modo[1], tengo que trabajar para mantener a la familia, así que no le dije nada al mayordomo[2].

Después del descanso de quince minutos, empezamos de nuevo. A mí me tocó subir a la máquina y empacar, pues cambiamos de trabajo a cada rato. Me alegré de no tener que seguir cortando, porque me molestaba mucho la cintura. Pero al subirme a la máquina—bueno, es que hay una plataforma donde se para uno delante de la banda, y la máquina tiene dos alas que se doblan y se levantan para hacerla más chica, y así la pueden remolcar de un campo a otro. Total, que al subirme al ala izquierda de la máquina, se desconectó, o no sé qué pasó, pero de repente el ala bajó y me caí. Traté de agarrarme de algo para no caerme, pero no pude. Me caí de pie, pero todavía se balanceaba el ala, y por poco me pega en la cabeza. La esquivé, pero como estaba tan lodoso, me resbalé y quedé boca arriba con un pie estirado adelante y el otro atrás. Además, caí sobre dos surcos, lo que me torció la espalda.

Y para colmo de desgracias, cuando vieron lo que me había pasado, de repente pararon la máquina y se me cayeron encima un montón de cajas que estaban en la banda. Una de ellas me pegó en la rodilla izquierda y quebró el hueso, y otra me quebró el tobillo derecho. Me

---

1 ni modo: I have no choice
2 mayordomo: foreman

parece que otra caja me pegó en la cabeza también, porque me desmayé. Cuando volví en mí, estaba en la ambulancia. Me llevaron al hospital, y allí me sacaron radiografías y luego me enyesaron las dos piernas. Me mandaron a casa, pero estaba completamente incapacitado. No podía andar sin las muletas, pero los brazos me dolían también porque estaba todo golpeado. Pasé una semana con todo el cuerpo adolorido, tomando pastillas para el dolor como quien come caramelos[1]. Pero al rato se calmó el dolor y empecé a caminar un poco. El doctor me paró del trabajo[2] durante seis semanas, pero luego me dio de alta y regresé al trabajo.

Ahora, a seis meses del accidente, todavía me molestan la rodilla y el tobillo, especialmente en el trabajo cuando tengo que caminar mucho en el campo, siguiendo la máquina y caminando entre surcos. Y cuando ando cortando, me duele mucho la cintura. Cuando llego del trabajo, estoy tan cansado y adolorido que apenas puedo caminar. Me baño y me acuesto, a veces ni como, nomás me echo en la cama y ya. Al otro día me siento un poco mejor, pero al llegar al trabajo, todo empieza de nuevo. Así estoy desde hace unos cuatro meses, sin mejora. He ido con el quiropráctico, pero no me alivia nada. Espero que alguien me pueda ayudar, porque necesito trabajar para mantener a la familia, no tengo otro remedio.

1 como quien come caramelos: like they were candy
2 me paró del trabajo: took me off work, disabled me

Simultaneous Lesson 8 (3B)

Directions: Shadow

(115 WPM)

Physical Changes During Pregnancy

Women go through many emotional and physical changes during the different stages of pregnancy. The most common signs of early pregnancy are the cessation of menstruation, accompanied by nausea and vomiting (especially in the morning), fatigue, increased frequency of urination, and swollen and tender breasts. All of these symptoms are caused by the hormonal changes that the body undergoes as it prepares to sustain and nurture the new life that is forming in the uterus. As the pregnancy progresses from the first to the second trimester, the expansion of the uterus causes crowding of the digestive organs, often resulting in constipation, hemorrhoids, and heartburn. Many women begin to notice changes in their skin: stretch marks on the abdomen and breasts, a dark line extending from the navel to the genital area, and sometimes brown blotches on the face. They may also experience varicose veins, calf cramps, edema or swelling of the hands and feet, and backache.

Maintaining good posture helps reduce the aches and pains associated with pregnancy, as well as the breathing problems. Pregnant women should make sure they get plenty of exercise to maintain good health and prepare for the rigors of childbirth, although strenuous activity should be avoided in the final trimester. It is very important for women to watch what they eat during pregnancy, as vitamin and mineral deficiencies can impede proper fetal development and can also lead to complications in the pregnancy. Gaining too much weight can also cause complications, but on the other hand, insufficient weight gain can result in low birth weight, giving the baby a poor start in life. Drug and alcohol consumption have also been shown to cause low birth weight, and should definitely be avoided during pregnancy.

Although many women feel more energetic and enthusiastic when they become pregnant, they may be subject to sudden mood swings. It may be difficult for them to accept the rapid changes in their bodies, and there may be conflicts with their husbands concerning sexual relations. As the pregnancy progresses, they may begin to feel some anxiety about the impending ordeal of childbirth and parenthood. For many women, this is a time when emotional support from family and friends becomes particularly important.

Directions: Interpret into English.

(140 WPM)

Embarazo

Ahora estoy en el quinto mes de embarazo. Pensé que se me iban a quitar las náuseas, pero todavía me siento mareada por las mañanas. Tengo que traer galletas en la bolsa cuando voy al trabajo, porque si no, estoy en el baño toda la mañana y la supervisora se enoja. Temo que me corran del trabajo, y no está trabajando mi esposo ahorita, así que necesito trabajar, aunque me sienta tan mal. Es que es un trabajo bastante pesado, tenemos que levantar a los pacientes de la cama para meterlos en la silla de ruedas o para bañarlos. Algunos de ellos pesan bastante, y hay otros que se resisten y hay que batallar un poco con ellos. Antes no me molestaba, me gustaba mucho el trabajo, pero ahora con los dolores de espalda y el cansancio, pues, no aguanto.

Otra cosa que he notado es que de repente me echo a llorar por nada, se me saltan las lágrimas cuando menos lo espero. Cuando eso me pasa en el trabajo me da mucha vergüenza. Además, me irrito muy fácilmente, por pequeñeces que antes no me molestaban. Les grito a los niños y hasta me tienen miedo. Eso me tiene muy deprimida, no quiero asustarlos pero se me viene esa rabia y no la puedo controlar. Creo que estoy un poco preocupada por algo que me pasó hace una quincena. Salimos a pasear en el campo, y vi un conejito. Mi suegra me dice que ahora la criatura va a salir con el labio cucho, y no sé, mis amigas me dicen que es puro mito, que no le va a pasar nada, pero de todos modos me pone a pensar. Otra cosa que me preocupa es que mi esposo se enoja conmigo porque no quiero estar con él, Ud. sabe, como hombre y mujer, porque temo que pueda ser dañino. El dice que no hace ningún daño a la criatura, pero mi suegra me dice que sí. No sé qué hacer.

Además de eso, estoy bastante bien. No tengo los dolores de cabeza que tenía antes, y la diabetes está más o menos controlada. Como bien, a pesar de las náuseas, aunque no he engordado tanto como con los otros embarazos. No como mucho por la mañana, sólo una tostada de pan que me trae mi esposo antes de levantarme, pero más tarde en el día tengo buen apetito. A veces los olores de la comida me dan basca cuando preparo algo muy grasoso para la familia. Trato de comer muchos vegetales y frutas. También tomo mucha leche, pero no como tanta carne como quisiera porque no tenemos mucho dinero ahora. Si como demasiado, me da agruras, así que tomo varias comidas pequeñas durante el día. Además, muchas veces me da gas y arrojo flatos. ¡Qué vergüenza! Y también se me han agravado las almorranas que empezaron con el primer embarazo, y tengo mucha picazón allí abajo.

Ahora que está pateando el bebé, a veces de repente necesito orinar y tengo que correr al baño, lo que resulta muy inconveniente en el trabajo. A veces me despierta por la noche. También a veces me da una sensación de ahogo, porque la criatura está creciendo y me pone mucha presión. Recuerdo que en los otros embarazos, eso se quitaba a medida que bajaba el bebé. Otra cosa que he notado es que se me hinchan los pies, especialmente después de un día pesado en el trabajo, cuando he tenido que caminar mucho. Cuando llego a casa, me acuesto en el sofá con las piernas sobre una almohada, y se me quita la hinchazón. No sé cuánto tiempo más podré trabajar, con tanta molestia. Pienso parar un mes antes de aliviarme, si puedo aguantarme hasta entonces.

Simultaneous Lesson 9 (3B)

Directions: Shadow

(130 WPM)

Auto Safety Tips

The automobile has become such a ubiquitous feature in American life that people take driving for granted. They regard it as being as natural as breathing or eating. Unfortunately, they often ignore the dangers inherent in sealing oneself in a two-ton metal capsule and hurtling down the road at seventy miles an hour. The sight of commuters shaving, applying make-up, eating meals, and talking on the phone is all too common on our freeways. Add to that the potent ingredient of alcohol or drugs, and you have an accident waiting to happen. Even without the influence of mind-altering substances, drowsy or distracted drivers can be a menace. And with the growth of the elderly population in this country, there is increasing concern about drivers who may not be as alert as they used to be, whose hearing and vision may be impaired, and who may suddenly lose control of their vehicle because of a stroke or heart attack.

When a pedestrian is run over by a car, usually the driver of the car is held responsible, but sometimes it is the pedestrian himself who is to blame. The admonition to "stop, look, and listen" that grade school children have been learning for generations seems to have been forgotten by many adults. The screeching of tires, the crunch of bumper locking with bumper, and the tinkling of broken glass tell us that once again, someone was in too much of a hurry to wait for the light to change or to walk to the corner crosswalk and instead blundered out into traffic.

Each year, nearly 20 million vehicles are involved in accidents, and over 30,000 occupants of those vehicles are killed. An additional 7,000 pedestrians lose their lives in car-related accidents. The nation's hospital emergency rooms treat many thousands more who are the lucky ones, the ones who survived. Not only are millions of dollars spent each year paying the medical bills of traffic accident victims, but the economy suffers from lost work time due to disability.

How can you avoid becoming another traffic accident statistic? The most obvious way is to observe the speed limit at all times, and to slow down when conditions are less than optimum, such as when visibility is hampered by fog, or when rain makes the streets slick. Another way is to stay alert at all times. Just because you drive your car every day doesn't mean you can put yourself on autopilot and devote your attention to other, more pressing matters. Assume that the guy behind the wheel of the other car is not nearly as attentive or quick-reacting as you are. Assume that the truck in front of you is going to turn without signaling, that the car on the corner is going to pull out without looking, that the pedestrian standing between cars is about to step out in front of you. In other words, drive defensively. Drive as if your life depended on it.

Directions: Interpret into English.

(145 WPM)

Accidente de Tránsito

¿Cómo pasó el accidente? Pues, iba cruzando la calle como a las dos, dos y media de la tarde, cuando vi que venía un coche. No me preocupaba porque estaba en la vía de peatones[1] y la luz estaba verde para mí, roja para él. Pero el tipo no se detuvo, siguió acercándose, inclusive aumentó la velocidad. Se comió la luz[2] y se me vino encima[3], creo que nunca me vio. Antes del choque oí un rechinido de llantas[4], pero fue del otro coche que venía en el otro sentido. Por supuesto, traté de correr a todo correr[5], pero no había para dónde, puesto que venía el otro coche, y no había tiempo para volver a la acera. Lo que pasó fue que el parachoques[6] del primer coche me pegó y me tumbó al suelo, y luego me arrastró unos metros. El otro coche, al tratar de evitarlo, dio un frenazo[7] e hizo un trompo[8], chocando con el primer coche. Es que estaba mojada la calle porque había llovido esa mañana. El impacto del otro coche hizo que me arrastrara aún más, pero esta vez hacia un lado.

Cuando el coche me atropelló, me golpeó primero en la cadera derecha, y cuando me caí, me pegué la cabeza. Luego cuando me arrastró, me golpeó en el hombro izquierdo y me raspó todo el lado izquierdo. Estaba consciente todo el tiempo, y lo vi todo. Ojalá hubiera perdido el conocimiento, porque ahora veo el accidente una y otra vez, como una película. No me lo puedo quitar de la cabeza. Me duele todo el cuerpo, no sé dónde me duele más. Tal vez por atrás, creo que me dañó los riñones o algo. Y cuando oriné hace un ratito, vi sangre. Tengo un dolor de cabeza muy feo, se me está borrando la vista.

Estoy todo rasguñado en los brazos, el torso, y las piernas, porque el coche me arrastró un buen trecho. Y tengo muchas cortadas porque el parabrisas se hizo añicos[9] y había vidrio por todas partes. Por eso había tanta sangre en el pavimento, y pensaron que yo estaba más

---

1 vía de peatones: crosswalk
2 se comió la luz: ran a red light
3 se me vino encima: came right at me
4 rechinido de llantas: squealing/screeching of tires
5 correr a todo correr: run like crazy, skedaddle out of there
6 parachoques: bumper
7 dio un frenazo: slammed on the brakes
8 hizo un trompo: spun out
9 el parabrisas se hizo añicos: the windshield shattered

lastimado de lo que en realidad resulté. Además, me está saliendo un moretón muy grande aquí, y no puedo doblar el codo.

Creo que se quebró el tanque de combustible del coche, porque había un gran charco de gasolina. Temiendo que una chispa o un cigarrillo hiciera estallar todo, traté de levantarme y huir, pero se me aflojaron las piernas y me caí. Logré escabullirme a gatas[1], empapado en gasolina. Todavía huelo a gasolina, aún después de quitarme la ropa.

Por fin llegó la ambulancia. Los paramédicos me pusieron en una camilla y me ataron tan fuerte que no me podía mover. Pensé que estaba paralizado, pero ahora puedo mover bien las piernas. Salvo que me duelen la cadera y el muslo. Creo que algo está quebrado o zafado ahí, probablemente aparezca en los rayos X. Se ve que está todo hinchado, y cuando fui al baño hace un ratito estaba cojeando. La enfermera se enojó y me dijo que no debiera andar solo, pero no había quién me ayudara y necesitaba orinar. Ahora, con este suero en el brazo, no puedo levantarme y tengo que usar la bacinilla.

Mi cuñada me dice que el chofer del coche era un viejito que sufrió un derrame cerebral y perdió el control del vehículo. No sé qué diablos le pasaría, pero claro que no me vio, ni tenía la menor intención de parar. Ahora estoy todo golpeado, no sé si me van a operar o qué. Probablemente tenga que pasar varios días aquí en el hospital. Pero gracias a Dios, estoy todavía con vida, me podía haber matado.

1 escabullirse a gatas: to scramble or crawl away

4 Terminology

This chapter contains the following sections:

- **Illustrations**
- **Specialized Word Lists**
  - ☐ Common Roots, Prefixes, and Suffixes
  - ☐ Neurology Terms
  - ☐ Cardiovascular Terms
  - ☐ Oncology Terms
  - ☐ Gynecology Terms
  - ☐ Orthopedic and Rheumatology Terms
  - ☐ Medical Instruments and Devices
  - ☐ Términos coloquiales relacionados con la medicina popular
- **Combined Medical Glossary**
  - ☐ English-Spanish
  - ☐ Spanish-English

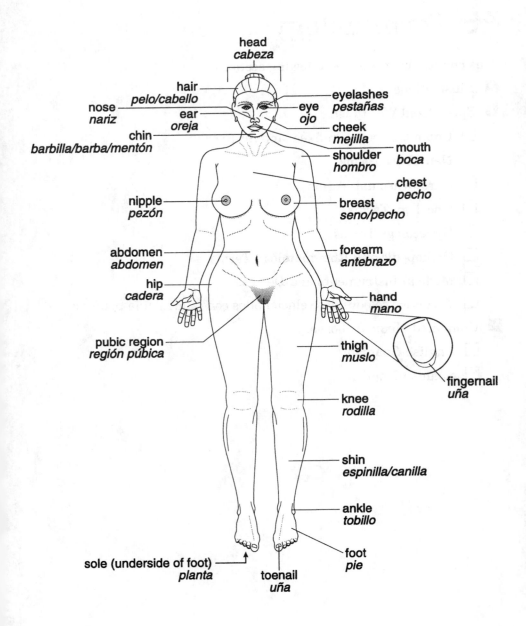

Figure 1. External Front View of Adult Female

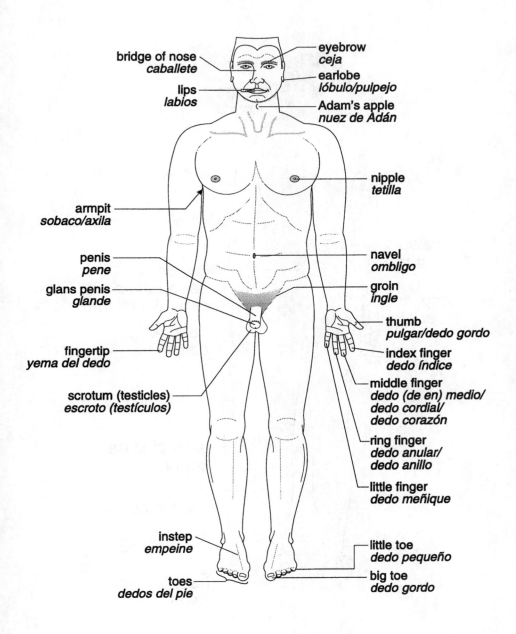

Figure 2. External Front View of Adult Male

ACEBO

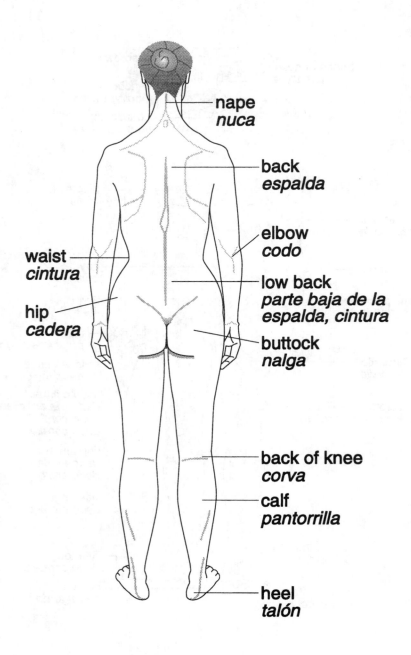

nape
nuca

back
espalda

elbow
codo

waist
cintura

low back
*parte baja de la
espalda, cintura*

hip
cadera

buttock
nalga

back of knee
corva

calf
pantorrilla

heel
talón

Figure 3. External Rear View of Adult Female

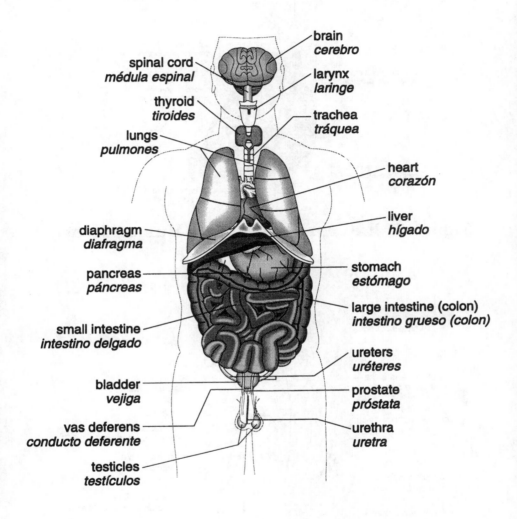

Figure 4. Internal Organs as Viewed from the Front (Male)

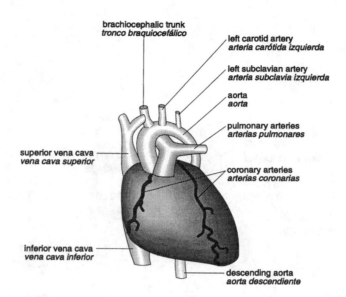

Figure 5. External View of the Human Heart

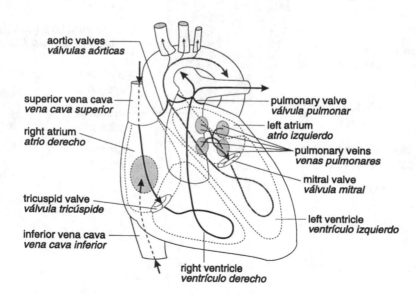

Figure 6. Blood Flow Through the Heart

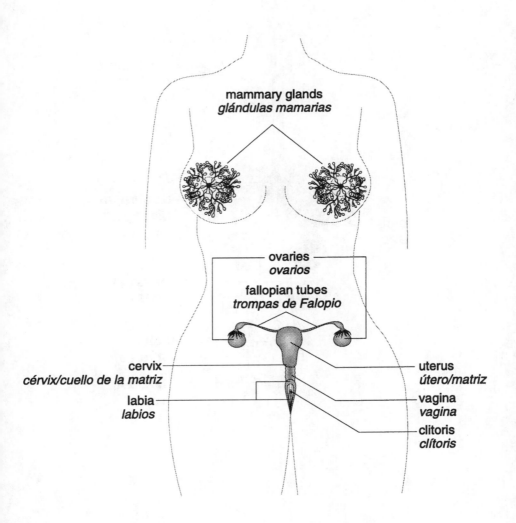

Figure 7. Female Reproductive Organs

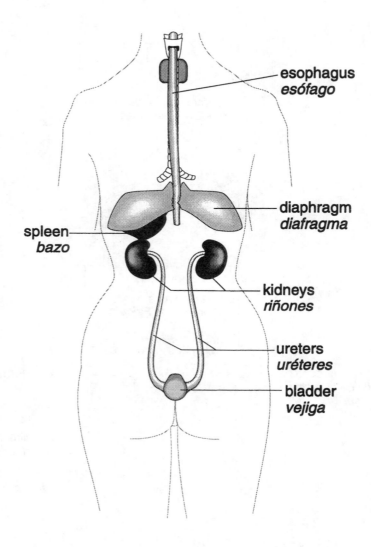

esophagus
esófago

diaphragm
diafragma

spleen
bazo

kidneys
riñones

ureters
uréteres

bladder
vejiga

Figure 8. Certain Internal Organs as Viewed from the Rear

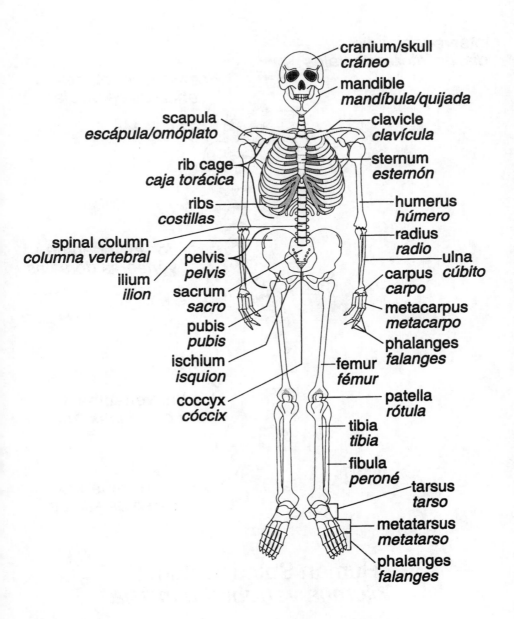

Figure 9. Major Bones of the Human Skeleton

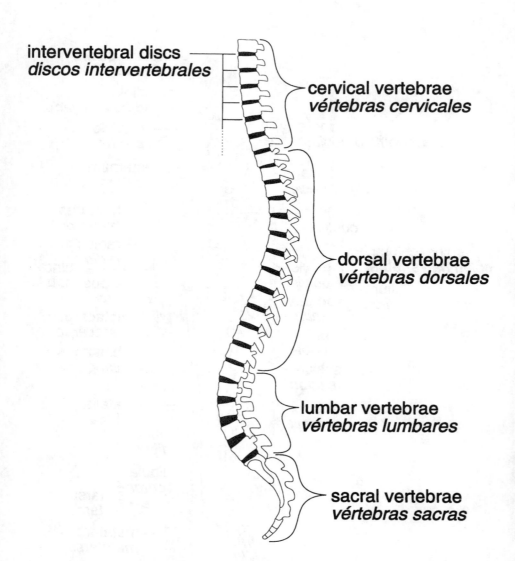

intervertebral discs
discos intervertebrales

cervical vertebrae
vértebras cervicales

dorsal vertebrae
vértebras dorsales

lumbar vertebrae
vértebras lumbares

sacral vertebrae
vértebras sacras

Human Spinal Column
Columna vertebral humana

Figure 10. Spinal Column

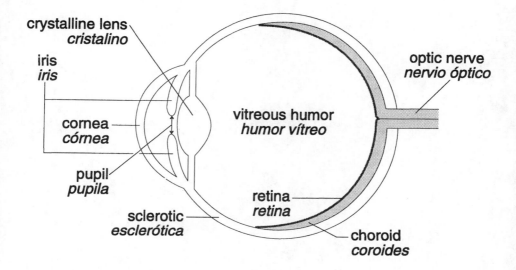

Figure 11. Simplified Cross Section of the Human Eye

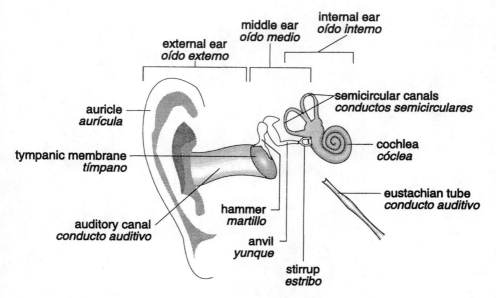

Figure 12. The Ear

Common Roots, Prefixes, and Suffixes

English	Spanish	Meaning
a-, ab-	a-, ab-	not, far from
a-, an-	a-, an-	without
abdomino	abdomin, abdomino	having to do with the abdomen
acr, acro	acr, acro	having to do with the extremities
aden, adeno	aden, adeno	having to do with glands
algesi, alge, algio, algo	algesia	having to do with pain
-algia	-algia	pain
angi, angio	angi, angio	having to do with the blood vessels
ante, anter, antero	ante, anter, antero	before or in front of
anti	anti	against
arterio	arteri, arterio, arter	having to do with the arteries
arthro	ar, artro	having to do with the joints
auto-	auto-	self
blast, blasto	blast, blasto	bud or budding, particularly of an early embrionic form
blephar, blepharo	blefar, blefaro	having to do with an eyelid or eyelash
brady-	bradi-	denotes slowness
bronchi, broncho	bronqui, bronquio, bronc, bronco	having to do with the air passages of the lungs
carcino	carcin, carcino	having to do with cancer
cardi, cardio	cardi, cardio	having to do with the heart
carp, carpo	carp, carpo	having to do with the wrist
caud, caudo	caud, caudo	having to do with a tail
centesis	centesis	perforation of
cephalo	cefal, cefalo	having to do with the head
cheilo, cheil	queil, queilo	having to do with the lip or with a liplike structure

English	Spanish	Meaning
chlor, chloro	clor, cloro	green
circum-	circum-, circun-	around
con	con	with
contra	contra	against
-clysis	-clisis	indicates irrigation or washing out of
col, colo	col, colo	having to do with the colon
core, coreo, coro	core, coreo, coro	having to do with the pupil or iris
corne, corneo	corne, corneo	having to do with the cornea
cost, costo	cost, costo	having to do with the ribs
crypt, crypto	cript, cripto	hidden
cranio	crane, craneo	having to do with the skull
cyan, cyano	cian, ciano	blue, bluish
cysto, cyst, cysti, cystido	cist, cisto, quist	having to do with a sac, a cyst, or a bladder, generally the urinary bladder
cyto	cit, cito	having to do with cells
dactyl, dactylo	dactil, dactilo	having to do with the fingers or toes
dent, dento	dent, dento	having to do with teeth
dermat, dermato, derm, dermo	dermat, dermato, derm, dermo	having to do with the skin
dexter, dextro, dextr	dextr, dextro	indicates the right side
diplo	dipl, diplo	double
dis	dis	free of
dorso, dorsi	dors, dorso	behind, or having to do with the back
dromo	drom, dromo	having to do with conduction or with running
dys-	dis-	denotes difficulty, pain, or abnormality
ectasia	ectasia	having to do with dilation or enlargement

English	Spanish	Meaning
ecto	ect, ecto	on the outside of
-ectomy	ectomía	surgical removal of
ectopic	ectópico	out of place
emes, emesis	emes, emesis	having to do with vomiting
end, endo	end, endo	inside of
enter, entero	enter, entero	having to do with the intestines
epi	epi	on top of, above
erythro	eritr, eritro	red
esophag, esophago	esofag, esofago	having to do with the esophagus
esthesio, aesthesio	estesia	having to do with the perception of physical sensations
ex-, extra-	ex-, extra-	outside of
fibr, fibro	fibr, fibro	having to do with fibers
gangli, ganglio	gangli, ganglio	a knot or knot-like structure
gastr, gastro	gastr, gastro	having to do with the stomach
-gen, -genesis	-gen, -genesis	denotes formation or development of the condition or entity described by the root to which this suffix is attached (e.g., carcino*gen*: a substance tending to promote the development of cancer)
gingive, gingivo	gingiv, gingivo	having to do with the gums
gloss, glosso	glos, gloso	having to do with the tongue
gluc, gluco	gluc, gluco	having to do with glucose (sugar)
-gnosis	-gnosis	indicates knowledge of
gyneco, gynaeco, gyn, gyne, gyno	ginec, gineco	having to do with women
hemi	hemi	half

English	Spanish	Meaning
hemo, haemo, hem, haem, hema, haema, hemat, hemato, haemato	hem, hemo, hemat, hemato	having to do with the blood
hepat, hepato	hepat, hepato	having to do with the liver
heter, hetero	heter, hetero	different
hom, homo	hom, homo	same
hydr, hydro	hidr, hidro	having to do with water or with hydrogen
hyper-	hiper-	over and above the normal
hypo-	hipo-	below, less than
hystero	hister, histero	having to do with the uterus or with hysteria
in-	en-	in
in-	in-	no
infra-	infra-	below, on the under side of
inter-	inter-	between, among
intra-	intra-	inside of
irid, irido	irid, irido, iro	having to do with the iris
iso	iso	equal
-itis	-itis	inflammation of
jejuno	yeyun, yeyuno	having to do with the jejunum
kerat, kerato	querat, querato	having to do with the cornea
kinesio, kine, cine	quinesi, quinesio	having to do with movement
lacri, lachry	lacrim, lacrimo	having to do with tears
lapar, laparo	lapar, laparo	having to do with the loin or with the wall of the abdomen
laryng, laryngo	laring, laringo	having to do with the larynx
later, latero	later, latero	having to do with the side
-lepsy	-lepsia	indicates an attack of
leuc, leuco, leuko	leuc, leuco	white, whitish
lumb, lumbo	lumb, lumbo	having to do with the lower back or loins

English	Spanish	Meaning
lyso	lis, liso	having to do with dissolution
macro-	macro-	denotes largeness
mal	mal	bad, poorly
-manual	-manual	having to do with the hand
megal, megalo	megal, megalo	large or enlarged
melano	melan, melano	black
men, meno	men, meno	having to do with menstruation
mes, meso	mes, meso	middle
-meter	-metro	denotes a measuring instrument
micro-	micro-	denotes smallness
mono-	mono-	one
multi-	multi-	many
myel, myelo	miel, mielo	having to do with bone marrow or with the spinal cord
myo, my	mi, mio	having to do with muscle
naso	nas, naso	having to do with the nose
necr, necro	necr, necro	having to do with death
nephro, nephr	nefr, nefro	having to do with the kidneys
neo-	neo-	new
neur, neuro	neur, neuro	having to do with nerves or the nervous system
noct, nocti	noct, nocti	having to do with the night
nulli-	nuli-	none
-oid	-oid	resembling
-ologist	-ólogo	specialist in
-ology	-ología	the study of
-oma	-oma	tumor of
omphalo	omfal, omfalo	having to do with the umbilicus
onych, onycho	onic, onico	having to do with the nails

English	Spanish	Meaning
ophthalm, ophthalmo	oftalm, oftalmo	having to do with the eye
orchio, orchi, orchido	orquid, orquido	having to do with the testicles
-osis	-osis	condition of
osteo	oste, osteo	having to do with bones
-ostomy	-ostomía	forming a new opening in
ot, oto	ot, oto	having to do with the ear
ovo, ovi, oo	oofor, ooforo	having to do with eggs or the ovaries
pancreato	pancreat, pancreato	having to do with the pancreas
para-	para-	close
-pedal	-pedal	having to do with the foot
pelv, pelvi	pelv, pelvi	having to do with the pelvis
peps, pepso, pepsia	peps, pepso, pepsia	having to do with the digestion
per-	per-	throughout
peri-	peri-	around
-pexy	-pexia	denotes fixation (physical)
phag, phago	fag, fago	having to do with eating
phalang, phalango	falang, falango	having to do with the bones of the fingers or toes
pharyng, pharyngo	faring, faringo	having to do with the pharynx
phleb, phlebo	fleb, flebo	having to do with the veins
phobia	fob, fobia	fear of
-plasm	-plasmo	formative or formed material
-plast	-plast, -plasto	having to do with any primitive living cell
-plegia, -plegic	-plegia, -plegico	having to do with paralysis or stroke
pleur, pleuro	pleur, pleuro	having to do with the pleura, the side, or a rib
pneo	pne, pneu	having to do with breathing
pneumo, pneumono	pneum, pneumo, pneumono	having to do with the lungs
pod, podo	pod, podo	having to do with the foot

English	Spanish	Meaning
poly-	poli-	denotes many
post-	post-	after
poster, postero	poster, postero	behind
pre-	pre-	before
pro-	pro-	indicates something that comes before something else or is a precursor to something else
proct, procto	proct, procto	having to do with the rectum and anus
psych, psycho	psic, psico	having to do with the mind
-ptosis	-ptosis	indicates downward displacement or inclination
pub, pubo	pub, pubo	having to do with the pubis
pyelo, pyel	piel, pielo	having to do with the pelvis of the kidney
pyr, pyro	pir, piro	having to do with fire or heat
rect, recto	rect, recto	having to do with the rectum
ren, reno	ren, reno	having to do with the kidney
retin, retino	retin, retino	having to do with the retina
retro	retr, retro	backward or behind
-rhaphy	-rrafia	denotes the joining of something in a seam or suture
-rhea	-rrea	denoting flow
rhino	rin, rino	having to do with the nose
-rrhage, -rrhagia	-rragia	denotes excessive flow
salpingo	salping, salpingo	having to do with tubes, specifically the Fallopian tubes
sclera	escler, esclero	having to do with the sclera (hard outer covering of the eyeball)
sclero	scler, sclero	denotes hardness
-scope	-scopio	indicates an instrument for viewing

English	Spanish	Meaning
semi-	semi-	half, partial
sinistro	sinistr, siniestro	indicates the left side
-sperm	-sperma	having to do with sperm or seed
spermato, spermo	espermat, espermato	having to do with sperm
splen, spleno	splen, spleno	having to do with the spleen
stomat, stomato	stomat, stomato	having to do with the mouth
sub-	sub-	below
super-, supra-	super- supra-	above, more than
syn-	sin-	indicates union or association
syphil, syphilo	sifil, sifilo	having to do with syphilis
-stasis	-stasis	indicates the maintenance of a constant level without increase or decrease
tachy-	taqui-	denotes speed, rapidity
therap, therapo	terap, terapo	having to do with treatment
therm, thermo	term, termo	having to do with heat
thorac, thoraco	torac, toraco	having to do with the chest
-tome, -tomy	-tomo, -tomía	denotes cutting, incision
trans	trans	throughout or from one side to the other
trauma	traumat, traumato	having to do with wounds and injuries
tri	tri	three
-tripsy	-tripsi	indicates the intentional crushing of a structure
troph, tropho	trof, trofo	having to do with nutrition
tympan, tympano	timpan, timpano	having to do with the tympanic membrane (the eardrum)
uni-	uni-	one
uretero	ureter, uretero	having to do with the ureters
urethro	uretr, uretro	having to do with the urethra

English	Spanish	Meaning
uro, ur, urono	ur, uro	having to do with urine
vas, vaso	vas, vaso	having to do with a vessel or duct
ventro, ventri	ventr, ventro	having to do with the belly
viscer, viscero	viscer, viscero	having to do with the contents of the abdomen
xantho	xant, xanto	yellow

Neurology Terms

absence seizure ausencia *f*, crisis *f* de ausencia
acetylcholine acetilcolina *f*
acoustic neuroma neuroma *m* acústico
akinesia acinesia *f*
akinetic seizure acceso *m* acinético
Alzheimer's disease enfermedad *f* de Alzheimer
amantadine hydrochloride clorhidrato *m* de amantadina
amitriptyline amitriptilina *f*
amygdala amígdala *f*
amyloid amiloideo
analgesia analgesia *f*
analgesic analgésico
anticholinergic agents agentes *m* anticolinérgicos
antidepressant antidepresivo
antiepileptic antiepiléptico
arteritis arteritis *f*
astrocytes astrocitos *m*
astrocytoma astrocitoma *m*
aura aura *f*
automatism automatismo *m*
autonomic nervous system sistema *m* nervioso autónomo
axon axón *m*
basal ganglia ganglios *m* basales
basilar artery migraine jaqueca *f* de la arteria basilar
benign exertional headache cefalalgia *f* benigna por esfuerzo
benserazide benseracida *f*
biofeedback biorretroalimentación *f*
biperiden biperidén *m*
bradykinesia bradicinesia *f*
brainstem tallo *m* cerebral
brainstem auditory evoked response test medición *f* de las respuestas evocadas auditivas del tallo cerebral
carbamazepine carbamacepina *f*
carbidopa carbidopa *f*

central vestibular disorder trastorno *m* central del aparato vestibular
cerebellum cerebelo *m*
cerebral cortex córtex *f*/corteza *f* cerebral
cerebral palsy parálisis *f* cerebral
cerebral ventricle ventrículo *m* cerebral
cerebrospinal fluid líquido *m* cerebrospinal
cerebrovascular cerebrovascular
cerebrum cerebrum *m*, cerebro *m*
cingulectomy cingulectomía *f*
cluster headache cefalea *f* en racimos/grupos/acúmulos
computed tomography (CT) tomografía *f* computarizada/computada
concussion concusión *f*, conmoción *f*
convulsion convulsión *f*
cordotomy cordotomía *f*
corpus callosum corpus *m* callosum
cortex corteza *f*, córtex *f*
Creutzfeldt-Jakob disease enfermedad *f*/síndrome *m* de Creutzfeldt-Jakob
cryothalamotomy destrucción *f* crioquirúrgica del tálamo
cyproheptadine ciproheptadina *f*
dementia demencia *f*
depression depresión *f*
dopamine dopamina *f*
dorsal root rhizotomy rizotomía *f* de la raíz dorsal
double vision vision *f*/vista *f* doble
dyskinesia discinesia *f*
electroencephalogram (EEG) electroencefalograma *m*
electromyography (EMG) electromiografía *f*
electronystagmography electronistagmografía *f*

endolymph endolinfa *f*
endorphin endorfina *f*
enkephalin encefalina *f*
ependymoma ependimoma *m*
epilepsy epilepsia *f*
epileptic focus foco *m* epiléptico
epileptiform epileptiforme
epinephrine epinefrina *f*
ergotamine tartrate tartrato *m* de
 ergotamina
extracerebral decarboxylase
 inhibitors inhibidores *m*
 extracerebrales de la descarboxilasa
festination festinación *f*
frontal lobe lóbulo *m* frontal
glial cells células *f* gliales
glioblastoma multiforme
 glioblastoma *m* multiforme
glioma glioma *m*
grand mal gran mal *m*
hemiplegic migraine jaqueca *f*
 hemipléjica
hippocampus hipocampo *m*,
 hippocampus *m*
Huntington's disease enfermedad
 f de Huntington
hydrocephalus hidrocéfalo *m*
hypothalamus hipotálamo *m*
infantile spasm espasmo *m* infantil
infarct dementia demencia *f* por
 infarto
L-dopa L-dopa *f*
labyrinth laberinto *m*
labyrinthectomy
 laberintectomía *f*
levodopa levodopa *f*
limbic system sistema *m* límbico
lumbar puncture punción *f* lumbar
magnetic resonance imaging
 (MRI) imágenes *f* por resonancia
 magnética, resonancia *f* magnética
 nuclear
mania manía *f*
manic-depressive
 maníaco-depresivo
meclizine meclicina *f*
medulla médula *f*

medulloblastoma
 meduloblastoma *m*
Ménière's disease enfermedad
 f/vértigo *m* de Ménière
meninges meninges *f*
meningioma meningioma *m*
meningitis meningitis *f*
methylphenidate metilfenidato *m*
migraine jaqueca *f*, migraña *f*
monoamine oxidase inhibitors
 (MAO) inhibidores *m* de la
 monoaminooxidasa
multi-infarct dementia demencia
 f por infartos múltiples
multiple sclerosis esclerosis *f*
 múltiple
multiple sensory deficit déficit *m*
 sensorial múltiple
myelin sheath vaina *f* de mielina
myelogram mielograma *m*
myoclonic seizure acceso *m*
 mioclónico, mioclonía *f*
nerve nervio *m*
nervous system sistema *m*
 nervioso
neuritis neuritis *f*
neurochemical neuroquímico
neurofibrillary tangles marañas *f*
 neurofibrilares
neurogenic pain dolor *m*
 neurogénico/neurógeno
neurological examination
 exploración *f* neurológica
neurologist neurólogo *m*
neurology neurología *f*
neuron neurona *f*
neurosurgeon neurocirujano *m*
neurotransmitter
 neurotransmisor *m*
nitrosourea nitrosourea *f*
nociceptor nociceptor *m*
nystagmus nistagmo *m*
occipital lobe lóbulo *m* occipital
ophthalmoplegic migraine
 jaqueca *f* oftalmopléjica
optical shingles herpes zoster *m*
 óptico

otoconia otoconia *f*
otoneurologist otoneurólogo *m*
palsy perlesía *f*, parálisis *f*
papaverine hydrochloride clorhidrato *m* de papaverina
parietal lobe lóbulo *m* parietal
Parkinson's disease enfermedad *f* de Parkinson
peripheral nerve neurotomy neurotomía *f* del nervio periférico
peripheral neuropathy neuropatía *f* periférica
peripheral vestibular disorder trastorno *m* periférico del aparato vestibular
petit mal petit mal *m*
phenobarbital fenobarbital *m*
phenytoin fenitoína *f*
Pick's disease enfermedad *f* de Pick
pituitary pituitario *m*
plaque placa *f*
pons pons *m*
positional vertigo vértigo *m* de posición
positron emission tomography (PET) tomografía *f* por emisión de positrones
postherpetic neuralgia neuralgia *f* posherpética
presenile dementia demencia *f* presenil
primary brain tumor tumor *m* cerebral primario
propranolol propranolol *m*
pseudodementia seudodemencia *f*
psychogenic pain dolor *m* psicogénico/psicógeno
psychogenic seizure acceso *m* psicogénico/psicógeno
psychometric psicométrico
psychomotor epilepsy epilepsia *f* psicomotora
reactive depression depresión *f* reactiva
reflex reflejo *m*
retropulsion retropulsión *f*
saccule sáculo *m*

Schwannoma Schwannoma *m*
secondary brain tumor tumor *m* cerebral secundario
seizure acceso *m*
semicircular canals conductos *m* semicirculares
senile dementia demencia *f* senil
senile plaque placa *f* senil
senility senilidad *f*
serotonin serotonina *f*
shingles herpes zoster *m*
single photon emission computed tomography (SPECT) tomografía *f* computada/computarizada por emisión de fotón único
spinal cord médula *f* espinal
spinal tap punción *f* lumbar
status migrainosus estado *m* jaquecoso
stimulation-produced analgesia (SPA) analgesia *f* producida por estímulos
substantia nigra substantia *f* nigra
sulci surcos *m*
temporal lobe lóbulo *m* temporal
thalamus tálamo *m*
thermocoagulation termocoagulación *f*
tic douloureux tic *m* doloroso
tonic-clonic seizure ataque *m* tónico-clónico
toxic headache cefalea *f* tóxica
transcutaneous electrical nerve stimulation (TENS) estimulación *f* eléctrica transcutánea de nervios, estimulación nerviosa transcutánea
transient ischemic attack (TIA) ataque *m* isquémico transitorio, ataque de isquemia transitoria
trigeminal neuralgia neuralgia *f* trigémina
trihexyphenidyl trihexifenidil *m*
tuberous sclerosis esclerosis *f* tuberosa
utricle utrículo *m*

vascular headache cefalea *f* vascular

vertigo vértigo *m*

vestibular labyrinth laberinto *m* vestibular

vestibular nerve section sección *f* del nervio vestibular

vestibular neuronitis neuronitis *f* vestibular

vestibule vestíbulo *m*

zoster zoster *m*

Cardiovascular Terms

abdominal aneurysm aneurisma
m abdominal
acute infarct scintigraphy
gammagrama *m* de infarto agudo
afterload carga *f* ulterior
aneurysm aneurisma *m*
angina angina *f*
angina pectoris angina *f* péctoris
angioplasty angioplastia *f*
angiotensin converting enzyme
(ACE) enzima *f* de conversión de
angiotensina
anticoagulant anticoagulante
antihypertensive
antihipertensivo *m*
aortic aneurysm aneurisma *m*
aórtico
aortic stenosis estenosis *f* aórtica
aortic valve válvula *f* aórtica
aphasia afasia *f*
arrhythmia arritmia *f*
arterial thrill estremecimiento *m*
arterial
arterioles arteriolas *f*
arteriosclerosis arteriosclerosis *f*
atherosclerosis aterosclerosis *f*
asymptomatic carotid bruit
soplo *m* asintomático de la carótida
atrial fibrillation fibrilación *f*
atrial
atrial flutter aleteo *m* auricular
atrial septal defect (ASD)
comunicación *f* interauricular (CIA)
atrioventricular node nudo *m*
atrioventricular
atrium atrio *m*
balloon angioplasty angioplastia *f*
con sonda balón/globo
beta blocker bloqueador *m* beta
blood pressure (BP) tensión *f*
arterial (TA)
blood stream torrente *m* sanguíneo
blood work análisis *f*/pruebas *f* de
sangre
bradycardia bradicardia *f*

bruit ruido *m*
bypass desviación *f*, derivación *f*,
injerto *m* de derivación
calcium antagonists antagonistas
f del calcio
cardiac catheterization
cateterización *f* cardiaca,
cateterismo *m* cardiaco
cardiac function función *f* cardiaca
cardiac monitor monitor *m*
cardiaco
cardiac output gasto *m* cardiaco
cardiomyopathy cardiomiopatía *f*
cardiopulmonary resuscitation
(CPR) resucitación *f*/reanimación *f*
cardiopulmonar (RCP)
cardiovascular disorder
padecimiento *m* cardiovascular
carotid endarterectomy
endarterectomía *f* carótida
carotid phonoangiography
fonoangiografía *f* de la carótida
cerebral embolism embolio *m*
cerebral
cerebral hemorrhage hemorragia
f cerebral
cerebral thrombosis trombosis *f*
cerebral
cholesterol colesterol *m*
chylomicron quilomicrón *m*
click chasquido *m*
collagen colágeno *m*
collateral circulation circulación *f*
colateral
congenital heart defect
cardiopatía *f* congénita
congestive heart failure
insuficiencia *f* cardiaca congestiva
contrast medium material *m* de
contraste
coronary arteriography
arteriografía *f* coronaria
coronary artery arteria *f* coronaria

coronary artery bypass graft
injerto *m* de derivación de la arteria
coronaria
coronary artery disease (CAD)
arteriopatía *f* coronaria
coronary heart disease (CHD)
cardiopatía *f* coronaria
coronary occlusion oclusión *f*
coronaria
coronary thrombosis trombosis *f*
coronaria
coronary vasodilator
vasodilatador *m* coronario
defibrillator desfibrilador *m*
diastole diástole *f*
diastolic diastólico
diastolic pressure presión *f*
diastólica
digital cardiac angiography
(DCA) angiografía *f* cardiaca digital
digital subtraction angiography
(DSA) angiografía *f* de
su(b)stracción digital
digitalis digital *f*, digitalis *f*
diuretic diurético *m*
Doppler ultrasound test examen
m ultrasónico Doppler,
ultrasonografía *f* Doppler
dysarthria disartria *f*
dysrhythmia disritmia *f*
echocardiography
ecocardiografía *f*
ejection fraction fracción *f* de
expulsión
electrocardiogram (ECG or EKG)
electrocardiograma *m*
electroencephalogram (EEG)
electroencefalograma *m*
embolism embolio *m*
endothelium endotelio *m*
essential hypertension
hipertensión *f* esencial
facial paresis paresia *f* facial
fibrillation fibrilación *f*
fibrin fibrina *f*
flutter aleteo *m* auricular

hardening of the arteries
endurecimiento *m* de las arterias
heart disease enfermedad *f* del
corazón
heart murmur soplo *m* cardiaco
heart rate frecuencia *f* cardiaca
heart transplant trasplante *m* del
corazón, trasplante cardiaco
high-density lipoprotein (HDL)
lipoproteína *f* de alta densidad
(LAD), lipoproteína de densidad
elevada
Holter monitor monitor *m* (de)
Holter
hypercholesterolemia
hipercolesterolemia *f*
hypertension hipertensión *f*
hypertriglyceridemia
hipertrigliceridemia *f*
interauricular septum tabique *m*
interauricular
intermediate-density lipoprotein
(IDL) lipoproteína *f* de media
densidad
intermittent claudication
claudicación *f* intermitente
interventricular septum tabique
m interventricular
ischemia isquemia *f*
laser angioplasty angioplastia *f*
por láser
left ventricular hypertrophy
hipertrofia *f* del ventrículo
izquierdo, ventrículo izquierdo
hipertrofiado
lipoprotein lipoproteína *f*
low-density lipoprotein (LDL)
lipoproteína *f* de baja densidad
(LBD)
lumen lumen *m*
magnetic resonance imaging
(MRI) imágenes *f* por resonancia
magnética, resonancia *f* magnética
nuclear
mitral stenosis estenosis *f* mitral
mitral valve válvula *f* mitral

myocardial infarction infarto *m* de(l) miocardio

myocardial ischemia isquemia *f* miocárdica

myocarditis miocarditis *f*

myocardium miocardio *m*

myxoma mixoma *m*

nitroglycerin nitroglicerina *f*

nuclear brain scan gammagrama *m* cerebral

ocular plethysmography (OPG) pletismografía *f* ocular

open heart surgery cirugía *f* de corazón abierto

opening snap/click chasquido *m* de apertura

pacemaker marcapaso *m*

palpitation palpitación *f*, latido rápido del corazón

percutaneous transluminal coronary angioplasty (PTCA) angioplastia *f* transluminal percutánea coronaria

perfusion imaging estudio *m* con perfusión (miocárdica con talio), prueba *f* de perfusión (del miocardio con talio)

pericarditis pericarditis *f*

peripheral vascular disease enfermedad *f* vascular periférica, trastorno *m* vascular periférico

phlebitis flebitis *f*

phospholipids fosfolípidos *m*

plaque placa *f*

platelet plaqueta *f*

preload carga *f* previa

premature atrial contraction (PAC) contracción *f* auricular prematura

premature ventricular contraction (PVC) contracción *f* ventricular prematura

prostaglandin prostaglandina *f*

pulmonary valve válvula *f* pulmonar

radionuclide imaging imágenes *f* diagnósticas por radionúclidos, estudio *m*/exploración *f* con radionúclidos

resting pulse pulso *m* en reposo

saphenous vein vena *f* safena

sclerotherapy escleroterapia *f*

secondary hypertension hipertensión *f* secundaria

silent ischemia isquemia *f* subclínica

sinoatrial node (SA node) nudo *m* sinoauricular

sphygmomanometer esfigmomanómetro *m*

sphygmomanometer cuff manguito *m*/abrazadera *f* de esfigmomanómetro

standby pacemaker marcapaso *m* de demanda

stenosis estenosis *f*

streptokinase estreptocinasa *f*

stress test prueba *f* del ejercicio/esfuerzo

stroke derrame *m* cerebral, embolia

subarachnoid hemorrhage hemorragia *f* subaracnoidea

sudden cardiac death (SCD) muerte *f* cardiaca repentina

sympathetic nerve inhibitors inhibidores *m* del sistema nervioso simpático

systole sístole *f*

systolic sistólico

systolic pressure presión *f* sistólica

tachycardia taquicardia *f*

thrill estremecimiento *m*

thrombolysis trombólisis *f*

thrombus trombo *m*

transient ischemic attack (TIA) ataque *m* de isquemia transitoria

tricuspid stenosis estenosis *f* tricúspide

tricuspid valve válvula *f* tricúspide

triglyceride triglicérido *m*

urokinase urocinasa *f*

varicose veins venas *f* varicosas

vasodilator vasodilatador *m*

ventricle ventrículo *m*

ventricular aneurysm aneurisma
m ventricular

ventricular fibrillation
fibrilación *f* ventricular

ventricular septal defect (VSD)
comunicación *f* interventricular
(CIV)

ventricular tachycardia
taquicardia *f* ventricular

venule vénula *f*

**very-low-density lipoprotein
(VLDL)** lipoproteína *f* de muy baja
densidad (LMBD)

wedged pulmonary pressure
presión *f* pulmonar en cuña

Oncology Terms

actinic keratosis queratosis *f* actínica

acute lymphoblast leukemia (ALL) leucemia *f* linfoblástica aguda

acute monoblast leukemia (AMOL) leucemia *f* monoblástica aguda

acute myeloblast leukemia (AML) leucemia *f* mieloblástica aguda

acute myelomonoblast leukemia (AMMOL) leucemia *f* mielomonoblástica aguda

adenocarcinoma adenocarcinoma *m*

adjuvant therapy terapia *f* adyuvante

angiogram angiograma *m*

areola aréola *f*

arteriogram arteriograma *m*

aspiration aspiración *f*

barium enema enema *f* de bario

barium sulfate sulfato *m* de bario

barium swallow deglución *f* de bario, bario *m* por vía bucal

basal cell carcinoma carcinoma *m* basocelular/de células basales

Bence-Jones proteins proteínas *f* de Bence-Jones

benign benigno

benign prostatic hypertrophy (BPH) hipertrofia *f* prostática benigna

benign prostatic hyperplasia hiperplasia *f* prostática benigna

biological therapy terapia *f* biológica, bioterapia *f*

biopsy biopsia *f*

bladder cancer cáncer *m* de (la) vejiga

blast cell hemoblasto *m*, hemocitoblasto *m*

bone marrow médula *f* ósea

bowel resection resección *f* del intestino

breast cancer cáncer *m* mamario, cáncer de (la) mama, cáncer de(l) seno, cáncer de(l) pecho

breast self-examination (BSE) autoexamen *m* de la mama/del seno, autoexploración *f* mamaria

bronchoscopy broncoscopia *f*

bulbs bulbos *m*

cancerous tissue tejido *m* canceroso

carcinogen carcinógeno *m*

carcinogenesis carcinogénesis *f*

carcinoma in situ carcinoma *m* in situ

catheter catéter *m*

cauterization cauterización *f*

chemoprevention quimioprofilaxia *f*

chemotherapy quimioterapia *f*

chronic granulocytic leukemia (CGL) leucemia *f* granulocítica crónica

chronic lymphocytic leukemia (CLL) leucemia *f* linfocítica crónica

clinical trial ensayo *m* clínico

cobalt treatment tratamiento *m* con cobalto

colonoscope colonoscopio *m*

colostomy colostomía *f*

colposcope colposcopio *m*

computed tomography (CT) tomografía *f* computada/computarizada

cone biopsy biopsia *f* en cono

conization conización *f*

creatinine creatinina *f*

cryosurgery criocirugía *f*

curette cureta *f*

cystectomy cistectomía *f*

cystoscope cistoscopio *m*

diethylstilbestrol (DES) dietilestilbestrol *m*

dilation and curettage (D&C) dilatación *f* y raspado *m*

discharge secreción *f*, exudado *m*

dysplasia displasia *f*

electrodessication
electrodesecación *f*

endoscopic retrograde cholangiopancreatogram (ERCP) colangiopancreatografía *f* retrógrada endoscópica

endometrial cancer cáncer *m* endometrial

endometriosis endometriosis *f*

endometrium endometrio *m*

epidermoid carcinoma carcinoma *m* epidermoide

erythrocytes eritrocitos *m*

estrogen receptor test prueba *f* de receptor de estrógeno

exploratory surgery cirugía *f* exploradora

fibroid mioma *m*, fibromioma *m*

fluoroscopy fluoroscopia *f*

granulocytes granulocitos *m*

granulocytic leukemia leucemia *f* granulocítica

granulocytopenia granulocitopenia *f*

hemoglobin hemoglobina *f*

histocompatibility histocompatibilidad *f*

hormone therapy terapia *f* hormonal, hormonoterapia *f*

hyperplasia hiperplasia *f*

hysterectomy histerectomía *f*

immunoglobulin inmunoglobulina *f*

immunotherapy inmunoterapia *f*

interferon interferón *m*

interstitial radiation therapy radioterapia *f* intersticial

intravenous pyelogram (IVP) urograma *m* excretorio, pielograma *m* intravenoso

invasive cervical cancer cáncer *m* invasor de la cérvix, carcinoma *m* cervical invasor, carcinoma invasor del cuello uterino

irradiation irradiación *f*

islet cell cancer cáncer *m* de célula(s) insular(es)

islets of Langerhans islotes *m* de Langerhans

laparotomy laparotomía *f*

large cell carcinoma carcinoma *m* de células grandes

leukemia leucemia *f*

leukocytes leucocitos *m*

lobes lóbulos *m*

lobules lobulillos *m*

lumpectomy lumpectomía *f*

lung cancer cáncer *m* de(l) pulmón, cáncer *m* pulmonar, carcinoma *m* de pulmón

luteinizing hormone-releasing hormone agonists (LHRH agonists) hormona *f* liberadora de hormona leuteinizante

lymph linfa *f*

lymph node ganglio *m* linfático

lymphangiogram linfangiograma *m*

lymphatic system sistema *m* linfático

lymphedema linfedema *m*

lymphocytic leukemia leucemia *f* linfocítica

lymphocytes linfocitos *m*

lymphoma linfoma *m*

magnetic resonance imaging (MRI) imágenes *f* por resonancia magnética, resonancia *f* magnética nuclear

malignant maligno

mammogram mamograma *m*

mastectomy mastectomía *f*

mediastinoscopy mediastinoscopia *f*

mediastinotomy mediastinotomía *f*

melanocytes melanocitos *m*

melanoma melanoma *m*

metastasis metástasis *f*

metastasize metastatizar

Moh's technique técnica *f* de Moh

monoclonal antibodies anticuerpos *m* monoclonales

myelocytic leukemia leucemia *f* mielocítica

myelogenous leukemia leucemia *f* mielógena

myelosis mielosis *f*

myometrium miometrio *m*

nephrectomy nefrectomía *f*

nephrotomography nefrotomografía *f*

neutrophils neutrófilos *m*

oat cell cancer carcinoma *m* de células en avena, carcinoma indiferenciado microcelular

orchiectomy orquiectomía *f*

palpation palpación *f*

Pap test/smear prueba *f*/examen *m*/tinción *f* de Papanicolaou

papillary tumor tumor *m* papilar

pathologist patólogo *m*

pelvic exam examen *m* pélvico

perineal surgery cirugía *f* perineal

plasmacyte plasmacito *m*

platelets plaquetas *f*

pneumonectomy neumonectomía *f*

polyp pólipo *m*

progesteron receptor test prueba *f* de receptor de progesterona

prostatic acid phosphatase (PAP) fosfatasa *f* ácida prostática

prosthesis prótesis *f*

radiation therapy radioterapia *f*

radical hysterectomy histerectomía *f* radical

radioactive isotope isótopo *m* radi(o)activo

radiotherapy radioterapia *f*

Reed-Sternberg cells células *f* de Reed-Sternberg

remission remisión *f*

renal cell cancer cáncer *m* de células renales

retropubic prostatectomy prostatectomía *f* retropúbica

salpingo-oophorectomy salpingooforectomía *f*

Schiller test prueba *f* de Schiller

side effect efecto *m* secundario

sigmoidoscope sigmoidoscopio *m*

sigmoidoscopy sigmoidoscopia *f*

skin cancer cáncer *m* de (la) piel, cáncer cutáneo

small cell lung cancer cáncer *m* pulmonar de células pequeñas

sonogram sonograma *m*

speculum espéculo *m*

squamous cell carcinoma carcinoma *m* de células escamosas, carcinoma espinocelular

stoma estoma *m*

suction curettage legrado *m*/raspado *m* por succión

sunscreen filtro *m* solar, protector *m* solar

systemic therapy terapia *f* sistémica

tamoxifen tamoxifén *m*

testicular self-examination (TSE) autoexamen *m* de los testículos

thermography termografía *f*

topical chemotherapy quimioterapia *f* tópica

transitional cell carcinoma carcinoma *m* de célula transicional

transrectal ultrasound ultrasonido *m* transrectal

transurethral resection (TUR) resección *f* transuretral

tumor tumor *m*

ultrasound ultrasonido *m*

ultraviolet radiation (UV) radiación *f* ultravioleta

wedge resection resección *f* en cuña

Whipple procedure técnica *f* de Whipple

white blood cell glóbulo *m* blanco, leucocito *m*

Gynecology and Obstetrics Terms

abortion aborto *m*
adenomyosis adenomiosis *f*
adnexal mass masa *f* anexial
amenorrhea amenorrea *f*
amniocentesis amniocentesis *f*
amniotic fluid líquido *m* amniótico
amniotic sac saco *m* amniótico
anemia anemia*f*
anemic anémico
anovulatory anovulatorio
bag of waters fuente *f*, bolsa *f* de
   las aguas
Bartholin cyst quiste *m* de
   Bartholin
Bartholin gland carcinoma
   carcinoma *m* de la glándula de
   Bartholin
basal body temperature graph
   gráfica *f* de la temperatura corporal
   basal
bicornuate uterus útero *m*
   bicórneo
birth control pill píldora *f*
   anticonceptiva
bottle feed alimentar con biberón
Bowen's disease enfermedad *f* de
   Bowen
breast engorgement ingurgitación
   f mamaria
breast feed amamantar, dar pecho,
   dar de mamar
breast tenderness mastalgia *f*
breech presentation presentación
   f de nalgas
candidiasis candidiasis *f*
carry to term llevar a término
cervical cap capuchón *m* cervical
cervical punch biopsy biopsia *f*
   cervical en sacabocados
cervical stenosis estenosis *f*
   cervical
cervicitis cervicitis *f*
cervix cuello *m* (de la matriz),
   cérvix *f*
cesarean section sección *f* cesárea

chancroid chancroide *m*
Chlamydia Chlamydia *f*
clitoris clítoris *f*
coitus coito *m*
cold knife conization conización *f*
   con cuchillo frío
colpocleisis colpocleisis *f*
colporrhaphy colporrafia *f*
condom condón *m*
condyloma acuminatum
   condiloma *m* acuminado
contraceptive anticonceptivo *m*.
   contraceptivo *m*
contraction contracción *f*. dolor *m*
   de parto
cornual pregnancy embarazo *m*
   cornual
corpus luteum cuerpo *m* amarillo,
   corpus *m* luteum
crowning aparición *f* de la cabeza
   fetal
cul-de-sac cul-de-sac *m*
culdocentesis culdocentesis *f*
culdoscopy culdoscopia *f*
cystic adenosis adenosis *f* cística
cystocele cistocele *m*
cystosarcoma phyllodes
   cistosarcoma *m* filodo
cystoscopy cistoscopia *f*
cystourethrocele
   cistouretrocele *m*
cytologic citológico
delivery parto *m*, expulsión *f* del
   feto
diaphragm diafragma *m*
diethylstilbestrol (DES)
   dietilestilbestrol *m*
dilated dilatado
dilation dilatación *f*
dilation and curettage (D&C)
   dilatación *f* y raspado *m*
dilation and evacuation (D&E)
   dilatación *f* y evacuación *f*
douche ducha *f*, lavada *f*, ducharse
due date fecha *f* estimada del parto

dysfunctional uterine bleeding (DUB) hemorragia *f* uterina disfuncional

dysmenorrhea dismenorrea *f*

dyspareunia dispareunia *f*

eclampsia eclampsia *f*

ectocervical ectocervical

ectopic pregnancy embarazo *m* ectópico

effacement of the cervix borramiento *m* del cuello

electroconization electroconización *f*

embryo embrión *m*

endocervical endocervical

endolymphatic stromal myosis miosis *f* endolinfática del estroma

endometrial carcinoma carcinoma *m* endometrial

endometrial cavity cavidad *f* endometrial

endometrial hyperplasia hiperplasia *f* endometrial

endometrial polyps pólipos *m* endometriales

endometriosis endometriosis *f*

endometrium endometrio *m*

enterocele enterocele *m*

episiotomy episiotomía *f*

estimated date of confinement (EDC) fecha *f* estimada del parto

estrogen estrógeno *m*

estrogen replacement therapy terapéutica *f* substitutiva de estrógenos

exocervix exocérvix *f*

fallopian tube trompa *f* de Falopio

fertilization fecundación *f*

fetal monitor monitor *m* (cardiaco) fetal

fetus feto *m*

fibrocystic disease enfermedad *f* fibroquística

fimbrial adhesion adherencia *f* de la fimbria

fistula fístula *f*

foam espuma *f*

follicle folículo *m*

footling presentation presentación *f* podálica

forceps fórceps *m*

fractional curettage raspado *m*/legrado *m* por fracciones

frank breech presentation presentación *f* franca de nalgas

Gartner duct cyst quiste *m* del conducto de Gartner

genital tuberculosis tuberculosis *f* genital

genital warts verrugas *f* genitales

glans clitoridis glande *m* clitoridis

gonadotropin gonadotropina *f*

gonorrhea gonorrea *f*

granuloma inguinale granuloma *m* inguinal

haemophilus ducreyi haemophylus *m* Ducrey, Hemophilus *m* ducreyi

hematocolpos hematocolpos *m*

hematometra hematómetra *f*

hermaphroditism hermafroditismo *m*

herpes genitalis herpes *m* genital

hidradenoma hidradenoma *m*

hirsutism hirsutismo *m*

hot flashes bochornos *m*

human chorionic gonadotropin (HCG) gonadotropina *f* coriónica humana

hydatidiform mole mola *f* hidatitiforme

hydronephrosis hidronefrosis *f*

hydrosalpinx hidrosalpinx *m*

hydroureter hidrouréter *m*

hymen himen *m*

hymenotomy himenotomía *f*

hypermenorrhea hipermenorrea *f*

hypoplastic vagina vagina *f* hipoplástica

hysterectomy histerectomía *f*

hysterography histerografía *f*

hysterosalpingography histerosalpingografía *f*

idiopathic uterine hypertrophy
hipertrofia *f* uterina idiopática
imperforate hymen himen *m*
imperforado
incompetent cervix cuello *f*
incompetente
intermenstrual bleeding
hemorragia *f* intermenstrual
intrauterine device (IUD)
dispositivo *m* intrauterino
intrauterine pregnancy
embarazo *m* intrauterino
iron deficiency anemia anemia *f*
ferropriva
labia majora labios *m* mayores
labia minora labios *m* menores
labor parto *m*, trabajo *m* de parto
lacerated cervix cuello *m*
desgarrado
laparoscopy laparoscopia *f*
latent syphilis sífilis *f* latente
leiomyoma leiomioma *m*
leiomyosarcoma
leiomiosarcoma *m*
leukorrhea leucorrea *f*
let-down reflex reflejo *m* del
chorro de leche
lochia loquios *m*
lumen lumen *m*
lymphogranuloma venereum
(LGV) linfogranuloma *m*
venéreo/inguinal
marsupialization
marsupialización *f*
meconium meconio *m*
menarche menarquía *f*,
menarca *f*
menopause menopausia *f*
menses menstruo *m*
menstrual period periodo *m*
(menstrual), regla *f*
menstruation menstruación *f*
mesonephric duct conducto *m*
mesonéfrico
micturition micción *f*
miscarriage aborto *m*
espontáneo/natural, malparto *m*

missed abortion aborto *m* fallido
moniliasis moniliasis *f*
morning sickness náuseas *f* del
embarazo
multipara multípara *f*
multiparous multípara
mycelium micelio *m*
myomectomy miomectomía *f*
myometrium miometrio *m*
nipple discharge exudado *m* por el
pezón
nipple inversion retracción *f* del
pezón
nulligravid nuligravida *f*
nulliparous nulípara
obstetric obstétrico
oral contraceptive anticonceptivo
m oral/bucal
os os *m*
ovarian agenesis agénesis *f*/
agenesia *f* ovárica
ovarian cyst quiste *m* ovárico
ovarian dysgenesis disgenesis
f/disgenesia *f* ovárica
ovaries ovarios *m*
ovisac ovisaco *m*
ovotestis ovotestis *m*
ovulation ovulación *f*
Paget's disease of the vulva
enfermedad *f* de Paget en la vulva
Pap smear prueba *f*/examen
f/tinción *f* de Papanicolaou
paracervical block bloqueo *m*
paracervical
paravaginal cystic mass masa *f*
quística paravaginal
pelvic examination examen *m*
pélvico
pelvic inflammatory disease
(PIV) enfermedad *f* inflamatoria
pélvica
pelvic peritonitis peritonitis *f*
pélvica
peritubal adhesion adherencia *f*
peritubárica
placenta previa placenta *f* previa

polycystic ovary ovario *m* poliquístico

polymenorrhea polimenorrea *f*

polyp pólipo *m*

portio vaginalis portio *m* vaginalis

postcoital poscoito

postcoital bleeding hemorragia *f* después del coito

postdatism posfecha *f*

postmaturity posmadurez *f*

postmenopausal posmenopáusico

post partum post partum, posparto

postpartum blues tristeza *f* posparto

preeclampsia preeclampsia *f*

pregnancy test prueba *f* de embarazo

premature labor parto *m* prematuro

premature separation of the placenta desprendimiento *m* prematuro de la placenta

premenopausal premenopáusico

premenstrual tension tensión *f* premenstrual

prepubescent prepubescente

preterm birth nacimiento *m* prematuro

primary syphilis sífilis *f* primaria

primipara primípara *f*

primiparous primípara

progesterone progesterona *f*

progestin progestina *f*

prolapsed uterus prolapso *m* del útero

prolapsed vagina prolapso *m* de la vagina

pruritis prurito *m*

pseudopolyp seudopólipo *m*

puberty pubertad *f*

rectocele rectocele *m*

rectovaginal fistula fístula *f* rectovaginal

rectovaginal septum tabique *m* rectovaginal

Rh incompatibility incompatibilidad *f* por Rh

ruptured tubo-ovarian abscess absceso *m* tubovárico roto

salpingitis salpingitis *f*

salpingolysis salpingólisis *f*

salpingo-oophorectomy salpingooforectomía *f*

salpingo-oophoritis salpingooforitis *f*

salpingostomy salpingostomía *f*

scar tissue tejido *m* cicatrizal

sebaceous cysts quistes *m* sebáceos

secondary syphilis sífilis *f* secundaria

sexually transmitted disease (STD) enfermedad *f* de transmisión sexual

speculum espéculo *m*

spermicidal foam espuma *f* espermaticida

spermicidal jelly jalea *f* espermaticida

spirochete espiroqueta *f*

spotting manchado *m*, sangrado *m* ligero

stirrups estribos *m*

stress incontinence incontinencia *f* de esfuerzo

subinvolution of the uterous subinvolución *f* del útero

suction curettage aspiración *f* con vacío

syphilis sífilis *f*

testicular feminization syndrome síndrome *m* de feminización testicular

toxemia toxemia *f*

trachelorrhaphy traquelorrafia *f*

transverse septum of the vagina tabique *m* vaginal transverso

Trichomonas vaginalis Trichomonas *f* vaginalis

trimester trimestre *m*

trophoblast trofoblasto *m*

tubal abortion aborto *m* tubárico

tubal ligation ligadura *f* de trompas

tubal pregnancy embarazo *m* tubárico
tuberculous salpingitis salpingitis *f* tuberculosa
tubo-ovarian abscess absceso *m* tuboovárico
twisted ovarian cyst quiste *m* ovárico torcido
ultrasound ultrasonido *m*
umbilical cord cordón *m* umbilical
ureteroneocystostomy ureteroneocistostomía *f*
ureteroureterostomy ureteroureterostomía *f*
ureterovaginal fistula fístula *f* ureterovaginal
urethrovaginal fistula fístula *f* uretrovaginal
urogenital sinus sinus *m* urogenital
uterine fundus fondo *m* del útero
uterine leiomyoma leiomioma *m* del útero
uterine retroflexion retroflexión *f* del útero
uterorectosacral ligaments ligamentos *m* uterorrectosacros
uterotubal insufflation insuflación *f* uterotubaria/ uterotubárica
uterus útero *m*
vagina vagina *f*
vaginal atresia atresia *f* vaginal
vaginectomy vaginectomía *f*
vaginitis vaginitis *f*
venereal venéreo
vesicovaginal fistula fístula *f* vesicovaginal
vulva vulva *f*
vulvectomy vulvectomía *f*
vulvitis vulvitis *f*
vulval elephantiasis elefantiasis *f* vulvar
yeast infection micosis *f* vaginal, infección *f* vaginal por hongos

Orthopedics and Rheumatology Terms

acromioclavicular joint
articulación *f* acromioclavicular
arthroscopy artroscopia *f*
acromion acromion *m*
acute hematogenous
osteomyelitis osteomielitis *f*
hematógena aguda
adolescent coxa vara coxa *f* vara
adolescente
amyloidosis amiloidosis *f*
angulated fracture fractura *f*
angulada
ankylosis anquilosis *f*
ankylosing spondylitis
espondilitis *f* anquilosante
appendicular bone hueso *m*
apendicular
arthritides artrítides *m*
arthrocentesis artrocentesis *f*
arthrodesis artrodesis *f*
arthroplasty artroplastia *f*
arthroscope artroscopio *m*
arthroscopic surgery cirugía *f*
artroscópica
arthrotomy artrotomía *f*
atlantoaxial dislocation
dislocación *f* atlantoaxoidea
atlas atlas *m*
avulsion fracture fractura *f*
avulsiva
axial compression compresión *f*
axial
azathioprine azatioprina *f*
back brace corsé *m* lumbosacro
bacterial arthritis artritis *f*
bacteriana
ball and socket joint cabeza *f* y
cavidad *f* articular
bone graft injerto *m* óseo
bone infarction infarto *m* óseo
bone tumor tumor *m* óseo
bony ankylosis anquilosis *f* ósea

Brodie's abscess absceso *m* de
Brodie
Brucella osteomyelitis
osteomielitis *f* provocada por
Brucella
bulge prominencia *f*,
abultamiento *m*
bunion juanete *m*
bursa bolsa *f*
bursitis bursitis *f*
calcaneus calcáneo *m*
cancellous canceloso
capitate bone hueso *m* capitado
capitellum capitellum *m*
carpal fracture fractura *f* carpiana
carpal tunnel syndrome
síndrome *m* del túnel carpiano
carpus carpo *m*
cartilage cartílago *m*
cast yeso *m*
cauda equina cauda *f* equina
cavitation cavitación *f*
cavus feet pies *m* cavos
cervical cervical
cervical collar collar *m* cervical
Charcot's joint articulación *f* de
Charcot
charley horse agujeta *f*
chiropractic therapy terapia
quiropráctica
chondroblastoma
condroblastoma *m*
chondromyxoid fibroma
condromixofibroma *m*
chondrosarcoma
condrosarcoma *m*
clavicle clavícula *f*
closed fracture fractura *f* cerrada
Clutton's joint articulación *f* de
Clutton
coccidioidomycosis
coccidioidomicosis *f*
coccygectomy coccigectomía *f*

coccyx cóccix *m*
collagen colágeno *m*
Colle's fracture fractura *f* de Colle
comminuted fracture fractura *f* conminuta
compound fracture fractura *f* expuesta/abierta
compression fracture fractura *f* por compresión
computed tomography (CT) tomografía *f* computada/computarizada
connective tissue tejido *m* conectivo
coracoid process apófisis *f* coracoides
corticosteroid corticosteroide *m*
cranial vault bóveda *f* craneal
cranium cráneo *m*, cranium *m*
cryptococcosis criptococosis *f*
crystal-induced arthritis artritis *f* por cristales
cuboid bone hueso *m* cuboideo
cuneiform bone hueso *m* cuneiforme
degenerative arthritis artritis *f* degenerativa
degenerative osteoarthritis osteoartritis *f* degenerativa
demineralization desmineralización *f*
diaphysectomy diafisectomía *f*
diaphysis diáfisis *f*
discoid lupus erythematosus lupus *m* eritematoso discoide
enchondroma encondroma *m*
epiphyseal plate lámina *f*/línea *f* epifisaria
epiphysis epífisis *f*
epiphysitis epifisitis *f*
erythrocyte sedimentation rate (sed rate) velocidad *f* de sedimentación globular
European blastomycosis blastomicosis *f* europea
Ewing's sarcoma sarcoma *m* de Ewing

extension dislocation dislocación *f* por extensión
femoral epiphyses epífisis *f* crural/femoral
femur fémur *m*
fenestration fenestración *f*
fibrosarcoma fibrosarcoma *m*
fibrous ankylosis anquilosis *f* fibrosa
fibula peroné *m*
flexion contracture contractura *f* de flexión
foam rubber pad almohadilla *f* de espuma de hule
fracture fractura *f*
fracture fracturar
friction rub frote *m*
frozen shoulder hombro *m* congelado
fusion fusión *f*
giant cell tumor tumor *m* de célula gigante
gibbus joroba *f*
Gilchrist's disease enfermedad *f* de Gilchrist
glenohumeral osteoarthritis osteoartritis *f* glenohumeral
glenoid glenoide
gold salts sales *f* de oro
gonorrheal arthritis artritis *f* gonorreica
gout gota *f*
grating ruido *m* raspante
greater trochanter trocánter *m* mayor
greater tuberosity tuberosidad *f* mayor
greenstick fracture fractura *f* en tallo/caña/rama verde
grinding rozamiento *m*
gumma goma *f*
hairline fracture fisura *f*
hamate bone hueso *m* ganchoso/unciforme
hammertoe deformity deformidad *f* de dedos en martillo

hamstring tendón *m* del hueso poplíteo
hamulus hamulus *m*
hematogenous arthritis artritis *f* hematógena
hematogenous osteomyelitis osteomielitis *f* hematógena
hemiarthroplasty hemiartroplastia *f*
herniated disk disco *m* herniado
hip capsule cápsula *f* de la cadera
histoplasmosis histoplasmosis *f*
housemaid's knee rodilla *f* de fregona
humerus húmero *m*
hydrocortisone hidrocortisona *f*
hydroxchloroquine hidroxicloroquina *f*
hyperextension hiperextensión *f*
hyperflexion hiperflexión *f*
hypertrophic arthritis artritis *f* hipertrófica
ilium ilion *m*
immunosuppressive drug fármaco *m* inmunosupresor
impacted fracture fractura *f* impactada, fractura con impacto
infectious arthritis artritis *f* infecciosa
interphalangeal joint articulación *f* interfalángica
intervertebral disk disco *m* intervertebral
intra-articular injection inyección *f* intraarticular
involucrum involucro *m*
ischium isquion *m*
joint articulación *f*
joint aspiration aspiración *f* articular
joint cavity cavidad *f* articular
joint replacement sustitución *f* protésica de la articulación
kyphosis cifosis *f*
lamina lámina *f*
laminagraphy laminografía *f*
laminectomy laminectomía *f*

lateral condyle cóndilo *m* lateral
lateral flexion flexión *f* lateral
lateral malleolus maléolo *m* lateral
lesser trochanter trocánter *m* menor
lesser tuberosity tuberosidad *f* menor
ligament ligamento *m*
limp cojear, renguear
limp cojera *f*
longitudinal fracture fractura *f* longitudinal
low back pain dolor *m* lumbar bajo
lumbar lumbar
lumbosacral lumbosacro
lunate bone hueso *m* semilunar
mandible mandíbula *f*
marble bones huesos *m* marmóreos
marrow médula *f* ósea
marrow thrombosis trombosis *f* medular
medial malleolus maléolo *m* interno
medial meniscus menisco *m* interno
medullary canal canal *m* medular
meniscus tear desgarro *m* de(l) menisco
metacarpus metacarpo *m*
metaphyseal infection infección *f* metafisaria
metaphysitis metafisitis *f*
metatarsal metatarsiano
methotrexate metotrexato *m*
midcarpal dislocation dislocación *f* mesocarpiana
midtarsal dislocation dislocación *f* mesotarsiana
miner's elbow codo *m* de minero
Minerva jacket corsé *m* Minerva
mixed connective tissue disease (MCTD) enfermedad *f* mixta de tejido conectivo
morning stiffness rigidez *f* matutina
muscle strain estiramiento *m*/ distensión *f* muscular

muscle tear desgarro *m* muscular
mycotic infection infección *f* micótica
myelography mielografía *f*
navicular navicular
necrosis necrosis *f*
necrotizing arteritis arteritis *f* necrosante
neurotrophic arthropathy artropatía *f* neurotrófica
nonsteroidal anti-inflammatory drug (NSAID) antiinflamatorio *m* no esteroide
North American blastomycosis blastomicosis *f* norteamericana
nucleus pulposus núcleo *m* pulposo
oblique fracture fractura *f* oblicua
obturator ring anillo *m* obturador
odontoid process apófisis *f* odontoides
olecranon olécranon *m*, olécrano *m*
open fracture fractura *f* abierta/expuesta
open reduction reducción *f* abierta
orthopedic support sostén *m* ortopédico
orthopedic surgeon cirujano *m* ortopédico
orthopedics ortopedia *f*
orthosis ortesis *f*
osseous dysplasia displasia *f* ósea
osteoarthrosis osteoartrosis *f*
osteoarticular focus foco *m* osteoarticular
osteoarticular lesion lesión *f* osteoarticular
osteoarticular tuberculosis tuberculosis *f* osteoarticular
osteochondroma osteocondroma *m*
osteoclastoma osteoclastoma *m*
osteogenic sarcoma sarcoma *m* osteógeno, osteosarcoma *m*
osteography osteografía *f*

osteoid osteoma osteoma *m* osteoide
osteolysis osteólisis *f*
osteomyelitis osteomielitis *f*
osteonecrosis osteonecrosis *f*
osteoperiostitis osteoperiostitis *f*
osteophytes osteófitos *m*
osteoporosis osteoporosis *f*
osteosclerosis osteosclerosis *f*
osteotomy osteotomía *f*
overlap syndrome síndrome *m* de superposición
patella rótula *f*, patela *f*
patellar retinaculum retináculo *m* rotuliano/patelar
patellofemoral joint articulación *f* femororrotuliana/rotulofemoral
pathologic fracture fractura *f* patológica
pelvis pelvis *f*
penicillamine penicilamina *f*
periosteum periostio *m*
periostitis periostitis *f*
phalanx (*pl* phalanges) falange *f*
plasma cell myeloma mieloma *m* de célula plasmática
polyarthralgia poliartralgia *f*
posterior extension splint férula *f* de extensión posterior
primary osteomyelitis osteomielitis *f* primaria
prosthesis prótesis *f*
pseudoarthrosis seudoartrosis *f*
pseudogout seudogota *f*
pubic symphysis sínfisis *f* del pubis
pubis pubis *m*
pyogenic arthritis artritis *f* piógena
pyogenic osteomyelitis osteomielitis *f* piógena
radial styloid process apófisis *f* estiloide radial
radiocarpal joint articulación *f* radiocarpiana
radioulnar joint articulación *f* radiocubital

radius radio *m*
range of motion amplitud *f* de movimiento
recalcitrant rebelde
reconstructive surgery cirugía *f* ortopédica reconstructora
retrosternal dislocation dislocación *f* retrosternal
rheumatology reumatología *f*
rheumatic fever fiebre *f* reumática
rheumatoid arthritis artritis *f* reumatoide
rheumatoid factor factor *m* reumatoide
rheumatoid nodules nódulos *m* reumatoides
rib cage caja *f* torácica
rotator cuff rotador *m* del hombro
ruptured disk disco *m* roto
saber shin tibia *f* en sable
sacroiliac sacroiliaco
sacrum sacro *m*
sagittal plane plano *m* sagital
Salmonella osteomyelitis osteomielitis *f* provocada por Salmonella
scaphoid bone escafoides *m*
scapula escápula *f*
sciatica ciática *f*
secondary osteomyelitis osteomielitis *f* secundaria
segmental resection resección *f* segmentaria
septic arthritis artritis *f* séptica
sequestrectomy secuestrectomía *f*
sequestrum secuestro *m*
sesamoid sesamoide
shoulder capsule cápsula *f* del hombro
skull fracture fractura *f* del cráneo
Smith's fracture fractura *f* de Smith
spinal column columna *f* vertebral
spinous process apófisis *f* espinosa
spiral fracture fractura *f* espiral/en espiral/espiroidea
splint férula *f*

spondylitis espondilitis *f*
spondylolisthesis espondilolistesis *f*
sprain esguince *m*
sprained ligament esguince *m* ligamentoso
spur espolón *m*
sternoclavicular dislocation dislocación *f* esternoclavicular
sternum esternón *m*
strapping inmobilización *f*
stress fracture fractura *f* de esfuerzo
subchondral bone hueso *m* subcondral
subcoracoid dislocation dislocación *f* subcoracoidea
subluxation subluxación *f*
subperiosteal abscess absceso *m* subperióstico
subtalar joint articulación *f* subastragalina
subtrochanteric fracture fractura *f* subtrocantérea
sulfasalazine salazosulfapiridina *f*
suppurative arthritis artritis *f* supurativa
supracondylar fracture fractura *f* supracondílea
suprapatellar pouch bolsa *f* suprarrotuliana
sustentaculum sustentaculum *m*
symphysis pubica sínfisis *f* púbica
synovectomy sinovectomía *f*
synovia sinovia *f*
synovial fluid líquido *m* sinovial
synovial membrane membrana *f* sinovial
synovitis sinovitis *f*
syphilitic osteitis osteítis *f* sifilítica
systemic lupus erythematosus lupus *m* eritematoso sistémico
tailor's bottom culo *m* de sastre
talofibular ligament ligamento *m* peroneoastragalino

talonavicular joint articulación *f* talonavicular

talus astrágalo *m*, talus *m*

tarsometatarsal dislocation dislocación *f* tarsometatarsiana

tendon sheath vaina *f* tendinosa

tendonitis tenonitis *f*

tennis elbow codo *m* de tenista

thoracic torácico

thoracolumbar junction unión *f* toracolumbar

tibia tibia *f*

tibial crest cresta *f* de la tibia

tibiofibular joint articulación *f* tibiofibular

tophus tofo *m*

torn ligament desgarro *m* ligamentoso

torsion torsión *f*

torulosis torulosis *f*

traction tracción *f*

transcutaneous electrical nerve stimulation (TENS) estimulación *f* eléctrica transcutánea de nervios, estimulación nerviosa transcutánea

transient synovitis sinovitis *f* transitoria

transverse fracture fractura *f* transversa

transverse process apófisis *f* transversa

traumatic arthritis artritis *f* traumática

trigger point of pain punto *m* desencadenante del dolor

triquetrum triquetro *m*

trochanter trocánter *m*

trochanteric fracture fractura *f* trocantérica

truss braguero *m*

tubercle tubérculo *m*

tuberculous arthritis artritis *f* tuberculosa

ulna cúbito *m*

unilateral dislocation dislocación *f* unilateral

unilateral subluxation subluxación *f* unilateral

vertebra vértebra *f*

weaver's bottom culo *m* de tejedor

whiplash lesión *f* de latigazo

whirlpool bath baño *m* de remolino

zygomatic arch arco *m* cigomático

-

Medical Instruments and Devices

arthroscope artroscopio *m*

back brace/support braguero *m*, corset *m* lumbosacro, corsé *m*, espaldera *f*, faja *f*

bandage envoltura *f*, venda *f*, vendaje *m*

bedpan bacinilla *f*

blood pressure cuff tensiómetro

cane (curved) bastón *m*

cane (straight) bordón *m*

cast yeso *m*, casco *m*

catheter catéter *m*

cervical collar collar *m* cervical, collarín *m*

clamp pinza(s) *f*

colonoscope colonoscopio *m*

colposcope colposcopio *m*

crutch muleta *f*

curette cureta *f*

cystoscope cistoscopio *m*

defibrillator desfibrilador *m*

disposable needle aguja *f* de un solo uso

disposable syringe jeringa *f* de un solo uso

dressing apósito *m*, venda *f*, vendaje *m*

ear scope otoscopio *m*

electrode electrodo *m*

examination couch mesa *f* de reconocimiento

eye scope oftalmoscopio *m*

eyedropper cuentagotas *f*

forceps fórceps *m*, pinzas *f*

height gauge talla *f*

hypodermic syringe jeringa *f* hipodérmica

ice pack bolsa *f* con hielo

inhaler inhalador *m*

intrauterine device dispositivo *m* intrauterino

kidney belt cinturón *m*, faja *f*

Minerva jacket corsé *m* Minerva

monitor monitor *m*

nebulizer nebulizador *m*

needle aguja *f*

operating table mesa *f* quirúrgica, mesa de operaciones

ophthalmoscope oftalmoscopio *m*

orthopedic brace férula *f* para miembros, soporte *m*

otoscope otoscopio *m*

pacemaker marcapasos *m*

percussor (reflex hammer) martillo *m* de reflejos

pipette pipeta *f*

posterior extension splint férula *f* de extensión posterior

rectoscope rectoscopio *m*

scalpel bisturí *m*

scissors tijeras *f*

scoop (curette) raspador *m*

sigmoidoscope sigmoidoscopio *m*

sliding-weight scale peso *m* de corredera

sling cabestrillo *m*, banda *f*, honda *f*

speculum espéculo *m*

sphygmomanometer tensiómetro, esfigmomanómetro

sphygmomanometer cuff manguito *m*/abrazadera *f* de esfigmomanómetro

spirometer espirómetro *m*

splint férula *f*, tablilla *f*

stethoscope estetoscopio *m*

stretcher camilla *f*

surgical needle aguja *f* para suturas

swab aplicador *m*, hisopo *m*

syringe jeringa *f*

thermometer termómetro

tongue blade/depressor abatelenguas *m*, bajalenguas *m*

tourniquet torniquete *m*

truss braguero *m*

tweezers pinzas *f*

urethroscope fibroscopio *m* urinario

vaginal speculum espéculo vaginal

vision chart cuadro *m* de agudeza
 visual
walker andadera *f*, andador *m*
weighing platform plataforma *f*
 del peso
wheelchair silla *f* de ruedas

Términos coloquiales relacionados con la medicina popular

Many of the terms in this word list are nonstandard and should be used with caution. Because of the nonstandard nature of many of the terms here, this word list is not included in its entirety in the Combined Medical Glossary.

A

acalenturado suffering from a mild fever
acedías *f* heartburn
achaque *m* systemic weakness
adormecimiento *m* numbness
agallas *f* tonsils
agallas, tener have tonsilitis or sore throat
agruras *f* heartburn
ahito *m* **(estar o quedarse)** indigestion (to have)
alambrito *m* coil, loop (IUD)
aldilla *f* groin
alferecía *f* epilepsy, febrile convulsions in children, any undefined nervous condition
aliviarse deliver, give birth
almareos *m* dizziness
almorragia *f* hemorrhage
almorranas *f* hemorrhoids
amodorrado drowsy
analis *m* analysis (mispronunciation of *análisis*)
andancia *f* epidemic of a mild illness
anginas *f* tonsils
anginas, tener have tonsilitis
ansia(s), tener to be anxious
aparatito *m* coil, loop (IUD)
apendis *m* appendix (mispronunciation of *apéndice*)
apostema *f* abcess
asentaderas *f* buttocks

ataque *m* convulsion, seizure, hysteric fit
aventado flatulent

B

baba *f* saliva, spittle
babaza *f* froth in the mouth
barriga *f* belly, stomach
basca *f* vomit
bilis *f* gall bladder disease
bilis, hacer to get sick because of an emotional upset
bilma *f* cast made of leaves
blanquillo *m* egg white (used in many home remedies)
boca *f* **del estómago** pit of the stomach
bola/bolita *f* lump
boquinete *m* cleft palate, harelip
buche *m* mouth, throat

C

cachete *m* buttock, cheek
cadera *m* hip (often used to refer to lumbo-sacral area)
calilla *f* suppository
cámara *f* stool, flatus
cambio *m* **de vida** change of life, menopause
campanilla *f* uvula
canicas *f* brain
canilla *f* shin, forearm
caño/cañón *m* urethra (particularly in men)
carnosidad *f* pterigium, fleshy growth
cataplasmo *m* medicated compress
celebro *m* back of the head, base of the skull (mispronunciation of *cerebro*)

cerebro *m* back of the head, base of the skull

cintura *f* low back, small of back

cirro *m* painless, hard tumor

coco *m* head, brain

coco *m* hurt, boo-boo (children)

cólico *m* crampy abdominal pains, infant colic, menstrual cramps

colita *f* tailbone

colti *m* stiff neck

columna *f* spine

comadrona *f* midwife

compañones *m* testicles

constipado congested, stuffed up, runny nose; sometimes used to mean constipated (*estreñido*)

costado, dolor del side stitch, any pain in the side, from the upper torso to the lower torso; archaic medical term for pneumonia

cóxis *m* coccyx (mispronunciation of *cóccix*)

coyontura *f* joint (mispronunciation of *coyuntura*)

criar con pecho breastfeed

cruda *f* hangover

cuadril *m* hip (animal term)

cuajarón *m* blood clot

cuajo *m* blood clot

cuarentena *f* 40-day period following childbirth during which activities and diet are restricted (also known as *la dieta*)

cuello *m* de la matriz cervix

cuero *m* skin

cuidarse use contraceptives

culequillas, estar en squat (mispronunciation of *cuclillas*)

CH

chamorro *m* calf

chanza *f* mumps

chichis *m* breasts

chichón *m* bump/lump on the head

chochero *m* medical practitioner in Mexico, similar to a homeopathist

D

daños *m* variety of symptoms that do not respond to treatment and are thus attributed to witchcraft

dar del cuerpo defecate, have a bowel movement

deponer vomit

deposición *f* bowel movement, stool, feces

deposiciones *f* diarrhea

desecho *m* discharge (vaginal)

desguanzado tired, run-down, light-headed

desguanzarse become tired, feel run down, feel faint

destornudar sneeze (mispronunciation of *estornudar*)

diabetis *f* diabetes (mispronunciation of *diabetes*)

dieta *f* 40-day period following childbirth during which activities and diet are restricted (also known as *la cuarentena*)

divieso *m* boil, furuncle

dolor *m* de sentidos earache

E

embolia *f* stroke

embolio *m* stroke

empacho *m* indigestion, constipation, any digestive symptom

empeine *m* herpes, skin disease

empeine *m* instep or dorsum of foot

empeine *m* lower part of abdomen, pubic region

empeine *m* ringworm

encarnado *m* healing wound; swelling due to a foreign body, such as a splinter

enchinarse (la piel) get goose bumps

encorar heal; swell (e.g., from a splinter)

enferma menstruating, on one's period

enfermedad *f* **de la sangre** syphilis

enfermedad *f* **endañada** disease resulting from an act of witchcraft

enfermedad *f* **secreta** venereal disease

engarrotar stiffen, go numb

entablazón *f* obstruction, severe constipation

entrepierna *f* crotch

entresijo *m* groin, genital region

entripado, estar have indigestion from overeating

entumido numb (mispronunciation of *entumecido*)

envarado extremely flatulent or bloated

envarado stiff or numb in the neck or extremities

erutar belch (mispronunciation of *eructar*)

escaldado, estar o sentirse have soreness of the mouth after eating sour fruit

escocimiento *m* burning pain, sting, smarting sensation

escozor *m* burning pain, sting, smarting sensation

espalda *f* back; often used to refer to the upper back (as opposed to *cintura*)

espinilla *f* blackhead, pimple

espinilla *f* shin

estar con have intercourse with, be intimate with

estómago *m* **sucio** dyspepsia, indigestion

F

falsear buckle, sprain (e.g., knee)

falseo *m* buckling, sprain (e.g., knee)

fenómeno *m* freak, monster (baby with multiple defects)

flujo *m* discharge (vaginal)

frialdad *f* impotence, infertility; vague sensation of uneasiness or emptiness

fríos *m* chills (usually due to malaria)

G

gargajos *m* mucus, phlegm, sputum

garras *f* fingernails (animal term)

gaznate *m* trachea, windpipe

golondrino *m* tumor under the armpit

goma *f* hangover

gómito *m* vomit (mispronunciation of *vómito*)

gorda pregnant

grano *m* pimple, sty (eye), any pustular lesion of the skin or scalp

grano *m* **enterrado** boil

gripa *f* flu

gripe *f* flu

H

hacer de las aguas urinate

hacer del cuerpo defecate

hacer uso de have intercourse with

héctico frail, consumptive

heder stink

herencia *f* hereditary disease

hervor *m* **de sangre** allergic reaction resulting in a rash

hético frail, consumptive

hierros *m* forceps

hocico *m* mouth, snout (animal term)

hormigueos *m* prickling, tingling

hoyito *m* **del chi** hole through which urine passes, meatus of the urethra

hueso *m* **de la rodilla** kneecap

hueso *m* **del pecho** breast bone

I

ijada *f* colic, pain in the side, side stitch

ijar *m* flank, space between floating ribs and iliac crests

incordio *m* any hardening of soft tissues, particularly in the form of a string; bubo, tumor in the groin; discomfort

inocente mentally retarded

J

jiote *m* skin lesion with scaling

jiricua *f* pie baldness

juntarse have intercourse

L

labio *m* **cucho** cleft palate, harelip

lamparones *m* pigmented or depigmented skin lesions

latido *m* gnawing sensation, presentiment; pulsation of the abdominal aorta

lomo *m* loin (animal term), upper part of the back (animal term)

lupia *f* encysted tumor

M

magulladura *f* bruise

mal *m* **de hiel** gall bladder disease

mal *m* **de ijar** flank pain

mal *m* **(de) ojo** evil eye

mal *m* **de orina** dysuria with dribbling, urinary tract infection

mal parto *m* miscarriage, spontaneous abortion

mala cama *f* miscarriage, spontaneous abortion

malo del corazón, estar to have a heart condition

mano *m* hand (often used to refer to the entire arm)

mareos *m* dizziness, nausea

maso *m* biceps, muscle (from the English pronunciation)

matriz *f* uterus, womb

mecos *m* semen

merolico *m* medicine man, quack

miembro *m* penis, member

mocos *m* nasal mucus, snot

mollera *f* fontanelle/fontanel, soft spot on a baby's head

mollera *f* **caída** fallen fontanelle/fontanel (condition resulting from dehydration)

mompers *m* mumps

moquera *f* nasal mucus, snot

N

nacido *m* pimple, pustule, furuncle (particularly on the scalp)

naturaleza *f* libido, sexual impulse

naturaleza, ser de ~ fuerte have intense sexual appetites

neurisma *m* aneurism (mispronunciation of *aneurisma*)

nube *f* **del ojo** cataract

nuez *f* **de Adán** Adam's apple

O

obrar defecate, move one's bowels

órgano *m* penis, member

orzuelo *m* **(del ojo)** sty

P

paleta *f* shoulder blade

panadizo *m* felon, whitlow, abscess of the fingertip

pano *m* chloasma, blotches on the skin resulting from pregnancy or use of contraceptive medication

panza *f* belly, stomach

parche *m* bandaid, plaster, poultice

partes *f* genitals, private parts

partes *f* **nobles** genitals, private parts

partes *f* **ocultas** genitals, private parts

partes *f* **privadas** genitals, private parts

pasmado slow-moving

pasmado, estar have a rash and swelling attributed to changing temperatures; have tetanus

pasmo *m* rash and swelling; rigidity and pain in the muscles, sudden spasm; tetanus

pasmo *m* **del parto** childbed fever

pasmo *m* **seco** infection, rash, or swelling attributed to changing temperatures

pata *f* foot (animal term)

pegajoso contagious

pepa *f* clitoris

perilla *f* **(del ojo)** sty (eye)

perlatico *m* palsy, paralysis

perlesía *f* palsy, paralysis

pescuezo *m* neck (animal term)

petacas *f* buttocks

pie *m* foot (often used to refer to the entire leg)

piocha *f* chin

postema *m* abscess

postemilla *f* abscess in the mouth

postilla *f* scab or crust on a wound

pujo *m* tenesmus, urge to evacuate rectum or bladder

pujos *m* tenesmus in infant caused by being touched by menstruating or newly delivered woman

punzada *f* side stitch; stabbing headache

purgación *f* gonorrhea, urethral discharge produced in men by gonorrhea

Q

quiscoltl *m* torticollis, stiff neck

R

rabadilla *f* coccyx, tailbone

redaños *m* guts

regla *f* menstrual flow, period

regüeldo *m* eructation, belch

repetir belch

resaca *f* hangover

restirar pull

resuello *m* breath, wheezing

resuello, no alcanzarle to be short of breath

retachar throb

retortijones *m* crampy abdominal pains often associated with diarrhea

rinconera *f* quack midwife

romadizo *m* head cold

roto, estar to have a hernia

S

sabañones *m* chilblains

sanar deliver, give birth

secas *f* buboes, swollen lymph nodes

secundinas *f* afterbirth

señorita *f* virgin

sentidos *m* ears

sieso *m* anus

sobaco *m* armpit

sobador *m* folk healer who gives massages

sobaquina *f* underarm odor

soltura *f* diarrhea

sonda *f* catheter

suero *m* IV (intravenous administration of a drug or fluid)

susto *m* fright, shock, trauma; folk belief that fright can cause physical damage

T

taba *f* ankle bone; kneecap

tabardillo *m* typhoid fever

tarantas *f* dizziness

tener agallas have tonsilitis or a sore throat

tener anginas have tonsilitis
tirarse gases pass gas
tirarse vientos pass gas
tiricia *f* jaundice; separation sorrow (languishing due to the absence of a loved one); any debilitating disease
tísico feeble, sickly
tis/tisis *f* tuberculosis, consumption
tlacotillo *m* perianal abscess
torzón *m* abdominal cramp
tragadero *m* throat
tragante *m* esophagus
tripa *f* catheter, intestine
tripa *f* **ida** locked intestine attributed to shock (see *susto*)
trompa *f* mouth

U

uñero *m* inflammation around the fingernail
usar have intercourse with

V

vagido *m* convulsive sob, cry of a newborn baby
vahido *m* vertigo, giddiness, dizziness
váris *f* varicose veins (mispronunciation of *várices*)
vello *m* body hair, pubic hair, fuzz
vergüenzas *f* genitals, private parts
verijas *f* pubic region
viento *m* expelled gas, flatus
visita, tener la menstruate, to be on one's period

Z

zaratanes *m* lumps in the breast attributed to trauma and believed to evolve into cancerous tumors

Combined Medical Terms

English → Spanish

A

abdomen abdomen *m*

abdominal aneurysm aneurisma *m* abdominal

abduction abducción *f*

abortion (induced) aborto *m*

abortion (miscarriage) mal parto *m*

abrasion escoriación *f*, raspadura *f*, abrasión *f*

abscess absceso *m*, hinchazón *f*

absence seizure ausencia *f*, crisis *f* de ausencia

absent-minded distraído, olvidadizo

acetylcholine acetilcolina *f*

ache dolencia *f*, dolor *m*, dolorcito *m*

acid ácido *m*

acne acné *m*

acoustic neuroma neuroma *m* acústico

acquired immune deficiency syndrome (AIDS) síndrome *m* de inmunodeficiencia adquirida (SIDA)

acromioclavicular joint articulación *f* acromioclavicular

acromion acromion *m*

actinic keratosis queratosis *f* actínica

acupuncture acupuntura *f*

acute agudo

acute hematogenous osteomyelitis osteomielitis *f* hematógena aguda

acute infarct scintigraphy gammagrama *m* de infarto agudo

acute lymphoblast leukemia (ALL) leucemia *f* linfoblástica aguda

acute monoblast leukemia (AMOL) leucemia *f* monoblástica aguda

acute myeloblast leukemia (AML) leucemia *f* mieloblástica aguda

acute myelomonoblast leukemia (AMMOL) leucemia *f* mielomonoblástica aguda

Adam's apple nuez *f* de Adán

adduction aducción *f*

adenocarcinoma adenocarcinoma *m*

adenomyosis adenomiosis *f*

adjustment (chiropractic) ajuste *m* (quiropráctico)

adjuvant therapy terapia *f* adyuvante

admissions ingresos *m*, internación *f*

admit (hospital) ingresar, internar

admitting (hospital department) admisión *f*, ingresos *m*

adnexal mass masa *f* anexial

adolescent coxa vara coxa *f* vara adolescente

adrenalin adrenalina *f*

afterbirth placenta *f*

afterload carga *f* ulterior

AIDS (acquired immunodeficiency syndrome) SIDA (síndrome *m* de inmunodeficiencia adquirida)

AIDS-related complex (ARC) complejo *m* asociado con el SIDA

airway vía *f* respiratoria

akinesia acinesia *f*

akinetic seizure acceso *m* acinético

allergy alergia *f*

Alzheimer's disease enfermedad *f* de Alzheimer

amantadine hydrochloride clorhidrato *m* de amantadina

amenorrhea amenorrea *f*

amitriptyline amitriptilina *f*

amniocentesis amniocentesis *f*

amniotic fluid líquido *m* amniótico
amniotic sac saco *m* amniótico
amputate amputar
amputation amputación *f*
amputee amputado/a *m* / *f*
amygdala amígdala *f*
amyloid amiloideo *m*
amyloidosis amiloidosis *f*
analgesia analgesia *f*
analgesic analgésico *m*
anaphylactic shock choque *m* anafiláctico
anemia anemia *f*
anemic anémico
anesthesia anestesia *f*
anesthetic anestésico *m*
aneurysm aneurisma *m*
angina angina *f*
angina pectoris angina *f* péctoris
angiogram angiograma *m*
angioplasty angioplastia *f*
angiotensin converting enzyme (ACE) enzima *f* de conversión de angiotensina
angulated fracture fractura *f* angulada
ankle tobillo *m*
ankle bone taba *f*
ankylosis anquilosis *f*
ankylosing spondylitis espondilitis *f* anquilosante
anorexia anorexia *f*
anovulatory anovulatorio
antacid antácido *m*
anterior anterior
antibody anticuerpo *m*
anticholinergic agents agentes *m* anticolinérgicos
anticoagulant anticoagulante
antidepressant antidepresivo *m*
antidote antídoto *m*
antiepileptic antiepiléptico *m*
antihistamine antihistamínico *m*
antihypertensive antihipertensivo *m*
anti-inflammatory antiinflamatorio

anti-psychotic antipsicótico
anus ano *m*
anxiety ansiedad *f*, desesperación *f*
anvil yunque *m*
aorta aorta *f*
aortic aneurysm aneurisma *m* aórtico
aortic stenosis estenosis *f* aórtica
aortic valve válvula *f* aórtica
aphasia afasia *f*
apoplexy apoplejía *f*
appendicitis apendicitis *f*
appendicular bone hueso *m* apendicular
appendix apéndice
arch arco *m*
areola aréola *f*
arm brazo *m*
armpit axila *f*, sobaco *m*
arrhythmia arritmia *f*
arterial thrill estremecimiento *m* arterial
arteriogram arteriograma *m*
arteritis arteritis *f*
arterioles arteriolas *f*
arteriosclerosis arteriosclerosis *f*
artery arteria *f*
arthritides artrítides *m*
arthritis artritis *f*
arthrocentesis artrocentesis *f*
arthrodesis artrodesis *f*
arthroplasty artroplastia *f*
arthroscope artroscopio *m*
arthroscopic surgery cirugía *f* artroscópica
arthroscopy artroscopia *f*
arthrotomy artrotomía *f*
artificial respiration respiración *f* artificial
artificial resuscitation resucitación *f* artificial
asphyxia asfixia *f*
aspiration aspiración *f*
aspirin aspirina *f*
asthenia astenia *f*
asthma asma *f*
astrocytes astrocitos *m*

astrocytoma astrocitoma *m*

asymptomatic carotid bruit
soplo *m* asintomático de la carótida

atheromatous plaque placa *f*
ateromatosa *f*

atherosclerosis aterosclerosis *f*

athletic supporter suspensorio *m*

atlantoaxial dislocation
dislocación *f* atlantoaxoidea

atlas atlas *m*

atrial fibrillation fibrilación *f*
atrial

atrial flutter aleteo *m* auricular

atrial septal defect (ASD)
comunicación *f* interauricular (CIA)

atrioventricular node nudo *m*
atrioventricular

atrium atrio *m*

attending physician médico *m*
adscrito

auditory canal conducto *m*
auditivo

aura aura *f*

auricle aurícula *f*

auto-immune disease enfermedad
f de autoinmunidad

automatism automatismo *m*

autonomic nervous system
sistema *m* nervioso autónomo

avulsion fracture fractura *f*
avulsiva

axial compression compresión *f*
axial

axon axón *m*

azathioprine azatioprina *f*

B

back espalda *f*

back brace/support braguero *m*,
corset *m* lumbosacro *m*, corsé *m*,
espaldera *f*, faja *f*

back, lower parte *f* baja de la
espalda, cintura *f Mex, USA*

back, upper espalda *f*, hombros *m*

backbone columna *f* vertebral,
espina *f* dorsal, espinazo *m*

bacterial bacteriano

bacterial arthritis artritis *f*
bacteriana

bag of waters fuente *f*, bolsa *f* de
las aguas

balance equilibrio *m*

baldness calvicie *f*

ball and socket joint cabeza *f* y
cavidad *f* articular

balloon angioplasty angioplastia *f*
con sonda balón/globo

bandage envoltura *f*, venda *f*,
vendaje *m*

bandaid curita *f*

barbiturate barbitúrico *m*

barium enema enema *f* de bario

barium sulfate sulfato *m* de bario

barium swallow deglución *f* de
bario, bario *m* por vía bucal

Bartholin cyst quiste *m* de
Bartholin

Bartholin gland carcinoma
carcinoma *m* de la glándula de
Bartholin

basal body temperature graph
gráfica *f* de la temperatura corporal
basal

basal cell carcinoma carcinoma *m*
basocelular/de células basales

basal ganglia ganglios *m* basales

basilar artery migraine jaqueca *f*
de la arteria basilar

bear down pujar

beat (heart) latido *m*

bed rest reposo *m*

bed, to stay in guardar cama

bedpan bacinilla *f*

bedridden postrado en cama

belly panza *f*, vientre *m*

belly button ombligo *m*

Bence-Jones proteins proteínas *f*
de Bence-Jones

bend agacharse, doblarse

bend doblar

benign benigno

benign exertional headache
cefalalgia *f* benigna por esfuerzo

benign prostatic hypertrophy (BPH) hipertrofia *f* prostática benigna

benign prostatic hyperplasia hiperplasia *f* prostática benigna

benserazide benseracida *f*

beta blocker bloqueador *m* beta

biceps bíceps *m*

bicornuate uterus útero *m* bicórneo

big toe dedo *m* gordo

bile bilis *f*, hiel *f*

bill cobro *m*, cuenta *f*

bind apretar

biofeedback biorretroalimentación *f*

biological therapy terapia *f* biológica, bioterapia *f*

biopsy biopsia *f*

biperiden biperidén *m*

birth nacimiento *m*, parto *m*

birth control control *m* de nacimiento/natalidad, planificación *f* familiar

birth control pill píldora *f* anticonceptiva

birth, give dar a luz

birthdate fecha *f* de nacimiento

birthplace lugar *m* de nacimiento

bite mordedura *f*, mordida *f*

bite down apretar los dientes

bite (insect) picadura *f*, piquete *m*

black and blue amoratado, morado

black eye ojo *m* morado

black out desmayarse

black widow spider araña viuda *f* negra

bladder vejiga *f*

bladder cancer cáncer *m* de (la) vejiga

bland diet régimen *m* de comida no picante

blast cell hemoblasto *m*, hemocitoblasto *m*

bleed sangrar

bleeding desangramiento *m*, hemorragia *f*, sangrado *m*, sangría *f*

blink parpadear

blister ampolla *f*, vejiga *f*

bloated envarado

bloating hinchazón *f*

blockage obstrucción *f*

blood sangre *f*

blood cell célula *f* sanguínea

blood count, blood-cell count biometría *f* hemática, recuento *m* sanguíneo

blood poisoning envenenamiento *m* de sangre

blood pressure (BP) presión *f* arterial, presión sanguínea, tensión *f* arterial (TA)

blood pressure cuff esfigmomanómetro *m*, tensiómetro *m*, abrazadera *f* hinchable

blood stream torrente *m* sanguíneo

blood test análisis *m* de sangre

blood type grupo *m* sanguíneo

blood vessel vaso *m* sanguíneo

blood work análisis *f*/pruebas *f* de sangre

bloodstream corriente *f* sanguínea, torrente *m* sanguíneo

bloody nose hemorragia *f* nasal, desangramiento *m* en las narices, sangrar por la nariz, sangramiento *m* por la nariz

bloody stool defecación *f* sanguinolenta

blotch mancha *f*, erupción *f*

blow soplar

blow one's nose sonarse la nariz

blurred vision vista *f* borrosa, vista empañada

BM (bowel movement) defecación *f*, evacuación *f*

bodily fluids fluidos *m* corporales

body cast yeso *m* troncal

boil absceso *m* (de la piel), furúnculo *m*

bone hueso *m*

bone graft injerto *m* óseo

bone infarction infarto *m* óseo

bone marrow médula *f* ósea
bone tumor tumor *m* óseo
bony ankylosis anquilosis *f* ósea
booster shot inyección *f* de
refuerzo, revacunación *f*
bottle, baby biberón *m*, teta *f*,
mamadera *f*
bottle feed alimentar con biberón
bottom (i.e., *buttocks*) nalgas *f*
bowel movement (BM) defecación
f, evacuación *f*
bowel movement, to have a
defecar, evacuar, obrar
bowel resection resección *f* del
intestino
bowels intestinos *m*, entrañas *f*,
tripas *f*
Bowen's disease enfermedad *f* de
Bowen
bow-legged patizambo, zambo,
cascorro
brace, back braguero *m*, corset *m*,
corsé *m*
brace, orthopedic férula *f* para
miembros, soporte *m*
braces, dental bandas *f*, frenos *m*
brachial artery arteria *f* braquial
brachiocephalic trunk tronco *m*
braquiocefálico
bradycardia bradicardia *f*
bradykinesia bradicinesia *f*
brain cerebro *m*
brains sesos *m*
brainstem tallo *m* cerebral
brainstem auditory evoked
response test medición *f* de las
respuestas evocadas auditivas del
tallo cerebral
break wind arrojar flatos
breast pecho *m*, seno *m*
breast bone esternón *m*, hueso *m*
del pecho
breast cancer cáncer *m* mamario,
cáncer de (la) mama, cáncer de(l)
seno, cáncer de(l) pecho
breast engorgement ingurgitación
f mamaria

breast feed amamantar, dar pecho,
dar de mamar
breast self-examination (BSE)
autoexamen *m* de la mama/del
seno, autoexploración *f* mamaria
breast tenderness mastalgia *f*
breath aliento *m*
breath, to hold aguantar/detener
la respiración
breathe respirar
breathe deeply respirar profundo
breathe in inspirar, tomar aire
breathing respiración *f*, resuello *m*
breech asentaderas *f*, nalgas *f*,
trasero *m*
breech birth/delivery
presentación *f* de nalgas,
presentación podálica
breech presentation presentación
f de nalgas
bridge (dental) puente *m* (dental)
bridge (nose) caballete *m*,
puente *m*
bring on causar, producir, provocar
Brodie's abscess absceso *m* de
Brodie
bronchitis bronquitis *f*,
inflamación *m* de los bofes
bronchoscopy broncoscopia *f*
brow frente *f*
Brucella osteomyelitis
osteomielitis *f* provocada por
Brucella
bruise cardenal *m*, magulladura *f*,
moretón *m*
bruit ruido *m*
brush one's teeth cepillarse los
dientes
bubo bubón *m*
bubonic plague peste *f* bubónica
buck teeth dientes *m* salidos
buckle (knee, leg) aflojarse,
falsear
build (i.e., body type) complexión
f, figura *f*, talle *m*, tipo *m*
buildup acumulación *f*, depósito *m*
bulbs bulbos *m*

bulge prominencia *f*, abultamiento *m*

bump chichón *m*, golpe *m*, hinchazón *f*, topetazo *m*

bump chocar, golpear, topar

bump (head, etc.) darse en (la cabeza, etc.)

bunion juanete *m*

burn quemadura *f*

burn quemar(se), arder

burning (pain) ardor *m*

burp eructar

burp (baby) hacer eructar

bursa bolsa *f*

bursitis bursitis *f*

burst reventar(se)

buttocks asentaderas *f*, cachetes *m*, nalgas *f*, trasero *m*

buzzing zumbido *m*

bypass desviación *f*, derivación *f*, injerto *m* de derivación

C

calcaneus calcáneo *m*

calcium antagonists antagonistas *f* del calcio

calf pantorrilla *f*, chamorro *m Mex, USA*

callus callo *m*

calorie caloría *f*

canal conducto *m*

cancellous canceloso

cancer cáncer *m*

cancerous tissue tejido *m* canceroso

candidiasis candidiasis *f*

cane (curved) bastón *m*

cane (straight) bordón *m*

canker sore afta *f*

capillary capilar *m*

capitate bone hueso *m* capitado

capitellum capitellum *m*

capsular sac saco *m* capsular

capsule cápsula *f*

carbamazepine carbamacepina *f*

carbidopa carbidopa *f*

carbon dioxide dióxido/bióxido *m* de carbono

carbon monoxide monóxido *m* de carbono

carbuncle carbúnculo *m*, carbunco *m*

carcinogen carcinógeno *m*

carcinogenesis carcinogénesis *f*

carcinoma in situ carcinoma *m* in situ

cardiac catheterization cateterización *f* cardiaca, cateterismo *m* cardiaco

cardiac function función *f* cardiaca

cardiac monitor monitor *m* cardiaco

cardiac output gasto *m* cardiaco

cardiomyopathy cardiomiopatía *f*

cardiopulmonary resuscitation (CPR) resucitación *f*/reanimación *f* cardiopulmonar (RCP)

cardiovascular disorder/problem padecimiento *m* cardiovascular

carie carie *f*

carotid artery arteria *f* carótida

carotid endarterectomy endarterectomía *f* carótida

carotid phonoangiography fonoangiografía *f* de la carótida

carpal fracture fractura *f* carpiana

carpal tunnel syndrome (CTS) síndrome *m* del túnel carpiano

carpus carpo *m*

carry to term llevar a término

cartilage cartílago *m*

cast yeso *m*, casco *m*

cast, in a estar enyesado

CAT scan (computerized axial tomography) (exploración *f* de) tomografía *f* axial computada/computarizada (TAC)

cataract catarata *f*

catheter catéter *m*, sonda *f*

cauda equina cauda *f* equina

cauterization cauterización *f*

cavitation cavitación *f*

cavity (dental) carie *f*, picadura *f*, diente *m* podrido
cavus feet pies *m* cavos
central vestibular disorder trastorno *m* central del aparato vestibular
cephalalgia cefalea *f*
cerebellum cerebelo *m*
cerebral cortex córtex *f*/corteza *f* cerebral
cerebral embolism embolio *m* cerebral
cerebral hemorrhage hemorragia *f* cerebral
cerebral palsy parálisis *f* cerebral
cerebral thrombosis trombosis *f* cerebral
cerebral ventricle ventrículo *m* cerebral
cerebrospinal fluid líquido *m* cerebrospinal
cerebrovascular cerebrovascular
cerebrum cerebrum *m*, cerebro *m*
cervical cervical
cervical cap capuchón *m* cervical
cervical collar collar *m* cervical, collarín *m*
cervical punch biopsy biopsia *f* cervical en sacabocados
cervical region región *f* cervical
cervical stenosis estenosis *f* cervical
cervical vertebra vértebra *f* cervical
cervicitis cervicitis *f*
cervix cuello *m* (de la matriz), cérvix *f*
cesarean section sección *f* cesárea
chancre chancro *m*
chancroid chancroide *m*
change of life cambio *m* de vida
chapped lips labios *m* agrietados/partidos
Charcot's joint articulación *f* de Charcot
charley horse agujeta *f*

chart expediente *m*
checkup chequeo *m*
Chlamydia Chlamydia *f*
chromosome cromosoma *m*
chloasma (blotches on the skin) pano *m*
chronic granulocytic leukemia (CGL) leucemia *f* granulocítica crónica
chronic lymphocytic leukemia (CLL) leucemia *f* linfocítica crónica
cheek cachete *m*, mejilla *f*
cheek bone pómulo *m*
chemoprevention quimioprofilaxia *f*
chemotherapy quimioterapia *f*
chest pecho *m*, tórax *m*
chew masticar
chewable masticable
chicken pox varicela *f*, viruela *f* de gallina, viruela loca
childbirth parto *m*
childhood illness enfermedad *f* de la infancia/niñez
chills escalofríos *m*
chin barba *f*/barbilla *f*, mentón *m*, piocha *f*
chiropractic therapy terapia *f* quiropráctica
chiropractor quiropráctico *m*
choke ahogarse, asfixiarse, sofocarse
choke (food) atragantarse
choking atragantamiento *m*, estrangulación *f*
cholera cólera *m*
cholesterol colesterol *m*
chondroblastoma condroblastoma *m*
chondromyxoid fibroma condromixofibroma *m*
chondrosarcoma condrosarcoma *m*
choroid coroides *f*
chylomicron quilomicrón *m*
cicatrized lesion herida *f* cicatrizada

cingulectomy cingulectomía *f*
cirrhosis cirrosis *f*
clammy viscoso, húmedo y frío
clamp pinza(s) *f*
clavicle clavícula *f*
clear up resolverse
cleft palate abertura *f* del paladar, boquinete *m*, labio *m* cucho, labio leporino
clench apretar
click chasquido *m*
clicking (noise made by joint) chasquido *m*, trueno *m*
climax orgasmo *m*
clinic clínica *f*
clinical radiographic examination revisión *f* clínica radiográfica
clinical trial ensayo *m* clínico
clitoris clítoris *m*
closed fracture fractura *f* cerrada
clot, blood coágulo *m*
clot coagular(se)
clotting coagulación *f*
cloudy urine orina *f* turbia
cloudy vision vista *f* nublada
cluster headache cefalea *f* en racimos/grupos/acúmulos
Clutton's joint articulación *f* de Clutton
cobalt treatment tratamiento *m* con cobalto
coccidioidomycosis coccidioidomicosis *f*
coccygectomy coccigectomía *f*
coccyx cóccix *m*
cochlea cóclea *f*
codeine codeína *f*
coitus coito *m*
cold catarro *m*, resfrío *m*
cold knife conization conización *f* con cuchillo frío
cold sore fuego *m* (úlcera en los labios)
colic cólico *m*
collagen colágeno *m*

collar bone clavícula *f*, hueso *m* del cuello
collateral circulation circulación *f* colateral
Colle's fracture fractura *f* de Colle
colon colon *m*
colonoscope colonoscopio *m*
color-blind daltónico
colostomy colostomía *f*
colpocleisis colpocleisis *f*
colporrhaphy colporrafia *f*
colposcope colposcopio *m*
coma coma *m*
come to volver en sí
comminuted fracture fractura *f* conminuta
communicable disease enfermedad *f* transmisible
complain quejarse
complaint malestar *m*, queja *f*
complexion cutis *m*, tez *f*
compound fracture fractura *f* expuesta/abierta
compress compresa *f*, parche *m*
compression fracture fractura *f* por compresión
computed tomography (CT) tomografía *f* computarizada/computada
concussion concusión *f*, conmoción *f*
condom condón *m*, hule *m*, preservativo *m*
condyloma acuminatum condiloma *m* acuminado
cone biopsy biopsia *f* en cono
confusion aturdimiento *m*
congenital heart defect cardiopatía *f* congénita
congestion congestión *f*, constipación *f*, inflamación *f*
congestive heart failure insuficiencia *f* cardiaca congestiva
conization conización *f*
connective tissue tejido *m* conectivo
consciousness, to lose perder el conocimiento

consciousness, to regain volver en sí

constipated estreñido

constipation estreñimiento *m*

constipation, severe entablazón *m*

contact lenses lentes *m* de contacto, pupilentes *m*

contagion contagio *m*

contraceptive anticonceptivo *m*, contraceptivo *m*

contraction contracción *f*, dolor *m* de parto

contraindication contraindicación *f*

contrast medium material *m* de contraste

convalescent hospital clínica *f* de reposo

convulsion ataque *m*, convulsión *f*

coracoid process apófisis *f* coracoides

cordotomy cordotomía *f*

corn callo *m*

cornea córnea *f*

cornual pregnancy embarazo *m* cornual

coronary arteriography arteriografía *f* coronaria

coronary artery arteria *f* coronaria

coronary artery bypass graft injerto *m* de derivación de la arteria coronaria

coronary artery disease (CAD) arteriopatía *f* coronaria

coronary heart disease (CHD) cardiopatía *f* coronaria

coronary occlusion oclusión *f* coronaria

coronary thrombosis trombosis *f* coronaria

coronary vasodilator vasodilatador *m* coronario

corpus callosum corpus *m* callosum

corpus luteum cuerpo *m* amarillo, corpus *m* luteum

cortex corteza *f*, córtex *f*

corticoids corticoides *m*

corticosteroids corticosteroides *m*

cortisone cortisona *f*

cotton algodón *m*

cotton ball bolita *f* de algodón, torunda *f*

cough tos *f*
  dry seca
  hacking fuerte
  persistent rebelde, persistente

cough up desgarrar, expectorar

counseling asesoramiento *m*, psicoterapia *f*, consejería *f*

counteract contrarrestar

CPR (cardiopulmonary resuscitation) resucitación *f*/reanimación *f* cardiopulmonar (RCP)

crack (noise made by joint) trueno *m*

crack (noise made by joint) tronar

cracked (skin) agrietado, partido, reventado

cramp (abdominal) retorcijón *m*

cramp (menstrual) cólico *m* (menstrual)

cramp (muscular) calambre *m*

cranial vault bóveda *f* craneal

cranium cráneo *m*, cranium *m*

craving antojos *m*

creatinine creatinina *f*

Creutzfeldt-Jakob disease enfermedad *f*/síndrome *m* de Creutzfeldt-Jakob

crick in the neck tortícolis *f*

crippled lisiado, tullido

crooked torcido, chueco

cross-eyed bizco, turnio

crotch bifurcación *f*, entrepiernas *f*, ingle *f*

croup garrotillo *m*, ronquera *f*

crown (dental) corona *f*

crowning (childbirth) aparición *f* de la cabeza fetal

crush aplastar, machucar

crushing aplastamiento *m*

crutch muleta *f*, sobaquera *f*
cryosurgery criocirugía *f*
cryothalamotomy destrucción *f* crioquirúrgica del tálamo
cryptococcosis criptococosis *f*
crystal-induced arthritis artritis *f* por cristales
crystalline lens cristalino *m*
CT scan (computed tomography) (exploración *f* de) tomografía *f* computada/computarizada (TC)
CTS (carpal tunnel syndrome) síndrome *m* del tunel carpiano
cuboid bone hueso *m* cuboideo
cul-de-sac cul-de-sac *m*
culdocentesis culdocentesis *f*
culdoscopy culdoscopia *f*
culture, blood hemocultivo *m*
culture, stool coprocultivo *m*
culture, urine urocultivo *m*
cuneiform bone hueso *m* cuneiforme
curettage curetaje *m*, legrado *m*, raspado *m*
curette cureta *f*, raspador *m*
curl encoger(se)
cut cortada
cut down (on) disminuir
cuticle cutícula *f*
cyproheptadine ciproheptadina *f*
cyst quiste *m*
cystectomy cistectomía *f*
cystic adenosis adenosis *f* cística
cystocele cistocele *m*
cystosarcoma phyllodes cistosarcoma *m* filodo
cystoscope cistoscopio *m*
cystoscopy cistoscopia *f*
cystourethrocele cistouretrocele *m*
cytologic citológico

D

D&C (dilation and curettage) dilatación *f* y legrado *m*
damage daño *m*

dandruff caspa *f*
dazed atarantado, aturdido
deaf sordo
deaf-mute sordomudo *m*
deafness sordera *f*
debridement desbridamiento *m*, debridación *f*
deceased difunto *m*
decongestant descongestivo *m*
defecate defecar
defibrillate desfibrilar
defibrillator desfibrilador *m*
deformed deformado
degenerative arthritis artritis *f* degenerativa
degenerative osteoarthritis osteoartritis *f* degenerativa
dehydration deshidratación *f*
delirious delirante
delirious, to be delirar
deliver, give birth dar a luz
deliver (mother) dar a luz
deliver (obstetrician) atender el parto
delivery parto *m*, expulsión *f* del feto
dementia demencia *f*
demineralization desmineralización *f*
dental checkup examen *m*/ chequeo *m* dental
dental floss hilo *m* dental
denture dentadura *f* postiza
dependency farmacodependencia *f*, dependencia *f*
Dependent Personality Disorder trastorno *m* de personalidad dependiente
depressed deprimido
depression depresión *f*
deranged demente, trastornado
descending aorta aorta *f* descendiente
despondent abatido, deprimido, desanimado
diabetes diabetes *f*
diagnosis diagnosis *f*, diagnóstico *m*

diagnostic imaging imágenes diagnósticas
diaphragm diafragma *m*
diaphysectomy diafisectomía *f*
diaphysis diáfisis *f*
diarrhea diarrea *f*
diastole diástole *f*
diastolic diastólico
diastolic pressure presión *f* diastólica
diphtheria difteria *f*
diuretic diurético *m*
diet dieta *f*, régimen *m*
diet, to be on a dieta, estar a
diethylstilbestrol (DES) dietilestilbestrol *m*
digestive tract vía *f* digestiva
digital cardiac angiography (DCA) angiografía *f* cardiaca digital
digital subtraction angiography (DSA) angiografía *f* de su(b)stracción digital
digitalis digital *f*, digitalis *f*
dilated dilatado
dilation dilatación *f*
dilation and curettage (D&C) dilatación *f* y raspado *m*
dilation and evacuation (D&E) dilatación *f* y evacuación *f*
dimple hoyuelo *m*
disability incapacidad *f*
disabled incapacitado
discharge secreción *f*, exudado *m*, derrame *m*
discharge dar de alta
discoid lupus erythematosus lupus *m* eritematoso discoide
discomfort malestar *m*, molestia *f*
disease enfermedad *f*, mal *m* (e.g., *mal de la vesícula*—gallbladder disease)
disk, herniated disco *m* herniado
disk, slipped disco *m* desplazado/zafado
dislocate dislocar(se), zafar(se)
dislocated zafado
dislocation dislocación *f*

disorder trastorno *m*
disposable needle aguja *f* de un solo uso
disposable syringe jeringa *f* de un solo uso
disorientation aturdimiento *m*
distal distal
distal end extremo *m* distal
distress aflicción *f*, angustia *f*
dizziness mareos *m*, vértigo *m*, atarantamiento *m*, tarantas *f*
DNA (deoxyribonucleic acid) ácido *m* desoxirribonucleico (ADN)
donate blood donar sangre
donor donante *m*
dopamine dopamina *f*
Doppler ultrasound test examen *m* ultrasónico Doppler, ultrasonografía *f* Doppler
dorsal neural arch arco *m* dorsal neural
dorsal root rhizotomy rizotomía *f* de la raíz dorsal
dorsal vertebra vértebra *f* dorsal
dosage dosificación *f*, dosis *f*, posología *f*
dose dosis *f*, medida *f*
double vision visión *f*/vista *f* doble
douche ducha *f*, lavada *f*, ducharse
drain drenar(se)
draw blood sacar sangre *f*
dressing apósito *m*, venda *f*, vendaje *m*
drill fresa *f*
drowsiness somnolencia *f*, modorra *f*
drowsy adormilado, somnoliento, soñoliento, amodorrado
drug dependency farmacodependencia *f*
drug interaction interacción *f* de fármacos
drug treatment program programa *m* de tratamiento de narcomanía/farmacodependencia
druggist boticario *m*, farmacéutico *m*

drugstore botica *f*, farmacia *f*
duct conducto *m*
due date fecha *f* estimada del parto
dull (pain) calmar
dull (pain) sordo, lento
dysarthria disartria *f*
dysentery disentería *f*
dysfunctional uterine bleeding (DUB) hemorragia *f* uterina disfuncional
dyskinesia discinesia *f*
dysmenorrhea dismenorrea *f*
dyspareunia dispareunia *f*
dysplasia displasia *f*
dysrhythmia disritmia *f*

E

ear (externally visible) oreja *f*
ear (inner) oído *m*
   external oído externo
   internal oído interno
   middle oído medio
ear scope otoscopio *m*
earache dolor *m* de oído
eardrum tímpano *m*
earlobe lóbulo *m* de la oreja, pulpejo
echocardiography ecocardiografía *f*
eclampsia eclampsia *f*
ectocervical ectocervical
ectopic pregnancy embarazo *m* ectópico
EEG (electroencephalogram) electroencefalograma (EEG) *m*
effacement of the cervix borramiento *m* del cuello
effusion derrame *m*
ejaculation, premature eyaculación *f* precoz
ejection fraction fracción *f* de expulsión
EKG (electrocardiogram) electrocardiograma (ECG) *m*
elbow codo *m*
electrocardiogram (EKG/ECG) electrocardiograma (ECG) *m*

electroconization electroconización *f*
electrode electrodo *m*
electrodesiccation electrodesecación *f*
electroencephalogram (EEG) electroencefalograma (EEG) *m*
electromyogram (EMG) electromiograma (EMG) *m*
electromyography (EMG) electromiografía *f*
electronystagmography electronistagmografía *f*
eliminate eliminar
embarrassed acomplejado
embolism embolio *m*
embryo embrión *m*
Emergency Room sala *f* de emergencia/de urgencias
EMG (electromyogram) electromiograma (EMG) *m*
emotional stress tensión *f* emocional, estrés *m*
enchondroma encondroma *m*
endocervical endocervical
endolymph endolinfa *f*
endolymphatic stromal myosis miosis *f* endolinfática del estroma
endometrial cancer cáncer *m* endometrial
endometrial carcinoma carcinoma *m* endometrial
endometrial cavity cavidad *f* endometrial
endometrial hyperplasia hiperplasia *f* endometrial
endometrial polyps pólipos *m* endometriales
endometriosis endometriosis *f*
endometrium endometrio *m*
endorphin endorfina *f*
endoscopic retrograde cholangiopancreatogram (ERCP) colangiopancreatografía *f* retrógrada endoscópica
endothelium endotelio *m*
enema enema *m*, lavativa *f*

enkephalin encefalina *f*
enterocele enterocele *m*
entry wound orificio *m* de entrada
ependymoma ependimoma *m*
epidermoid carcinoma carcinoma *m* epidermoide
epigastric epigástrico
epilepsy acceso *m*, ataque *m*, epilepsia *f*
epileptic epiléptico
epileptic convulsion/seizure convulsión *f* epiléptica
epileptic focus foco *m* epiléptico
epileptiform epileptiforme
epinephrine epinefrina *f*
epiphyseal plate lámina *f*/línea *f* epifisaria
epiphysis epífisis *f*
epiphysitis epifisitis *f*
episiotomy episiotomía *f*
erection erección *f*
erection, to have enderezar (el miembro), parar (el miembro)
ergotamine tartrate tartrato *m* de ergotamina
erythrocyte eritrocito *m*
erythrocyte sedimentation rate (sed rate) velocidad *f* de sedimentación globular
esophagus esófago *m*
essential hypertension hipertensión *f* esencial
estimated date of confinement (EDC) fecha *f* estimada del parto
estrogen estrógeno *m*
estrogen receptor test prueba *f* de receptor de estrógeno
estrogen replacement therapy terapéutica *f* substitutiva de estrógenos
etiology etiología
European blastomycosis blastomicosis *f* europea
eustachian tube conducto *m* auditivo
evacuate (bowels) vaciar (las entrañas)

Ewing's sarcoma sarcoma *m* de Ewing
examination examen *m*, revisión *f*, reconocimiento *m*, exploración *f*
examining table, examination table mesa *f* de exploración/reconocimiento
excise extirpar
exercise hypotension hipotensión *f* de esfuerzo
exertion esfuerzo *m*
exhaustion agotamiento *m*, fatiga *f*
exit wound orificio *m* de salida
exocervix exocérvix *f*
expiration date fecha *f* de caducidad/claudicación/vencimiento
expire (breathe out) espirar
expire (die) expirar, fallecer
expire (prescription) vencer, caducar, claudicar
exploratory surgery cirugía *f* exploradora
extension extensión *f*
extension dislocation dislocación *f* por extensión
extracerebral decarboxylase inhibitors inhibidores *m* extracerebrales de la descarboxilasa
extract (a tooth) sacar, extraer
extreme unction santos óleos *m*
extremity extremidad *f*
   lower extremidad inferior
   upper extremidad superior
exudation exudación *f*
eye ojo *m*
eye, corner of ángulo *m* del ojo
eye scope oftalmoscopio *m*
eye, white of blanco *m* del ojo
eyeball globo *m* del ojo
eyebrow ceja *f*
eyedropper cuentagotas *f*
eyeglasses anteojos *m*, espejuelos *m*, gafas *f*, lentes *m*
eyelash pestaña *f*
eyelid párpado *m*

F

face cara *f*
face-down boca abajo
face-up boca arriba
facial paresis paresia *f* facial
failure (organ) insuficiencia *f*
faint desmayarse
faint débil
fainting desmayo *m*
fainting spell desmayo *m*
fallopian tube trompa *f* de Falopio
family doctor médico *m* de cabecera, doctor *m* de planta *Mex, USA*
family planning planificación *f* familiar
family practice medicina *f* familiar
farsighted hipermétrope, présbite
fart arrojar flatos
fast ayunar
fatigue fatiga *f*
feces excremento *m*, heces *f*
fee honorario *m*
femoral epiphyses epífisis *f* crural/femoral
femur fémur *m*
fenestration fenestración *f*
fertilization fecundación *f*
fester enconarse
festination festinación *f*
fetal development desarrollo *m* del feto
fetal monitor monitor *m* (cardiaco) fetal
fetus feto *m*
fever calentura *f*, fiebre *f*
fever blister fuego *m* (ampolla en los labios)
fiber fibra *f*, residuo *m*
fibrillation fibrilación *f*
fibrin fibrina *f*
fibrocystic disease enfermedad *f* fibroquística
fibroid mioma *m*, fibromioma *m*
fibrosarcoma fibrosarcoma *m*
fibrous fibroso

fibrous ankylosis anquilosis *f* fibrosa
fibula peroné *m*
file expediente *m*
fill (prescription) surtir
fill (tooth) obturar, empastar
filling empaste *m*
fimbrial adhesion adherencia *f* de la fimbria
finding hallazgo *m*
finger dedo *m*
  index dedo índice
  little dedo meñique
  middle (dedo) corazón, dedo cordial, dedo de en medio
  ring dedo anular/anillo
fingernail uña *f*
fingertip yema *f* del dedo
first aid primeros auxilios *m*
first aid kit botiquín *m*
fist puño
fist, to make apretar el puño, cerrar la mano
fistula fístula *f*
flabby flojo, fláccido
flaccid fláccido
flake escama *f*
flap colgajo *m*
flare up agravar(se)
flatulent envarado
flex doblarse, flexionarse
flexion contracture contractura *f* de flexión
floss limpiar con hilo dental
flu gripa *f*, gripe *f*, flu *m* (*USA*)
fluid líquido *m*
flunitrazepam flunitracepam *m*
fluoroscopic fluoroscópico
fluoroscopy fluoroscopia *f*
fluoxetine hydrochloride clorhidrato *m* de fluoxetina
flush ruborizarse, sonrojarse
flushed (face) ruborizado, asombrado
flutter aleteo *m* auricular
foam espuma *f*

foam rubber pad almohadilla *f* de espuma de hule

follicle folículo *m*

follow-up control *m*, seguimiento *m*

follow-up visit visita *f* de vigilancia

fontanel/fontanelle fontanela *f*, mollera *f*

foot pie *m*

footling presentation presentación *f* podálica

foramen foramen *f*

forceps fórceps *m*, pinzas *f*

forearm antebrazo *m*

forehead frente *f*

fractional curettage raspado *m*/ legrado *m* por fracciones

fracture fractura *f*, quebradura *f*

fracture fracturar

frail débil, héctico, hético

frank breech presentation presentación *f* franca de nalgas

friction rub frote *m*

frontal lobe lóbulo *m* frontal

frostbite congelación *f*

frozen shoulder hombro *m* congelado

fungus hongo *m*

fusion fusión *f*

G

gag sentir náusea(s)

gain weight aumentar de peso, engordar

gallbladder vesícula *f* biliar

gallstone cálculo *m* biliar

gargle hacer gárgaras

Gartner duct cyst quiste *m* del conducto de Gartner

gas, to pass pasar gas, tirarse gases

gash tajo *m*

gastritis gastritis *f*

gauze gasa *f*

general anesthetic anestesia *f* general

general practitioner médico *m* general

genetic counseling asesoría *f* genética

genetic predisposition predisposición *f* genética

genital tuberculosis tuberculosis *f* genital

genital warts verrugas *f* genitales

germ germen *m*, microbio *m*

German measles rubéola *f*, sarampión *m* alemán

giant cell tumor tumor *m* de célula gigante

gibbus joroba *f*

Gilchrist's disease enfermedad *f* de Gilchrist

gingivitis gingivitis *f*

gland glándula *f*

glans penis glande *m*

glenohumeral osteoarthritis osteoartritis *f* glenohumeral

glenoid glenoide

glial cells células *f* gliales

glioblastoma multiforme glioblastoma *m* multiforme

glioma glioma *m*

glucose solution solución *f* glucosa

go away (pain) quitarse

goggles lentes *m* protectores

goiter bocio *m*, buche *m*

gold salts sales *f* de oro

gonadotropin gonadotropina *f*

gonorrhea gonorrea *f*, purgación *f*

gonorrheal arthritis artritis *f* gonorreica

goose bumps/pimples piel *f* de gallina

gout gota *f*

gown (hospital) bata

graft injerto *m*

graft, skin injerto *m* cutáneo

grand mal gran mal *m*

granulocytes granulocitos *m*

granulocytic leukemia leucemia *f* granulocítica

granulocytopenia
granulocitopenia *f*
granuloma inguinale granuloma
m inguinal
grasp prensión *f*
grasp agarrar
grate (noise made by joint)
rechinar
grating (noise made by a joint)
rechinido *m*, ruido *m* raspante
greater trochanter trocánter *m*
mayor
greater tuberosity tuberosidad *f*
mayor
greenstick fracture fractura *f* en
tallo/caña/rama verde
grief duelo *m*
grinding rozamiento *m*
grip prensión *f*
grip agarrar, apretar
grit (teeth) rechinar (dientes)
groin empeine *m*, ingle *f*, aldilla *f*
gumma goma *f*
gums encías *f*, gingivas *f*
gunshot balazo *m*, tiro *m*
gunshot wound balazo *m*, herida *f*
de arma de fuego
guts tripas *f*

H

haemophilus ducreyi
haemophylus *m* Ducrey,
Hemophilus *m* ducreyi
hair cabello *m*, pelo *m*
hair (on body) vello *m*
hair follicle folículo *m* piloso
hairline fracture fisura *f*
hamate bone hueso *m*
ganchoso/unciforme
hammer martillo *m*
hammertoe deformity
deformidad *f* de dedos en martillo
hamstring tendón *m* del hueso
poplíteo, tendón de la corva
hamulus hamulus *m*
hand, back of dorso *m* de la mano

hand, fleshy part of pulpejo *m*
hangnail uñero *m*, padrastro *m*
hard of hearing medio sordo
hardening of the arteries
endurecimiento *m* de las arterias
harelip labio *m* cucho, labio *m*
leporino
harmful dañino, nocivo
harmful effect efecto *m* nocivo
harmless inocuo
HDL (high-density lipoprotein)
LAD (lipoproteína *f* de alta
densidad)
headache dolor *m* de cabeza,
cefalea *f*
heal curar(se), sanar, encorar
health care atención *f* médica,
servicios *m* médicos
health insurance seguro *m* médico
healthcare center centro *m* de
salud
hearing audición *f*, oído *m*
heart corazón *m*
heart attack ataque *m* cardiaco,
infarto *m*
heart disease enfermedad *f* del
corazón
heart murmur soplo *m* cardiaco
heart rate frecuencia *f* cardiaca
heart transplant trasplante *m* del
corazón, trasplante cardiaco
heartburn acedía *f*, agruras *f*
heating pad almohada *f* eléctrica,
cojín *m* eléctrico
heel talón *m*
height gauge talla *f*
hematocolpos hematocolpos *m*
hematogenous arthritis artritis *f*
hematógena
hematogenous osteomyelitis
osteomielitis *f* hematógena
hematoma hematoma *m*,
moretón *m*
hematometra hematómetra *f*
hemiarthroplasty
hemiartroplastia *f*

hemiplegic migraine jaqueca *f* hemipléjica
hemoglobin hemoglobina *f*
hemorrhage desangramiento *m*, hemorragia *f*
hemorrhoids almorranas *f*, hemorroides *f*
hepatitis hepatitis *f*
hermaphroditism hermafroditismo *m*
hernia hernia *f*, rotura *f*
herniate herniarse
herniated disk disco *m* herniado
herpes herpes *m*, zona *f*
herpes genitalis herpes *m* genital
hiccup hipo *m*
hickey chupete *m*, chupón *m*
hidradenoma hidradenoma *m*
high blood pressure alta presión *f* sanguínea, presión *f* alta
high-density lipoprotein (HDL) lipoproteína *f* de alta densidad (LAD), lipoproteína de densidad elevada
high-fiber diet dieta *f* de mucha fibra, régimen *m* de mucho residuo
hip cadera *f*
hip capsule cápsula *f* de la cadera
hippocampus hipocampo *m*, hippocampus *m*
hirsutism hirsutismo *m*
histocompatibility histocompatibilidad *f*
histoplasmosis histoplasmosis *f*
histrionic histriónico
HIV (human immunodeficiency virus) virus *m* de inmunodeficiencia humana (VIH)
hives ronchas *f*, urticaria *f*
hoarse ronco
hoarseness ronquera *f*
hobby pasatiempo *m*
hold one's breath aguantar la respiración, detener la respiración
Holter monitor monitor *m* (de) Holter

hormone therapy terapia *f* hormonal, hormonoterapia *f*
hospice asilo *m* (para pacientes con enfermedades terminales)
hospitalized internado, hospitalizado
host huésped *m*
hot flashes bochornos *m*, calores *m*
household cleansers agentes *m* de limpieza, productos *m* de limpieza
housemaid's knee rodilla *f* de fregona
human chorionic gonadotropin (HCG) gonadotropina *f* coriónica humana
humeral artery arteria *f* humeral
humerus húmero *m*
hurt badly doler feo
Huntington's disease enfermedad *f* de Huntington
hydatidiform mole mola *f* hidatitiforme
hydrated hidratado
hydrocephalus hidrocéfalo *m*
hydrocortisone hidrocortisona *f*
hydronephrosis hidronefrosis *f*
hydrosalpinx hidrosalpinx *m*
hydrotherapy hidroterapia *f*
hydroureter hidrouréter *m*
hydroxchloroquine hidroxicloroquina *f*
hymen himen *m*
hymenotomy himenotomía *f*
hypercholesterolemia hipercolesterolemia *f*
hyperextension hiperextensión *f*
hyperflexion hiperflexión *f*
hypermenorrhea hipermenorrea *f*
hyperplasia hiperplasia *f*
hypersensitivity hipersensibilidad *f*
hypertension hipertensión *f*, presión *f* alta
hypertriglyceridemia hipertrigliceridemia *f*

hypertrophic arthritis artritis *f* hipertrófica
hypodermic syringe jeringa *f* hipodérmica, aguja *f* de inyecciones
hypoplastic vagina vagina *f* hipoplástica
hypothalamus hipotálamo *m*
hysterectomy histerectomía *f*
hysterography histerografía *f*
hysterosalpingography histerosalpingografía *f*

I

ice pack bolsa *f* con hielo
ICU (intensive care unit) unidad *f* de cuidados intensivos
id ello *m*
idiopathic uterine hypertrophy hipertrofia *f* uterina idiopática
ilium ilion *m*
immobilization inmovilización *f*
immune inmune
immune system sistema *m* inmunológico
immunization inmunización *f*, vacuna *f*
immunoglobulin inmunoglobulina *f*
immunosuppressive drug fármaco *m* inmunosupresor
immunotherapy inmunoterapia *f*
impacted impactado
impacted fracture fractura *f* impactada, fractura con impacto
imperforate hymen himen *m* imperforado
impetigo empétigo *m*
in a cast enyesado
incised wound herida *f* incisa
incision cortada *f*, incisión *f*
incompetent cervix cuello *m* incompetente
index finger dedo *m* índice
indigestion indigestión *f*, estómago *m* sucio
indigestion, to have ahito, estar

industrial injury lesión *f* de trabajo
infantile spasm espasmo *m* infantil
infarct dementia demencia *f* por infarto
infectious arthritis artritis *f* infecciosa
infectious disease enfermedad *f* infecciosa
influenza gripa *f*, gripe *f*, influenza *f*, flu *USA*
ingrown nail uña *f* encarnada/enterrada
inhaler inhalador *m*
injection inyección *f*, "chat" *m USA*
injure lastimar(se), lesionar(se)
injured herido, lastimado, lesionado
injury lastimadura *f*, lesión *f*
insane demente, loco
insect bite mordedura *f* de insecto, piquete *m* de insecto
insole plantilla *f*
insomnia insomnio *m*
instep empeine *m*
insulin insulina *f*
insurance seguro *m*, aseguranza *f USA*
insured asegurado
intensive care cuidados *m* intensivos, terapia *f* intensiva, vigilancia *f* intensiva
intensive care unit (ICU) unidad *f* de cuidados intensivos
interaction interacción *f*
interauricular septum tabique *m* interauricular
intercourse coito *m*
interferon interferón *m*
intermediate-density lipoprotein (IDL) lipoproteína *f* de media densidad
intermenstrual bleeding hemorragia *f* intermenstrual
intermittent claudication claudicación *f* intermitente

internal bleeding hemorragia *f* interna

interphalangeal interfalángico

interphalangeal joint articulación *f* interfalángica

interstitial radiation therapy radioterapia *f* intersticial

interventricular septum tabique *m* interventricular

intervertebral disk disco *m* intervertebral

intestine, large intestino *m* grueso/mayor

intestine, small intestino *m* delgado/pequeño

intestines intestinos *m*, tripas *f*

intra-articular injection inyección *f* intraarticular

intrauterine device (IUD) dispositivo *m* intrauterino

intrauterine pregnancy embarazo *m* intrauterino

intravenous endovenoso, intravenoso

intravenous pyelogram (IVP) urograma *m* excretorio, pielograma *m* intravenoso

invasive cervical cancer cáncer *m* invasor de la cérvix, carcinoma *m* cervical invasor, carcinoma invasor del cuello uterino

involucrum involucro *m*

iodine yodo *m*

iris iris *m*

iron deficiency anemia anemia *f* ferropriva

irradiation irradiación *f*

ischemia isquemia *f*

ischium isquion *m*

islet cell cancer cáncer *m* de célula(s) insular(es)

islets of Langerhans islotes *m* de Langerhans

itch comezón *f*, picazón *f*, sauna *f*

itch picar

itchy con comezón *f*

IUD (intrauterine device) dispositivo *m* intrauterino (DIU)

IV (intravenous administration of medication) administración *f* intravenosa/endovenosa de medicamentos (IV)

J

jab picar

jabbing punzante

jar sacudir

jarring movement jalón *m*, movimiento *m* brusco, sacudida *f*

jaundice ictericia *f*, enfermedad *f* amarilla, piel *f* amarilla

jaw mandíbula *f*, quijada *f*

joint articulación *f*, coyuntura *f*

joint aspiration aspiración *f* articular

joint cavity cavidad *f* articular

joint replacement sustitución *f* protésica de la articulación

jugular vein vena *f* yugular

K

kidney (*n*) riñón *m*

kidney (*adj*) renal

kidney belt cinturón *m*, faja *f*

kidney dialysis diálisis *f* renal

kidney stone cálculo *m* renal, piedra *f* renal

knee rodilla *f*

knee, back of corva *f*

kneecap rótula *f*, hueso *m* de la rodilla

knuckle nudillo *m*

kyphosis cifosis *f*

L

label etiqueta *f*

labia labios *m* (de la vagina)

labia majora labios *m* mayores

labia minora labios *m* menores

labor parto *m*, trabajo *m* de parto

labor pain dolor *m* de parto
laboratory study/test estudio *m* de gabinete
labyrinth laberinto *m*
labyrinthectomy laberintectomía *f*
lacerated cervix cuello *m* desgarrado
laceration cortada *f*, laceración *f*
lame cojo
lamina lámina *f*
laminagraphy laminografía *f*
laminectomy laminectomía *f*
laparoscopy laparoscopia *f*
laparotomy laparotomía *f*
large cell carcinoma carcinoma *m* de células grandes
larva larva *f*
larynx laringe *f*
laser angioplasty angioplastia *f* por láser
last rites santos óleos *m*
latent syphilis sífilis *f* latente
lateral condyle cóndilo *m* lateral
lateral flexion flexión *f* lateral
lateral malleolus maléolo *m* lateral
lavage lavado *m*
laxative laxante *m*, purga *f*, purgante *m*
LDL (low-density lipoprotein) LBD (lipoproteína *f* de baja densidad)
L-dopa L-dopa *f*
lean forward inclinarse hacia adelante
left-handed zurdo
left ventricular hypertrophy hipertrofia *f* del ventrículo izquierdo, ventrículo izquierdo hipertrofiado
leg pierna *f*
leiomyoma leiomioma *m*
leiomyosarcoma leiomiosarcoma *m*
leprosy lepra *f*
lesser trochanter trocánter *m* menor

lesser tuberosity tuberosidad *f* menor
let-down reflex reflejo *m* del chorro de leche
lethal mortal
leukemia leucemia *f*
leukocytes leucocitos *m*
leukorrhea leucorrea *f*
levodopa levodopa *f*
libido libido *f*
lice piojos *m*
lift alzar, levantar
ligament ligamento *m*
lightheaded mareado
lightheadedness mareo *m*
limb extremidad *f*, miembro *m*
    lower extremidad inferior
    upper extremidad superior
limbic system sistema *m* límbico
limp cojera *f*
limp cojear, renguear/renquear
lining revestimiento *m*
lip labio *m*
    lower labio inferior
    upper labio superior
lipoprotein lipoproteína *f*
liquid contrast medio *m* de contraste
lithium litio *m*
little finger dedo *m* meñique
little toe dedo *m* pequeño
liver hígado *m*
lobe lóbulo *m*
lobule lobulillo *m*
local anesthetic anestesia *f* local
lochia loquios *m*
lock (joint) atorar, entesar, trabar
lock-jaw pasmo *m* seco, trismo *m*
longitudinal fracture fractura *f* longitudinal
lose weight bajar de peso
low back pain dolor *m* lumbar bajo
low-density lipoprotein (LDL) lipoproteína *f* de baja densidad (LBD)
low back parte *f* baja de la espalda, cintura *f*

low-density lipoprotein (LDL) lipoproteína *f* de baja densidad (LBD)

lumbar lumbar

lumbar puncture punción *f* lumbar

lumbar vertebra vértebra *f* lumbar

lumbosacral lumbosacro

lumen lumen *m*

lump bola/bolita *f*, chichón *m*, hinchazón *f*

lumpectomy lumpectomía *f*

lunate bone hueso *m* semilunar

lung pulmón *m*, bofe *m*

lung cancer cáncer *m* de(l) pulmón, cáncer pulmonar, carcinoma *m* de pulmón

lung function función pulmonar

luteinizing hormone-releasing hormone agonists (LHRH agonists) hormona *f* liberadora de hormona leuteinizante

luxation luxación *f*

lymph linfa *f*

lymph node ganglio *m* linfático

lymphangiogram linfangiograma *m*

lymphatic system sistema *m* linfático

lymphedema linfedema *m*

lymphocytic leukemia leucemia *f* linfocítica

lymphocytes linfocitos *m*

lymphogranuloma venereum (LGV) linfogranuloma *m* venéreo/inguinal

lymphoma linfoma *m*

M

magnetic resonance imaging (MRI) imágenes *f* por/de resonancia magnética, resonancia *f* magnética nuclear

malaria malaria *f*, paludismo *m*

malignant maligno

malnutrition desnutrición *f*

malpractice negligencia *f* médica

mammary glands glándulas *f* mammarias

mammogram mamograma *m*

mandible mandíbula *f*/quijada *f*

mania manía *f*

manic-depressive maníaco-depresivo

marble bones huesos *m* marmóreos

marrow médula *f* ósea

marrow thrombosis trombosis *f* medular

marsupialization marsupialización *f*

massage dar masaje, sobar

mastectomy mastectomía *f*

measles sarampión *m*

meclizine meclicina *f*

meconium meconio *m*

medial medio

medial malleolus maléolo *m* interno

medial meniscus menisco *m* interno

median nerve nervio *m* mediano

mediastinoscopy mediastinoscopia *f*

mediastinotomy mediastinotomía *f*

medical history antecedentes *m* médicos, historia *f* clínica

medical practitioner facultativo(a) *m* / *f* médico(a)

medical records expediente *m* médico

medicated compress cataplasmo *m*

medication medicamento *m*

medulla médula *f*

medullary canal canal *m* medular

medulloblastoma meduloblastoma *m*

melancholy melancolía *f*

melanocytes melanocitos *m*

melanoma melanoma *m*

member (penis) miembro *m*

membrane membrana *f*

menarche menarquía *f*, menarca *f*

Ménière's disease enfermedad *f*/ vértigo *m* de Ménière

meninges meninges *f*

meningioma meningioma *m*

meningitis meningitis *f*

meniscus tear desgarro *m* de(l) menisco

menopause menopausia *f*, cambio *m* de vida

menses menstruo *m*

menstrual period periodo *m* (menstrual), regla *f*

menstruation menstruación *f*

mental hospital manicomio *m*, hospital *m* psiquiátrico

mesonephric duct conducto *m* mesonéfrico

metabolize metabolizar

metacarpus metacarpo *m*

metaphyseal infection infección *f* metafisaria

metaphysitis metafisitis *f*

metastasis metástasis *f*

metastasize metastatizar

metatarsal metatarsiano

metatarsus metatarso *m*

methotrexate metotrexato *m*

methyldopa metildopa *f*

methylphenidate metilfenidato *m*

micturition micción *f*

midcarpal dislocation dislocación *f* mesocarpiana

middle finger (dedo) corazón, dedo *m* cordial, dedo de en medio

midstream specimen muestra *f* de orina rocogida a la mitad de la micción

midtarsal dislocation dislocación *f* mesotarsiana

midwife partera *f*

migraine headache jaqueca *f*, migraña *f*

mild (pain) leve, ligero (dolor)

miner's elbow codo *m* de minero

Minerva jacket corsé *m* Minerva

miocardial infarction ataque *m* cardiaco, infarto *m* del miocardio

miscarriage aborto *m* espontáneo/natural, malparto *m*

missed abortion aborto *m* fallido

misstep, to take a pisar en falso, pisar mal

mitral stenosis estenosis *f* mitral

mitral valve válvula *f* mitral

mixed connective tissue disease (MCTD) enfermedad *f* mixta de tejido conectivo

moan gemir

Moh's technique técnica *f* de Moh

molar muela *f*

mole lunar *m*

mole (mass in uterus) mola *f*

moniliasis moniliasis *f*

monitor monitor *m*, pantalla *f*

monitor vigilar, controlar

monoamine oxidase inhibitors (MAO) inhibidores *m* de la monoaminooxidasa

monoclonal antibodies anticuerpos *m* monoclonales

mood estado *m* de ánimo, humor *m*

mood swing cambio *m* abrupto del estado de ánimo

morning sickness náuseas *f* del embarazo

morning stiffness rigidez *f* matutina

mouth boca *f*

mouth, by por vía bucal

MRI (magnetic resonance imaging) imágenes *f* por/de resonancia magnética, resonancia magnética nuclear

mucous membrane membrana *f* mucosa

mucus (nasal) mocos *m*

mucus (phlegm) flema *f*

multi-infarct dementia demencia *f* por infartos múltiples

multipara multípara *f*

multiparous multípara

multiple sclerosis esclerosis *f* múltiple

multiple sensory deficit déficit *m* sensorial múltiple

mumps paperas *f*, parótidas *f*, chanza *f*

muscle músculo *m*

muscle pull tirón *m*

muscle relaxant relajante *m* muscular

muscle strain estiramiento *m* muscular

muscle tear desgarro *m* muscular

mycelium micelio *m*

mycotic infection infección *f* micótica

myelin sheath vaina *f* de mielina

myelocytic leukemia leucemia *f* mielocítica

myelogenous leukemia leucemia *f* mielógena

myelography mielografía *f*

myelogram mielograma *m*

myelosis mielosis *f*

myelotomography mielotomografía *f*

myometrium miometrio *m*

myocardial infarction infarto *m* de(l) miocardio

myocardial ischemia isquemia *f* miocárdica

myocarditis miocarditis *f*

myocardium miocardio *m*

myoclonic seizure acceso *m* mioclónico, mioclonía *f*

myomectomy miomectomía *f*

myometrium miometrio *m*

myxoma mixoma *m*

N

nape (of neck) nuca *f*

nausea náusea *f*, asco *m*, basca *f*, mareos *m*

navel ombligo *m*

navicular navicular

nearsighted miope

nebulizer nebulizador *m*

neck cuello *m*

necrosis necrosis *f*

necrotizing arteritis arteritis *f* necrosante

needle aguja *f*

nephrectomy nefrectomía *f*

nephrotomography nefrotomografía *f*

nerve nervio *m*

nervous breakdown crisis *f* nerviosa

nervous system sistema *m* nervioso

nervousness nerviosidad *f*, nerviosismo *m*

neuritis neuritis *f*

neurochemical neuroquímico

neurofibrillary tangles marañas *f* neurofibrilares

neurogenic pain dolor *m* neurogénico/neurógeno

neurological examination exploración *f* neurológica

neurologist neurólogo *m*

neurology neurología *f*

neuron neurona *f*

neurosurgeon neurocirujano *m*

neurotransmitter neurotransmisor *m*

neurotrophic arthropathy artropatía *f* neurotrófica

neutrophils neutrófilos *m*

newborn recién nacido *m*

newborn nursery sala *f* de cuneros

night sweats sudores *m* nocturnos

nipple (of a bottle) tetilla/teta *f*

nipple (of a breast) pezón *m* (de la mujer), tetilla *f* (del hombre)

nipple discharge exudado *m* por el pezón

nipple inversion retracción *f* del pezón

nitroglycerin nitroglicerina *f*

nitrosourea nitrosourea *f*

nociceptor nociceptor *m*

nonsteroidal anti-inflammatory drug (NSAID) antiinflamatorio *m* no esteroide

North American blastomycosis blastomicosis *f* norteamericana

nose nariz *f*
  bridge of caballete *m*, puente *f*
  tip of punta de la nariz
  to blow sonarse la nariz
  to pick limpiarse la nariz con el dedo, meterse el dedo en la nariz

nosebleed desangramiento *m* en las narices, hemorragia *f* nasal, sangramiento *m* por la nariz, sangrar por la nariz

nostril narices *f*, ventana *f* de la nariz, ventanilla *f*

noxious nocivo

nuclear brain scan gammagrama *m* cerebral

nucleus pulposus núcleo *m* pulposo

nulligravid nuligravida *f*

nulliparous nulípara

numb adormecido, entumecido, entumido

numb, to go engarrotar

numbness adormecimiento *m*, entumecimiento *m*

nurse (breast feed) amamantar, dar de mamar, dar pecho

nursing station puesto *m* de enfermeras/enfermería

nystagmus nistagmo *m*

O

oat cell cancer carcinoma *m* de células en avena, carcinoma indiferenciado microcelular

obesity obesidad *f*

oblique fracture fractura *f* oblicua

observation, under vigilancia *f* (bajo), observación *f* (en)

obstetric obstétrico

obturator ring anillo *m* obturador

occipital lobe lóbulo *m* occipital

ocular plethysmography (OPG) pletismografía *f* ocular

odontoid process apófisis *f* odontoides

office consultorio *m*, consulta *f*

office hours horas *f* de consulta

ointment pomada *f*, ungüento *m*

olecranon olécranon *m*, olécrano *m*

one-armed manco

one-eyed tuerto

one-handed manco

onset comienzo *m*, principio *m*

open fracture fractura *f* abierta/expuesta

open heart surgery cirugía *f* de corazón abierto

open reduction reducción abierta

opening snap/click chasquido *m* de apertura

operating room (OR) quirófano *m*, sala *f* de operaciones

operating table mesa *f* quirúrgica, mesa de operaciones

ophthalmoplegic migraine jaqueca *f* oftalmopléjica

ophthalmoscope oftalmoscopio *m*

optic nerve nervio *m* óptico

optical shingles herpes zoster *m* óptico

OR (operating room) quirófano *m*, sala *f* de operaciones *f*

oral contraceptive anticonceptivo *m* oral/bucal

orally por vía bucal

orchiectomy orquiectomía *f*

organism organismo *m*

orgasm orgasmo *m*

orthodontic work ortodoncia *f*

orthopedic surgeon cirujano *m* ortopédico

orthopedic support sostén *m*/soporte *m* ortopédico

orthopedics ortopedia *f*

orthosis ortesis *f*

os os *m*

osseous dysplasia displasia *f* ósea

osteoarthrosis osteoartrosis *f*
osteoarticular focus foco *m*
  osteoarticular
osteoarticular lesion lesión *f*
  osteoarticular
osteoarticular tuberculosis
  tuberculosis *f* osteoarticular
osteochondroma
  osteocondroma *m*
osteoclastoma osteoclastoma *m*
osteogenic sarcoma sarcoma *m*
  osteógeno, osteosarcoma *m*
osteography osteografía *f*
osteoid osteoma osteoma *m*
  osteoide
osteolysis osteólisis *f*
osteomyelitis osteomielitis *f*
osteonecrosis osteonecrosis *f*
osteoperiostitis osteoperiostitis *f*
osteophytes osteófitos *m*
osteoporosis osteoporosis *f*
osteosclerosis osteosclerosis *f*
osteotomy osteotomía *f*
OTC (over-the-counter) que no
  requiere receta, sin receta, de venta
  libre
otoconia otoconia *f*
otoneurologist otoneurólogo *m*
otoscope otoscopio *m*
outpatient paciente *m*
  externo/ambulatorio
outpatient services servicios *m* de
  consulta externa
outpatient surgical suite
  quirófano *m* de pacientes externos
ovarian agenesis agénesis *f*/
  agenesia *f* ovárica
ovarian cyst quiste *m* ovárico
ovarian dysgenesis disgenesis *f*/
  disgenesia *f* ovárica
ovary ovario *m*
**over-the-counter medication
  (OTC)** medicamento *m* que no
  requiere receta/sin receta, de venta
  libre
overlap syndrome síndrome *m* de
  superposición

overweight pasado de peso
ovisac ovisaco *m*
ovotestis ovotestis *m*
ovulation ovulación *f*

P

pacemaker marcapaso(s) *m*
Paget's disease of the vulva
  enfermedad *f* de Paget en la vulva
pain dolor *m*
  burning ardor *m*
  dull lento, sordo
  jabbing punzante
  mild leve, ligero
  persistent insistente
  piercing quelante
  severe fuerte
  sharp agudo
  shooting punzante
  slight leve, ligero
  stabbing picante, que clava
  throbbing punzante
  unbearable insoportable
pain killer medicamento *m* para
  quitar el dolor
palate paladar *m*
palpation palpación *f*
palpitation palpitación *f*, latido *m*
  rápido del corazón
palsy perlesía *f*, parálisis *f*
pancreas páncreas *m*
pang punzada *f*
pant jadear, resollar
Pap test/smear prueba *f*/examen *m*/
  tinción *f* de Papanicolaou
papaverine hydrochloride
  clorhidrato *m* de papaverina
papillary tumor tumor *m* papilar
paracervical block bloqueo *m*
  paracervical
parasitic parasítico
paravaginal cystic mass masa *f*
  quística paravaginal
parietal lobe lóbulo *m* parietal
Parkinson's disease enfermedad *f*
  de Parkinson

partial plate placa *f* de la
  dentadura postiza
pass gas arrojar flatos
pass out desmayarse
passive-dependent
  pasivo-dependiente
patella rótula *f*, patela *f*
patellar retinaculum retináculo
  m rotuliano/patelar
patellofemoral joint articulación *f*
  femororrotuliana/rotulofemoral
pathogenic patogénico, patógeno
pathologic fracture fractura *f*
  patológica
pathologist patólogo *m*
paunch barriga *f*, panza *f*
peepee, to go hacer pipí
pelvic examination examen *m*
  pélvico
pelvic inflammatory disease
  (PIV) enfermedad *f* inflamatoria
  pélvica
pelvic peritonitis peritonitis *f*
  pélvica
pelvis pelvis *f*
penicillamine penicilamina *f*
penis pene *m*
percussor (reflex hammer)
  martillo *m* de reflejos
percutaneous transluminal
  coronary angioplasty (PTCA)
  angioplastia *f* transluminal
  percutánea coronaria
perfusion imaging estudio *m* con
  perfusión (miocárdica con talio),
  prueba *f* de perfusión (del miocardio
  con talio)
pericarditis pericarditis *f*
perineal surgery cirugía *f* perineal
periosteum periostio *m*
periostitis periostitis *f*
peripheral nerve neurotomy
  neurotomía *f* del nervio periférico
peripheral neuropathy
  neuropatía *f* periférica

peripheral vascular disease
  enfermedad *f* vascular periférica,
  trastorno *m* vascular periférico
peripheral vestibular disorder
  trastorno *m* periférico del aparato
  vestibular
period (menstrual) período *m*,
  regla *f*
peritubal adhesion adherencia *f*
  peritubárica
persistent pain dolor *m* insistente
perspiration transpiración *f*
perspire sudar, transpirar
PET (positron emission
  tomography) tomografía por/de
  emisión de positrones (TEP)
petit mal petit mal *m*
phalanx (*pl* phalanges) falange *f*
pharmacist boticario *m*,
  farmacéutico *m*
pharmacokinetics farmacocinética
pharmacy botica *f*, farmacia *f*
phenobarbital fenobarbital *m*
phenytoin fenitoína *f*
phlebitis flebitis *f*
phlegm flema *f*
phospholipids fosfolípidos *m*
physical (exam) reconocimiento *m*
  médico
physical handicap minusvalía *f*,
  incapacidad *f*
physical therapy fisioterapia *f*
physician médico *m*
pick one's nose limpiarse la nariz
  con el dedo, meterse el dedo en la
  nariz
Pick's disease enfermedad *f* de Pick
piercing (pain) quelante (dolor)
pill pastilla *f*, píldora *f*
pimple espinilla *f*, barro *m*, grano
  m, granito *m*
pinch pellizcar
pinched nerve nervio *m*
  atrapado/aplastado/oprimido
pins and needles hormigueo *m*
pipette pipeta *f*
pituitary pituitario *m*

placenta placenta *f*
placenta previa placenta *f* previa
plantar dorsiflexion dorsiflexión *f* plantar
plaque placa *f*
plaque (dental) sarro *m*, placa *f*
plasma plasma *f*
plasma cell myeloma mieloma *m* de célula plasmática
plasmacyte plasmacito *m*
platelet plaqueta *f*
pleurisy pleuresía *f*, pleuritis *f*, inflamación *f* de los bofes,
pneumonectomy neumonectomía *f*
pneumonia pulmonía *f*
poison ivy hiedra *f* venenosa
poison (man-made) veneno *m*
poison (natural) ponzoña *f*
poison oak encina *f* venenosa, roble venenoso
poison sumac zumaque *m* venenoso
poisoning envenenamiento *m*
polyarthralgia poliartralgia *f*
polycystic ovary ovario *m* poliquístico
polymenorrhea polimenorrea *f*
polyp pólipo *m*
pons pons *m*
poopoo, to go hacer caca
popping (noise made by a joint) crujido *m*, trueno *m*
portio vaginalis portio *m* vaginalis
positional vertigo vértigo *m* de posición
positron emission tomography (PET) tomografía *f* por/de emisión de positrones (TEP)
postcoital poscoito
postcoital bleeding hemorragia *f* después del coito
postdatism posfecha *f*
posterior extension splint férula *f* de extensión posterior
postherpetic neuralgia neuralgia *f* posherpética

postmaturity posmadurez *f*
postmenopausal posmenopáusico
post partum post partum, posparto
postpartum blues tristeza *f* posparto
postural hypotension hipotensión *f* postural
postural restriction restricción *f* postural
preeclampsia preeclampsia *f*
pregnancy embarazo *m*
pregnancy test prueba *f* de embarazo
pregnant embarazada
preload carga *f* previa
premature atrial contraction (PAC) contracción *f* auricular prematura
premature labor parto *m* prematuro
premature separation of the placenta desprendimiento *m* prematuro de la placenta
premature ventricular contraction (PVC) contracción *f* ventricular prematura
premenopausal premenopáusico
premenstrual tension tensión *f* premenstrual
prenatal care atención *f* prenatal
prepubescent prepubescente
prescribe recetar
prescription receta *f*
presenile dementia demencia *f* presenil
preterm birth nacimiento *m* prematuro
prick pinchazo *m*, piquete *m*
prick pinchar, picar
prickly con hormigueo, con picazón
primary brain tumor tumor *m* cerebral primario
primary osteomyelitis osteomielitis *f* primaria
primary syphilis sífilis *f* primaria
primipara primípara *f*
primiparous primípara

procedure procedimiento *m*
progesterone progesterona *f*
progesteron receptor test prueba
 f de receptor de progesterona
progestin progestina *f*
prognosis pronóstico *m*
prolapsed uterus prolapso *m* del
 útero
prolapsed vagina prolapso *m* de la
 vagina
prone boca abajo, prono
propranolol propranolol *m*
prostaglandin prostaglandina *f*
prostate próstata *f*
prostatic acid phosphatase (PAP)
 fosfatasa *f* ácida prostática
prosthesis prótesis *f*
prostrate postrado, boca abajo
proximal proximal
pruritis prurito *m*
pseudoarthrosis seudoartrosis *f*
pseudodementia seudodemencia *f*
pseudogout seudogota *f*
pseudopolyp seudopólipo *m*
psychogenic pain dolor *m*
 psicogénico/psicógeno
psychogenic seizure acceso *m*
 psicogénico/psicógeno
psychological counseling
 psicoterapia *f*
psychometric psicométrico
psychomotor agitation agitación
 f psicomotora
psychomotor epilepsy epilepsia *f*
 psicomotora
psychomotor retardation retardo
 m psicomotor
psychosomatic psicosomático
psychotherapy psicoterapia *f*
puberty pubertad *f*
pubic region verijas *f*
pubic symphysis sínfisis *f* del
 pubis
pubis pubis *m*
pull jalar, tirar

pull (a muscle) desgarrar,
 desgarrarse un músculo, estirarse
 un músculo, sufrir un tirón
pulmonary artery arteria *f*
 pulmonar
pulmonary valve válvula *f*
 pulmonar
pulmonary veins venas *f*
 pulmonares
pulse pulso *m*
punch punzón *m*
puncture puntura *f*, punzada *f*
puncture wound herida *f* punzante
pupil (of the eye) niña *f* del ojo,
 pupila *f*
pus materia *f*, pus *m*
push empujar
push (childbirth) pujar
push-up plancha *f*, lagartija *f*
pyogenic arthritis artritis *f*
 piógena
pyogenic osteomyelitis
 osteomielitis *f* piógena

Q

quack charlatán *m*, matasanos *m*,
 medicastro *m*, medicucho *m*,
 mediquillo *m*
quarantine cuarentena *f*
queasy con un poco de náusea

R

rabid rabioso
rabies rabia *f*
radial artery arteria *f* radial
radial styloid process apófisis *f*
 estiloide radial
radiation therapy radioterapia *f*
radical hysterectomy
 histerectomía *f* radical
radioactive isotope isótopo *m*
 radi(o)activo
radiocarpal joint articulación *f*
 radiocarpiana
radiologist radiólogo *m*

radionuclide imaging imágenes *f* diagnósticas por radionúclidos, estudio *m*/exploración *f* con radionúclidos

radiotherapy radioterapia *f*

radioulnar joint articulación *f* radiocubital

radius radio *m*

raise alzar, levantar

range of motion amplitud *f* de movimiento, capacidad *f* de movimiento

rash erupción *f*, salpullido *m*

reactive depression depresión *f* reactiva

recalcitrant rebelde

reconstructive surgery cirugía *f* ortopédica reconstructora

recover recuperarse, restablecerse, sanarse

rectal examination tacto *m* rectal

rectocele rectocele *m*

rectoscope rectoscopio *m*

rectovaginal fistula fístula *f* rectovaginal

rectovaginal septum tabique *m* rectovaginal

rectum recto *m*

red blood cell hematíe *m*

reddening enrojecimiento *m*

redness enrojecimiento *m*, inflamación *f*, rubor *m*

Reed-Sternberg cells células *f* de Reed-Sternberg

refer (to a specialist) mandar (a un especialista)

referral (to a specialist) recomendación *f* (de un especialista)

reflex reflejo *m*

relapse recaída *f*

release dar de alta

relieve (pain) calmar

remission remisión *f*

renal blood flow flujo sanguíneo renal

renal cell cancer cáncer *m* de células renales

renal function función *f* renal

respiratory failure insuficiencia *f* respiratoria

rest reposo *m*

rest descansar

resting pulse pulso *m* en reposo

restlessness inquietud *f*, agitación *f*

retropubic prostatectomy prostatectomía *f* retropúbica

retropulsion retropulsión *f*

retrosternal dislocation dislocación *f* retrosternal

Rh incompatibility incompatibilidad *f* por Rh

rheumatic fever fiebre *f* reumática

rheumatoid arthritis artritis *f* reumatoide

rheumatoid factor factor *m* reumatoide

rheumatoid nodule nódulo *m* reumatoide

rheumatology reumatología *f*

rib costilla *f*, arco *m* costal

rib cage caja *f* torácica

right-handed derecho

ring finger dedo *m* anular/anillo

ringing (ears) zumbido *m*

ringworm tiña *f*

root canal canal *m* en la raíz

rotational movement movimiento *m* rotativo, giratorio

rotator cuff rotador *m* del hombro

rounds, to make hacer rondas, pasar visita

rubella rubéola *f*, sarampión *m* alemán

run-down agotado, debilitado

runny nose nariz *f* tapada/tupida, secreciones *f* por la nariz

runny nose, to have fluirle la nariz

ruptured disk disco *m* roto

ruptured tubo-ovarian abscess absceso *m* tuboovárico roto

S

saber shin tibia *f* en sable
saccule sáculo *m*
sacral vertebra vértebra *f* sacra
sacroiliac sacroiliaco *m*
sacrum sacro *m*
safe sex relaciones *f* sin riesgo
safe sex, to have tomar
  precauciones durante el coito
sagittal plane plano *m* sagital
saliva saliva *f*, babas *f*
Salmonella osteomyelitis
  osteomielitis *f* provocada por
  Salmonella
salpingitis salpingitis *f*
salpingolysis salpingólisis *f*
salpingo-oophorectomy
  salpingooforectomía *f*
salpingo-oophoritis
  salpingooforitis *f*
salpingostomy salpingostomía *f*
salve ungüento *m*
sample muestra *f*
saphenous vein vena *f* safena
scab costra *f*, postilla *f*
scalp cuero *m* cabelludo, casco *m* de
  la cabeza
scalpel bisturí *m*
scan exploración *f*, imagen *f*
  diagnóstica
scaphoid bone escafoides *m*
scapula escápula *f*, omóplato *m*
scapular region región *f* escapular
scar cicatriz *f*
scar tissue tejido *m* cicatrizal
scarlet fever fiebre *f* escarlatina
Schiller test prueba *f* de Schiller
Schwannoma Schwannoma *m*
sciatica ciática *f*
scissors tijeras *f*
sclera esclerótica *f*
sclerotherapy escleroterapia *f*
scoop (curette) raspador *m*
scratch arañazo *m*, rasguño *m*
scratch arañar, rasguñar
scream chillar, gritar

screen (oscilloscope) pantalla *f*
screen examen *m* de detección
screening detección *f*
scrotum escroto *m*
sebaceous cysts quistes *m* sebáceos
secondary brain tumor tumor *m*
  cerebral secundario
secondary hypertension
  hipertensión *f* secundaria
secondary osteomyelitis
  osteomielitis *f* secundaria
secondary syphilis sífilis *f*
  secundaria
secretion secreción *f*, exudación *f*
sedation sedación *f*
sedative calmante *m*, sedante *m*
segmental resection resección *f*
  segmentaria
seizure acceso *m*, ataque *m*,
  convulsión *f*
semen semen *m*
semicircular canals conductos *m*
  semicirculares
senile dementia demencia *f* senil
senile plaque placa *f* senil
senility senilidad *f*
sensitive sensible
septic arthritis artritis *f* séptica
septum tabique *m*
sequestrectomy secuestrectomía *f*
sequestrum secuestro *m*
serotonin serotonina *f*
sesamoid sesamoide
severe agudo, grave
severe hepatic insufficiency
  insuficiencia *f* hepática grave
severe liver failure insuficiencia *f*
  hepática grave
sex coito *m*, sexo *m*
sex drive libido *f*
sexual dysfunction disfunción *f*
  sexual
sexual relations relaciones *f*
  íntimas/sexuales
sexual relations, to have cumplir
  con la mujer, estar con la mujer/el
  marido, hacer uso de la mujer

sexually transmitted disease (STD) enfermedad *f* de transmisión sexual

shake temblar

shake (liquid medicine) agitar

shaking temblor *m*

sharp (instrument) afilado

sharp (pain) agudo

shin canilla *f*, espinilla *f*, tibia *f*

shingles herpes *m*, zona *f*, zoster *m*

shock (fright) sobresalto *m*, susto *m*

shock (syndrome) choque *m*, shock *m*

shock therapy/treatment terapia *f* electroconvulsiva

short of breath, to be faltarle la respiración

shortness of breath sensación *f* de ahogo, falta *f* de aire

shot (injection) inyección *f*, "chat" *m USA*

shotgun vitamin therapy vitaminoterapia *f* en escopetazo

shoulder hombro *m*

shoulder blade escápula *f*, omóplato *m*

shoulder capsule cápsula *f* del hombro

shriek chillar

side effect efecto *m*/reacción *f* secundario, efecto colateral

side stitch aire *m*, dolor *m* de bazo, dolor de costado, ijada *f*

sigmoidoscope sigmoidoscopio *m*

sigmoidoscopy sigmoidoscopia *f*

sign (of illness) signo *m* (de enfermedad)

silent ischemia isquemia *f* subclínica

single photon emission computed tomography (SPECT) tomografía *f* computada/computarizada por emisión de fotón único

sinoatrial node (SA node) nudo *m* sinoauricular

sinus seno *m*

sip sorbo *m*

sit down sentarse

sit up incorporarse, levantarse

sitzbath baño *m* de asiento

skeleton esqueleto *m*

skin cancer cáncer *m* de (la) piel, cáncer cutáneo

skin rash salpullido *m*, sarpullido *m*, erupción *f*

skull cráneo *m*, calavera *f*

skull fracture fractura *f* del cráneo

sliding-weight scale peso *m* de corredera

slight leve, ligero

sling cabestrillo *m*, banda *f*, honda *f*

slip resbalón *m*

slip resbalarse

slippage deslizamiento *m*, estiramiento *m*

slipped zafado

small cell lung cancer cáncer *m* pulmonar de células pequeñas

smallpox viruela *f*, viruela *f* negra

smart escocer, picar

smelling salts sales *f* aromáticas

smear frotis *m*

Smith's fracture fractura *f* de Smith

sneeze estornudar

socket (eye) cuenca *m*

socket (tooth) alvéolo *m*

soft tissue tejido *m* blando

sole (of foot) planta *f*

Somatoform Pain Disorder trastorno *m* de dolor somatiforme

somatic somático

sonogram sonograma *m*

sore adolorido

sore llaga *f*

sore throat dolor *m* de garganta, garganta *f* inflamada

specimen espécimen *m*, muestra *f*

speculum espéculo *m*

spell ataque *m* (de una enfermedad)

spermicidal foam espuma *f* espermaticida

spermicidal jelly jalea *f* espermaticida

sphygmomanometer esfigmomanómetro *m*, tensiómetro *m*

sphygmomanometer cuff abrazadera *f*/manguito *m* de esfigmomanómetro

spinal anesthetic anestesia *f* espinal

spinal canal conducto *m* espinal

spinal column columna *f* vertebral

spinal cord médula *f* espinal

spinal tap punción *f* lumbar

spine espina *f* dorsal

spinous process apófisis *f* espinosa

spiral fracture fractura *f* espiral/en espiral/espiroidea

spirits estado *m* de ánimo

spirochete espiroqueta *f*

spirometer espirómetro *m*

spleen bazo *m*

splint férula *f*, tablilla *f*

splint colocar una férula, entablillar

spondylitis espondilitis *f*

spondylolisthesis espondilolistesis *f*

sponge bath baño de esponja

spotting manchado *m*, sangrado *m* ligero, goteo *m* (intermenstrual)

sprain esguince *m*, dislocación *f*, falseo *m*, torcedura *f*

sprain torcer

sprained ligament esguince *m* ligamentoso

spread diseminar(se), propagar(se)

spur (bone) espolón *m*, esquince *m*, rebaba *f*

sputum esputo *m*, flema *f*

squamous cell carcinoma carcinoma *m* de células escamosas, carcinoma espinocelular

squat acuclillarse, ponerse en cuclillas, agacharse *S Amer*

squeeze apretar

squint entrecerrar (los ojos), fruncir la vista, mirar entrecerrado

stab wound cuchillada *f*/cuchillazo *m*, herida *f* de arma blanca

stabbing/piercing pain dolor *m* quelante

stabbing/poking/jabbing pain dolor *m* picante

stanch restañar

standby pacemaker marcapaso(s) *m* de demanda

staple grapa *f*

stare (at) fijar la vista (en)

state of mind estado *m* de ánimo

status migrainosus estado *m* jaquecoso

stay in bed guardar cama

stenosis estenosis *f*

sterile estéril

sternoclavicular dislocation dislocación *f* esternoclavicular

sternum esternón *m*, hueso *m* del pecho

steroid esteroide *m*

stethoscope estetoscopio *m*

stiff rígido, tieso

stiff neck colti *m*

stiffen engarrotar

stiffness rigidez *f*

stillborn nacido muerto

stimulation-produced analgesia (SPA) analgesia *f* producida por estímulos

sting arder, picar

stirrup *m* estribo *m*

stitch, side aire *m*, dolor *m* del costado

stitches puntadas *f*, suturas *f*

stoma estoma *m*

stomach estómago *m*

stomach ache dolor *m* de estómago

stomach cramp retorcijón *m*/retortijón *m*

stomach upset estómago *m* revuelto

stone cálculo *m*, piedra *f*

stool excremento *m*

stoop agacharse, doblarse
straighten enderezar(se), estirar, extender
strain a muscle desgarrarse un músculo
strain (at stool) hacer esfuerzos (estreñimiento), pujar (por estreñimiento)
strain (muscle) distensión *f* (muscular)
strapping inmobilización *f*
strenuous activity actividad *f* fuerte, esfuerzo *m*
streptokinase estreptocinasa *f*
stress tensión *f*, estrés *m*
stress fracture fractura *f* de esfuerzo
stress incontinence incontinencia *f* de esfuerzo
stress test prueba *f* del ejercicio/esfuerzo
stretch alargar, estirar(se), extender
stretch mark estría *f*
stretcher camilla *f*
stroke ataque *m* de parálisis, derrame *m* cerebral, embolia *f*, embolio *m*
stuffy nose nariz *f* tapada/tupida
stuttering tartamudeo
sty (eye) orzuelo *m*
subarachnoid hemorrhage hemorragia *f* subaracnoidea
subchondral bone hueso *m* subcondral
subclavian artery arteria *f* subclavia
subcoracoid dislocation dislocación *f* subcoracoidea
subinvolution of the uterus subinvolución *f* del útero
subluxation subluxación *f*
subperiosteal abscess absceso *m* subperióstico
substance abuse abuso *m* de substancias tóxicas
substantia nigra substantia *f* nigra

subtalar joint articulación *f* subastragalina
subtrochanteric fracture fractura *f* subtrocantérea
suction curettage legrado *m*/raspado *m* por succión, aspiración *f* con vacío
sudden repentino, súbito
sudden cardiac death (SCD) muerte *f* cardiaca repentina
suffocation ahogo *m*
suicidal ideation ideas suicidas
suicide attempt intento *m* de suicidio
sulci surcos *m*
sulfasalazine salazosulfapiridina *f*
sunscreen filtro *m* solar, protector *m* solar
supine boca arriba, supino
suppository supositorio *m*, calía *f*
suppository (vaginal) óvulo *m*
suppurative arthritis artritis *f* supurativa
supracondylar fracture fractura *f* supracondílea
suprapatellar pouch bolsa *f* suprarrotuliana
surgeon cirujano *m*
surgery cirugía *f*
surgical needle aguja *f* para suturas
sustentaculum sustentaculum *m*
suture sutura *f*, puntada *f*, punto *m* de sutura
swab aplicador *m*, hisopo *m*
sweat sudor *m*
sweat sudar
sweat glands glándulas *f* sudoríparas
sweating sudoración *f*
swell hinchar, encorar
swelling hinchazón *f*, recuperación *f*, restablecimiento *m*
swollen hinchado
sympathetic nerve inhibitors inhibidores *m* del sistema nervioso simpático

symphysis pubica sínfisis *f* púbica

symptom malestar *m*, síntoma *m*, seña *f*, padecimiento *m*

syndrome síndrome *m*

synovectomy sinovectomía *f*

synovia sinovia *f*

synovial fluid líquido *m* sinovial

synovial membrane membrana *f* sinovial

synovitis sinovitis *f*

syphilitic osteitis osteítis *f* sifilítica

syphilis sífilis *f*

syringe jeringa *f*

systemic lupus erythematosus lupus *m* eritematoso sistémico

systemic therapy terapia *f* sistémica

systole sístole *f*

systolic sistólico

systolic pressure presión *f* sistólica

T

tablet tableta *f*, comprimido *m*

tachycardia taquicardia *f*

tailbone cóccix *m*, colita *f*

tailor's bottom culo *m* de sastre

talofibular ligament ligamento *m* peroneoastragalino

talonavicular joint articulación *f* talonavicular

talus astrágalo *m*, talus *m*

tamoxifen tamoxifén *m*

tapeworm solitaria *f*

tardive dyskinesia discinesia *f* tardía

tarsometatarsal dislocation dislocación *f* tarsometatarsiana

tarsus tarso *m*

tartar sarro *m*

tear (muscle, ligament) desgarrar(se)

temple sien *f*

temporal lobe lóbulo *m* temporal

temporal mandibular joint (TMJ) articulación *f* temporomandibular (ATM)

temperature, to take tomar la temperatura *f*

tender adolorido, sensible (al tacto)

tenderness dolor *m* (al tocar)

tendon tendón *m*

tendon sheath vaina *f* tendinosa

tendonitis tenonitis *f*

tennis elbow codo *m* de tenista

test análisis *m*, estudio *m*, prueba *f*

testicles testículos *m*

testicular feminization syndrome síndrome *m* de feminización testicular

testicular self-examination (TSE) autoexamen *m* de los testículos

tetanus tétanos *m*

thalamus tálamo *m*

thermocoagulation termocoagulación *f*

thermography termografía *f*

thermometer termómetro *m*

thickening engrosamiento *m*

thigh muslo *m*

thoracic torácico

thoracolumbar junction unión *f* toracolumbar

thorax tórax *m*

thrill estremecimiento *m*

throat garganta *f*.

throb palpitar, pulsar, retachar

throbbing latido *m*

throbbing/stabbing pain dolor *m* punzante

thrombolysis trombólisis *f*

thrombus trombo *m*

throw up arrojar, devolver, deponer (*Mex*), vomitar

thumb dedo *m* gordo, dedo pulgar

thymus timo *m*

thyroid tiroides *f*

tibia tibia *f*

tibial crest cresta *f* de la tibia

tibiofibular joint articulación *f* tibiofibular

tic douloureux tic *m* doloroso
tightness tirantez *f*
tingle enchinar, hormiguear
tingling hormigueo *m*
tissue (flesh) tejido *m*
tissue (paper) gasa *f*, tejido *m* fino
TMJ (temporal mandibular joint) ATM (artículación *f* temporomandibular)
toe dedo *m* del pie
　big dedo gordo del pie
　little dedo pequeño del pie
toenail uña *f*
tongue lengua *f*
tongue blade abatelenguas *m*, bajalenguas *m*
tongue depressor abatelenguas *m*, bajalenguas *m*
tonic-clonic seizure ataque *m* tónico-clónico
tonsils amígdalas *f*, agallas *f*
tooth (incisor) diente *m*, colmillo *m*
tooth (molar) muela *f*
toothache dolor *m* de muelas/dientes
toothpaste pasta *f* dental/dentífrica
tophus tofo *m*
topical chemotherapy quimioterapia *f* tópica
torn ligament desgarro *m* ligamentoso
torsion torsión *f*
torulosis torulosis *f*
tourniquet torniquete *m*
toxemia toxemia *f*
toxic headache cefalea *f* tóxica
toxic substance substancia *f* tóxica
toxin toxina *f*
trachea tráquea *f*
trachelorrhaphy traquelorrafia *f*
tract tracto *m*, vía *f*
traction tracción *f*
tranquilizer tranquilizante *m*
transcutaneous electrical nerve stimulation (TENS) estimulación *f* eléctrica transcutánea de nervios, estimulación nerviosa transcutánea

transfusion transfusión *f*
transient ischemic attack (TIA) ataque *m* isquémico transitorio, ataque de isquemia transitoria
transient synovitis sinovitis *f* transitoria
transitional cell carcinoma carcinoma *m* de célula transicional
transrectal ultrasound ultrasonido *m* transrectal
transurethral resection (TUR) resección *f* transuretral
transverse transverso
transverse fracture fractura *f* transversa
transverse process apófisis *f* transversa
transverse septum of the vagina tabique *m* vaginal transverso
traumatic arthritis artritis *f* traumática
traumatology traumatología *f*
treating physician médico *m* que atiende/trata (al paciente)
tremor temblor *m*
Trichomonas vaginalis Trichomonas *f* vaginalis
tricuspid stenosis estenosis *f* tricúspide
tricuspid valve válvula *f* tricúspide
trigeminal neuralgia neuralgia *f* trigémina
trigger point of pain punto *m* desencadenante del dolor
triglyceride triglicérido *m*
trihexyphenidyl trihexifenidil *m*
trimester trimestre *m*
triquetrum triquetro *m*
trochanter trocánter *m*
trochanteric fracture fractura *f* trocantérica
trophoblast trofoblasto *m*
truss braguero *m*
tubal abortion aborto *m* tubárico
tubal ligation ligadura *f* de trompas

tubal pregnancy embarazo *m* tubárico

tube (anatomical) conducto *m*, trompa *f*, tubo *m*

tube (instrument) manguera *f*, sonda *f*

tubercle tubérculo *m*

tuberculosis tisis *f*, tuberculosis *f*

tuberculous arthritis artritis *f* tuberculosa

tuberculous salpingitis salpingitis *f* tuberculosa

tuberous sclerosis esclerosis *f* tuberosa

tubo-ovarian abscess absceso *m* tuboovárico

tummy barriguita *f*

tumor tumor *m*

turn (around) dar la vuelta, voltear(se)

tweezers pinzas *f*

twinge punzada *f*

twist torcer(se)

twisted ovarian cyst quiste *m* ovárico torcido

twitch contracción *f* espasmódica, movimiento *m* espasmódico

twitch crisparse

tympanic membrane tímpano *m*

typhoid fever fiebre *f* tifoidea

U

ulcer úlcera *f*

ulcerated ulcerado

ulna cúbito *m*

ultrasound ultrasonido *m*

ultraviolet radiation (UV) radiación *f* ultravioleta

umbilical cord cordón *m* umbilical

unbearable pain dolor *m* insoportable

unconscious inconsciente

unilateral dislocation dislocación *f* unilateral

unilateral subluxation subluxación *f* unilateral

upper arm parte *f* superior del brazo

upper GI studies análisis *f*/ estudios *m* del tubo digestivo superior

upset alterado, trastornado

upset (stomach) revuelto

ureter uréter *m*

ureteroneocystostomy ureteroneocistostomía *f*

ureteroureterostomy ureteroureterostomía *f*

ureterovaginal fistula fístula *f* ureterovaginal

urethra uretra *f*

urethroscope fibroscopio *m* urinario

urethrovaginal fistula fístula *f* uretrovaginal

urinalysis análisis *m* de orina

urinary tract disorder trastorno *m* del tracto urinario

urine orina *f*, orines *m*

urogenital sinus sinus *m* urogenital

urokinase urocinasa *f*

uterine fundus fondo *m* del útero

uterine leiomyoma leiomioma *m* del útero

uterine retroflexion retroflexión *f* del útero

uterorectosacral ligaments ligamentos *m* uterorrectosacros

uterotubal insufflation insuflación *f* uterotubario/ uterotubárico

uterus matriz *f*, útero *m*

utricle utrículo *m*

V

vaccinate vacunar

vaccination vacunación *f*, vacuna *f*

vagina vagina *f*

vaginal atresia atresia *f* vaginal

vaginal speculum espéculo *m* vaginal

vaginectomy vaginectomía *f*
vaginitis vaginitis *f*
varicose vein vena *f* varicosa, várices *f*
vas deferens conducto *m* deferente
vascular headache cefalea *f* vascular
vasectomy vasectomía *f*
vasodilator vasodilatador *m*
vasomotor disorder trastorno *m* vasomotor
vector vector *m*
vein vena *f*
vein, jugular vena *f* yugular
vein stripping extracción *f* de várices
vein, varicose vena *f* varicosa, várices *f*
vena cava vena *f* cava
venereal venéreo
venom veneno *m*
ventilation ventilación *f*
ventral ventral
ventricle ventrículo *m*
ventricular aneurysm aneurisma *m* ventricular
ventricular fibrillation fibrilación *f* ventricular
ventricular septal defect (VSD) comunicación *f* interventricular (CIV)
ventricular tachycardia taquicardia *f* ventricular
venule vénula *f*
vertebra vértebra *f*
vertigo vértigo *m*
very-low-density lipoprotein (VLDL) lipoproteína *f* de muy baja densidad (LMBD)
vesicovaginal fistula fístula *f* vesicovaginal
vessel vaso *m* (sangíneo)
vestibular labyrinth laberinto *m* vestibular
vestibular nerve section sección *f* del nervio vestibular

vestibular neuronitis neuronitis *f* vestibular
vestibule vestíbulo *m*
viral vírico, viral
virus virus *m*
vision vista *f*
vision chart cuadro *m* de agudeza visual
visiting hours horas *f* de visita
vital signs signos *m* vitales
vocal cord cuerda *f* vocal
void (bladder) vaciar, evacuar
volar volar
vulva vulva *f*
vulvectomy vulvectomía *f*
vulvitis vulvitis *f*
vulval elephantiasis elefantiasis *f* vulvar

W

waist cintura *f*
waiting room sala *f* de espera
walker andadera *f*, andador *m*
ward sala *f*
wart verruga *f*, mezquino *m*
weakness debilidad *f*
wear off pasar
weaver's bottom culo *m* de tejedor
wedge resection resección *f* en cuña
wedged pulmonary pressure presión *f* pulmonar en cuña
weighing platform plataforma *f* del peso
weight gain aumento *m* de peso
weight loss pérdida *f* de peso
wheelchair silla *f* de ruedas
wheelchair access acceso *m* para silla de ruedas
wheeze silibancia *f*
wheeze chillarle el pecho, silbarle el pecho
wheezing chiflido *m*, chillido *m*
whiplash desnucamiento *m*, lesión *f* de latigazo

Whipple procedure técnica *f* de
Whipple
whirlpool bath baño *m* de remolino
whistling (lungs) chiflido *m*,
chillido *m*
white blood cell glóbulo *m* blanco,
leucocito *m*
whooping cough tos *f* ferina
windpipe gaznate *m*
wipe enjugar
wipe oneself asearse, limpiarse
wisdom tooth muela *f* del juicio
womb matriz *f*, vientre *m*
work-related injury lesión *f*
relacionada con el trabajo
worthlessness, feeling of
autodesvalorización *f*
wound herida *f*
wound, entry orificio *m* de entrada
wound, exit orificio *m* de salida
wound, gunshot herida *f* de arma
de fuego
wound, incised herida *f* incisa
wound, puncture herida *f*
punzante
wound, stab herida *f* de arma
blanca
wrist muñeca *f*

X

X-rays radiografías *f*, rayos *m* X

Y

yawn bostezar
yeast infection micosis *f* vaginal,
infección *f* vaginal por hongos
yellow fever fiebre *f* amarilla

Z

zoster zoster *m*
zygomatic arch arco *m* cigomático

Español → Inglés

A

abatelenguas *m* tongue blade, tongue depressor

abatido *m* despondent

abdomen *m* abdomen

abducción *f* abduction

abertura *f* **del paladar** cleft palate

aborto *m* abortion (induced)

aborto *m* **espontáneo/natural** miscarriage

aborto *m* **fallido** missed abortion

aborto *m* **tubárico** tubal abortion

abrasión *f* abrasion

abrazadera *f* **hinchable de esfigmomanómetro** blood pressure cuff, sphygmomanometer cuff

absceso *m* abscess

absceso *m* **(de la piel)** boil

absceso *m* **de Brodie** Brodie's abscess

absceso *m* **subperióstico** subperiosteal abscess

absceso *m* **tuboovárico** tubo-ovarian abscess

absceso *m* **tuboovárico roto** ruptured tubo-ovarian abscess

abultamiento *m* bulge

abuso *m* **de substancias tóxicas** substance abuse

acceso *m* seizure, epilepsy, attack, fit

acceso *m* **acinético** akinetic seizure

acceso *m* **mioclónico** myoclonic seizure

acceso *m* **psicogénico/psicógeno** psychogenic seizure

acceso *m* **para silla de ruedas** wheelchair access

acedía *f* heartburn

acetilcolina *f* acetylcholine

ácido *m* acid

ácido *m* **desoxirribonucleico (ADN)** *m* DNA (deoxyribonucleic acid)

acinesia *f* akinesia

acné *m* acne

acomplejado embarrassed

acromion *m* acromion

actividad *f* **fuerte** strenuous activity

acuclillarse squat

acumulación *f* buildup

acupuntura *f* acupuncture

achaque systemic weakness

adenocarcinoma *m* adenocarcinoma

adenomiosis *f* adenomyosis

adenosis *f* **cística** cystic adenosis

adherencia *f* **de la fimbria** fimbrial adhesion

adherencia *f* **peritubárica** peritubal adhesion

ajuste *m* **(quiropráctico)** adjustment (chiropractic)

administración *f* **intravenosa/endovenosa de medicamentos (IV)** intravenous administration of medication (IV)

admisión *f* **(departamento del hospital)** admitting

adolorido sore, tender

adormecido numb

adormecimiento *m* numbness

adormilado drowsy

adrenalina *f* adrenalin

aducción *f* adduction

afasia *f* aphasia

afilado (instrumento) sharp

aflicción *f* distress

aflojarse buckle (knee, leg)

afta *f* canker sore

agacharse bend, stoop; squat (*S Amer*)

agallas *f* tonsils

agarrar grasp, grip

agentes *m* **anticolinérgicos** anticholinergic agents

agentes *m* **de limpieza** household cleansers
agitar (medicina líquida) shake
agotado run-down
agotamiento *m* exhaustion
agravar(se) flare up
agrietada (piel) cracked
agruras *f* heartburn
aguantar la respiración hold one's breath
agudo acute, sharp (pain)
aguja *f* needle
aguja *f* **de inyecciones** hypodermic syringe
aguja *f* **de un solo uso** disposable needle
aguja *f* **para suturas** surgical needle
agujeta *f* charley horse
agénesis *f*/**agenesia** *f* **ovárica** ovarian agenesis
agitación *f* restlessness
agitación *f* **psicomotora** psychomotor agitation
ahincarse to kneel
ahito, estar to have indigestion
ahogarse choke
ahogo *m* suffocation
ahogo *m*, **sensación de** shortness of breath
aire *m* side stitch
alargar stretch
aldilla *f* groin
alergia *f* allergy
aleteo *m* **auricular** atrial flutter
algodón *m* cotton
aliento *m* breath
alimentar con biberón to bottle feed
almohada *f* **eléctrica** heating pad
almohadilla *f* **de espuma de hule** foam rubber pad
almorranas *f* hemorrhoids
alta presión *f* **sanguínea** high blood pressure
alterado upset
alvéolo *m* **(diente)** socket (tooth)

alzar lift, raise
amamantar breastfeed, nurse
amenorrea *f* amenorrhea
amiloideo *m* amyloid
amiloidosis *f* amyloidosis
amitriptilina *f* amitriptyline
amniocentesis *f* amniocentesis
amodorrado drowsy
amoratado black and blue
amplitud *f* **de movimiento** range of motion
ampolla *f* blister
amputación *f* amputation
amputado *m* amputee
amputar amputate
amígdala *f* amygdala
amígdalas *f* tonsils
analgesia *f* analgesia
analgesia *f* **producida por estímulos** stimulation-produced analgesia (SPA)
analgésico analgesic
análisis *m* **de orina** urinalysis
análisis *m* **del tubo digestivo superior** upper GI studies
andadera *f* walker
andador *m* walker
anemia *f* anemia
anemia *f* **ferropriva** iron deficiency anemia
anestesia *f* anesthesia
anestesia *f* **espinal** spinal anesthesia
anestesia *f* **general** general anesthesia
anestesia *f* **local** local anesthesia
anestésico *m* anesthetic
aneurisma *m* aneurysm
aneurisma *m* **abdominal** abdominal aneurysm
aneurisma *m* **aórtico** aortic aneurysm
aneurisma *m* **ventricular** ventricular aneurysm
angina *f* angina
angina *f* **péctoris** angina pectoris
angiograma *m* angiogram

angiografía *f* **cardiaca digital**
digital cardiac angiography (DCA)
angiografía *f* **de su(b)stracción**
digital digital subtraction
angiography (DSA)
angioplastia *f* angioplasty
angioplastia *f* **con sonda**
balón/globo balloon angioplasty
angioplastia *f* **por láser** laser
angioplasty
angioplastia *f* **transluminal**
percutánea coronaria
percutaneous transluminal
coronary angioplasty (PTCA)
ángulo *m* **del ojo** corner of the eye
angustia distress
anillo *m* **obturador** obturator ring
anovulatorio anovulatory
ano *m* anus
anorexia *f* anorexia
anquilosis *f* ankylosis
anquilosis *f* **fibrosa** fibrous
ankylosis
anquilosis *f* **ósea** bony ankylosis
ansiedad anxiety
antácido *m* antacid
antagonistas *f* **del calcio** calcium
antagonists
antebrazo *m* forearm
antecedentes *m* **médicos** medical
history
anteojos *m* eyeglasses
anticoagulante anticoagulant
anticonceptivo *m* contraceptive
anticonceptivo *m* **oral/bucal** oral
contraceptive
anticuerpo *m* antibody
anticuerpos *m* **monoclonales**
monoclonal antibodies
antidepresivo *m* antidepressant
antídoto *m* antidote
antiepiléptico *m* antiepileptic
antihipertensivo *m*
antihypertensive
antihistamínico *m* antihistamine
antiinflamatorio *m*
anti-inflammatory

antiinflamatorio *m* **no esteroide**
nonsteroidal anti-inflammatory
drug (NSAID)
antipsicótico anti-psychotic
antojos *m* craving
anémico anemic
análisis *m* test
análisis *m* **de sangre** blood test,
blood work
aorta *f* aorta
aorta *f* **descendiente** descending
aorta
aparición *f* **de la cabeza fetal**
crowning
apéndice appendix
apendicitis *f* appendicitis
aplastamiento *m* crushing
aplastar crush
aplicador *m* swab
apoplejía *f* apoplexy
apretar bind, clench, grip, squeeze
apretar el puño to make a fist
apretar los dientes bite down
apófisis *f* **coracoides** coracoid
process
apófisis *f* **espinosa** spinous process
apófisis *f* **estiloide radial** radial
styloid process
apófisis *f* **odontoides** odontoid
process
apófisis *f* **transversa** transverse
process
apósito *m* dressing
araña *f* **viuda negra** black widow
spider
arañar scratch
arañazo *m* scratch
arco *m* arch
arco *m* **cigomático** zygomatic arch
arco *m* **costal** rib
arco *m* **dorsal neural** dorsal
neural arch
arder sting, burn
ardor *m* burning (pain)
arritmia *f* arrhythmia
arrojar to throw up

arrojar flatos to fart, pass gas, break wind
arteria *f* artery
arteria *f* **braquial** brachial artery
arteria *f* **carótida** carotid artery
arteria *f* **coronaria** coronary artery
arteria *f* **humeral** humeral artery
arteria *f* **pulmonar** pulmonary artery
arteria *f* **radial** radial artery
arteria *f* **subclavia** subclavian artery
arteriografía *f* **coronaria** coronary arteriography
arteriograma *m* arteriogram
arteriolas *f* arterioles
arteriopatía *f* **coronaria** coronary artery disease (CAD)
arteriosclerosis *f* arteriosclerosis
arteritis *f* **necrosante** necrotizing arteritis
arteritis *f* arteritis
articulación *f* joint
articulación *f* **acromioclavicular** acromioclavicular joint
articulación *f* **de Charcot** Charcot's joint
articulación *f* **de Clutton** Clutton's joint
articulación *f* **femororrotuliana** patellofemoral joint
articulación *f* **interfalángica** interphalangeal joint
articulación *f* **radiocarpiana** radiocarpal joint
articulación *f* **radiocubital** radioulnar joint
articulación *f* **rotulofemoral** patellofemoral joint
articulación *f* **subastragalina** subtalar joint
articulación *f* **talonavicular** talonavicular joint
articulación *f* **temporomandibular (ATM)** temporal mandibular joint (TMJ)

articulación *f* **tibiofibular** tibiofibular joint
artrítides arthritides
artritis *f* arthritis
artritis *f* **bacteriana** bacterial arthritis
artritis *f* **degenerativa** degenerative arthritis
artritis *f* **gonorreica** gonorrheal arthritis
artritis *f* **hematógena** hematogenous arthritis
artritis *f* **hipertrófica** hypertrophic arthritis
artritis *f* **infecciosa** infectious arthritis
artritis *f* **piógena** pyogenic arthritis
artritis *f* **por cristales** crystal-induced arthritis
artritis *f* **reumatoide** rheumatoid arthritis
artritis *f* **supurativa** suppurative arthritis
artritis *f* **séptica** septic arthritis
artritis *f* **traumática** traumatic arthritis
artritis *f* **tuberculosa** tuberculous arthritis
artrocentesis *f* arthrocentesis
artrodesis *f* arthrodesis
artropatía *f* **neurotrófica** neurotrophic arthropathy
artroplastia *f* arthroplasty
artroscopia *f* arthroscopy
artroscopio *m* arthroscope
artrotomía *f* arthrotomy
aréola *f* areola
asco *m* nausea
asearse wipe oneself
asegurado insured
aseguranza *f* *(USA)* insurance
asentaderas *f* breech, buttocks
asesoramiento *m* counseling
asesoría *f* **genética** genetic counseling
asfixia *f* asphyxia

asfixiarse choke
asilo *m* **(para pacientes con enfermedades terminales)** hospice
asma *f* asthma
asombrado (cara) flushed
aspiración *f* aspiration
aspiración *f* **articular** joint aspiration
aspiración *f* **con vacío** suction curettage
aspirina *f* aspirin
astenia *f* asthenia
astrocitoma *m* astrocytoma
astrocitos *m* astrocytes
astrágalo *m* talus
ataque *m* convulsion, epilepsy, seizure
ataque *m* **cardiaco** heart attack, miocardial infarction
ataque *m* **de isquemia transitoria** transient ischemic attack (TIA)
ataque *m* **de parálisis** stroke
ataque *m* **(de una enfermedad)** spell
ataque *m* **isquémico transitorio** transient ischemic attack (TIA)
ataque *m* **tónico-clónico** tonic-clonic seizure
atarantado dazed
atarantamiento *m* dizziness
atención *f* **médica** health care
atención *f* **prenatal** prenatal care
atender el parto (obstétrico) deliver
aterosclerosis *f* atherosclerosis
atlas *m* atlas
atorar (coyuntura) lock
atragantamiento *m* choking
atragantarse choke (food)
atresia *f* **vaginal** vaginal atresia
atrio *m* atrium
aturdido dazed
aturdimiento *m* confusion, disorientation
audición *f* hearing
aumentar de peso gain weight

aumento *m* **de peso** weight gain
aura *f* aura
aurícula *f* auricle
ausencia *f* absence seizure
autodesvalorización *f* feelings of worthlessness
autoexamen *m* **de la mama/del seno** breast self-examination (BSE)
autoexamen *m* **de los testículos** testicular self-examination (TSE)
autoexploración *f* **mamaria** breast self-examination (BSE)
automatismo *m* automatism
axila *f* armpit
axón *m* axon
ayunar fast
azatioprina *f* azathioprine

B

babas *f* saliva
bacinilla *f* bedpan
bacteriano bacterial
bajalenguas *m* tongue depressor, tongue blade
bajar de peso lose weight
balazo *m* gunshot, gunshot wound
banda *f* sling
bandas *f* braces (dental)
barba *f*/**barbilla** *f* chin
barbitúrico *m* barbiturate
bario *m* **por vía bucal** barium swallow
barriga *f* paunch
barriguita *f* tummy
barro *m* pimple
basca *f* nausea
bastón *m* cane (curved)
bazo *m* spleen
baño *m* **de asiento** sitzbath
baño *m* **de esponja** sponge bath
baño *m* **de remolino** whirlpool bath
bata *f* gown (hospital)
benigno benign
benseracida *f* benserazide
biberón *m* baby bottle

bifurcación *f* crotch
bilis *f* bile
biometría *f* **hemática** blood count
biopsia *f* biopsy
biopsia *f* **cervical en sacabocados** cervical punch biopsy
biopsia *f* **en cono** cone biopsy
biorretroalimentación *f* biofeedback
bioterapia *f* biological therapy
bióxido *m* **de carbono** carbon dioxide
biperidén *m* biperiden
bisturí *m* scalpel
bizco cross-eyed
blanco *m* **del ojo** white of the eye
blastomicosis *f* **europea** European blastomycosis
blastomicosis *f* **norteamericana** North American blastomycosis
bloqueador *m* **beta** beta blocker
bloqueo *m* **paracervical** paracervical block
boca *f* mouth
boca abajo face-down, prone
boca arriba face-up, supine
bochornos *m* hot flashes
bocio *m* goiter
bofe *m* lung
bola *f*/**bolita** *f* lump
bolita *f* **de algodón** cotton ball
bolsa *f* bursa
bolsa *f* **con hielo** ice pack
bolsa *f* **de las aguas** bag of waters
bolsa *f* **suprarrotuliana** suprapatellar pouch
boquinete *m* cleft palate
bordón *m* cane (straight)
borramiento *m* **del cuello** effacement of the cervix
bostezar yawn
boticario *m* druggist, pharmacist
botica *f* drugstore, pharmacy
botiquín *m* first aid kit
bradicardia *f* bradycardia
bradicinesia *f* bradykinesia

braguero *m* back brace/support, truss
brazo *m* arm
broncoscopia *f* bronchoscopy
bronquitis *f* bronchitis
bubón *m* bubo
bucal, por vía by mouth
buche *m* goiter
bulbos *m* bulbs
bursitis *f* bursitis
bíceps *m* biceps
bóveda *f* **craneal** cranial vault

C

caballete *m* bridge of the nose
cabello *m* hair
cabestrillo *m* sling
cabeza *f* **y cavidad** *f* **articular** ball and socket joint
caca, hacer to go poopoo
cachetes *m* buttocks
cachete *m* cheek
cadera *f* hip
caducar (receta) expire
caja *f* **torácica** rib cage
calambre *m* cramp (muscular)
calavera *f* skull
calcáneo *m* calcaneus
cálculo *m* stone
cálculo *m* **biliar** gallstone
cálculo *m* **renal** kidney stone
calentura *f* fever
callo *m* callus, corn
calmante *m* sedative
calmar (dolor) dull, relieve
calores *m* hot flashes
caloría *f* calorie
calía *f* suppository
calvicie *f* baldness
cambio *m* **de vida** change of life, menopause
camilla *f* stretcher
canal *m* **en la raíz** root canal
canal *m* **medular** medullary canal
canceloso cancellous
cáncer *m* cancer

cáncer *m* **cutáneo** skin cancer
cáncer *m* **de célula(s) insular(es)** islet cell cancer
cáncer *m* **de células renales** renal cell cancer
cáncer *m* **de (la) mama** breast cancer
cáncer *m* **de (la) piel** skin cancer
cáncer *m* **de (la) vejiga** bladder cancer
cáncer *m* **de(l) pecho** breast cancer
cáncer *m* **de(l) seno** breast cancer
cáncer *m* **endometrial** endometrial cancer
cáncer *m* **invasor de la cérvix** invasive cervical cancer
cáncer *m* **mamario** breast cancer
cáncer *m* **pulmonar de células pequeñas** small cell lung cancer
cáncer *m* **pulmonar/de(l) pulmón** lung cancer
candidiasis *f* candidiasis
canilla *f* shin; wrist (*Mex, USA*)
capilar *m* capillary
capitellum *m* capitellum
cápsula capsule
cápsula *f* **de la cadera** hip capsule
cápsula *f* **del hombro** shoulder capsule
capuchón *m* **cervical** cervical cap
cara *f* face
carbamacepina *f* carbamazepine
carbidopa *f* carbidopa
carbunco *m* carbuncle
carbúnculo *m* carbuncle
carcinogénesis *f* carcinogenesis
carcinoma *m* **basocelular/de células basales** basal cell carcinoma
carcinoma *m* **cervical invasor** invasive cervical cancer
carcinoma *m* **de célula transicional** transitional cell carcinoma
carcinoma *m* **de células en avena** oat cell cancer

carcinoma *m* **de células escamosas** squamous cell carcinoma
carcinoma *m* **de células grandes** large cell carcinoma
carcinoma *m* **de la glándula de Bartholin** Bartholin gland carcinoma
carcinoma *m* **de pulmón** lung cancer
carcinoma *m* **endometrial** endometrial carcinoma
carcinoma *m* **epidermoide** epidermoid carcinoma
carcinoma *m* **espinocelular** squamous cell carcinoma
carcinoma *m* **in situ** carcinoma in situ
carcinoma *m* **indiferenciado microcelular** oat cell cancer
carcinoma *m* **invasor del cuello uterino** invasive cervical cancer
carcinógeno *m* carcinogen
cardenal *m* bruise
cardiomiopatía *f* cardiomyopathy
cardiopatía *f* **congénita** congenital heart defect
cardiopatía *f* **coronaria** coronary heart disease (CHD)
carie *f* carie, cavity (dental)
carga *f* **previa** preload
carga *f* **ulterior** afterload
carie *f* cavity (dental)
carpo *m* carpus
cartílago *m* cartilage
casco *m* **de la cabeza** scalp
cascorro bow-legged
casco *m* cast
caspa *f* dandruff
cataplasmo *m* medicated compress
catarata *f* cataract
catarro *m* cold
catéter *m* catheter
cateterismo *m* **cardiaco** cardiac catheterization
cateterización *f* **cardiaca** cardiac catheterization

cauda *f* **equina** cauda equina
causar cause, bring on, produce
cauterización *f* cauterization
cavidad *f* **articular** joint cavity
cavidad *f* **endometrial**
  endometrial cavity
cavitación *f* cavitation
cefalalgia *f* **benigna por esfuerzo**
  benign exertional headache
cefalea *f* headache, cephalalgia
cefalea *f* **en**
  racimos/grupos/acúmulos
  cluster headache
cefalea *f* **tóxica** toxic headache
cefalea *f* **vascular** vascular
  headache
ceja *f* eyebrow
células *f* **de Reed-Sternberg**
  Reed-Sternberg cells
células *f* **gliales** glial cells
células *f* **sanguíneas** blood cells
centro *m* **de salud** healthcare
  center
cepillarse los dientes to brush
  one's teeth
cerebelo *m* cerebellum
cerebrovascular cerebrovascular
cerebro *m* brain; cerebrum; base of
  skull, back of head (*Mex, USA*)
cerebrum *m* cerebrum
cerrar la mano to make a fist
cervical cervical
cervicitis *f* cervicitis
cerviz *f* cervix
ciática *f* sciatica
cicatriz *f* scar
cifosis *f* kyphosis
cingulectomía *f* cingulectomy
cintura *f* waist; lower back (*Mex,
  USA*)
cinturón *m* kidney belt
ciproheptadina *f* cyproheptadine
circulación *f* **colateral** collateral
  circulation
cirro *m* hard, painless tumor
cirrosis *f* cirrhosis
cirugía *f* surgery

cirugía *f* **artroscópica**
  arthroscopic surgery
cirugía *f* **de corazón abierto** open
  heart surgery
cirugía *f* **exploradora** exploratory
  surgery
cirugía *f* **ortopédica**
  reconstructora reconstructive
  surgery
cirugía *f* **perineal** perineal surgery
cirujano *m* surgeon
cirujano *m* **ortopédico** orthopedic
  surgeon
cistectomía *f* cystectomy
cistocele *m* cystocele
cistosarcoma *m* **filodo**
  cystosarcoma phyllodes
cistoscopia *f* cystoscopy
cistoscopio *m* cystoscope
cistouretrocele *m* cystourethrocele
citológico cytologic
claudicación *f* **intermitente**
  intermittent claudication
claudicar (receta) expire
clavícula *f* clavicle, collar bone
clínica clinic
clínica de reposo convalescent
  hospital
clítoris *m* clitoris
clorhidrato *m* **de amantadina**
  amantadine hydrochloride
clorhidrato *m* **de fluoxetina**
  fluoxetine hydrochloride
clorhidrato *m* **de papaverina**
  papaverine hydrochloride
coagulación *f* clotting
coagular(se) clot
coágulo *m* blood clot
cobro *m* bill
coccidioidomicosis *f*
  coccidioidomycosis
coccigectomía *f* coccygectomy
cóccix *m* coccyx, tailbone
cóclea *f* cochlea
codeína *f* codeine
codo *m* elbow
codo *m* **de minero** miner's elbow

codo *m* **de tenista** tennis elbow
coito *m* coitus, intercourse, sex
cojear to limp
cojera *f* limp
cojín *m* **eléctrico** heating pad
cojo lame
colágeno *m* collagen
colangiopancreatografía *f*
 retrógrada endoscópica
 endoscopic retrograde
 cholangiopancreatogram (ERCP)
cólera *m* cholera
colesterol *m* cholesterol
colgajo *m* flap
cólico *m* colic
cólico *m* **(menstrual)** cramp
colita *f* tailbone
colmillo *m* tooth (incisor)
colocar una férula splint
colon *m* colon
colonoscopio *m* colonoscope
colostomía *f* colostomy
colpocleisis *f* colpocleisis
colporrafia *f* colporrhaphy
colposcopio *m* colposcope
colti *m* stiff neck
columna *f* **vertebral** backbone,
 spinal column
collar *m* **cervical** cervical collar
collarín *m* cervical collar
coma *f* coma
comezón *m* itch
comienzo *m* onset
complejo *m* **asociado con el SIDA**
 AIDS-related complex (ARC)
complexión *m* build
compresa *f* compress
compresión *f* **axial** axial
 compression
comprimido *m* tablet
comunicación *f* **interauricular**
 (CIA) atrial septal defect (ASD)
comunicación *f* **interventricular**
 (CIV) ventricular septal defect
 (VSD)
con comezón *f* itchy
con hormigueo *m* prickly

con picazón *f* prickly
con un poco de náusea queasy
concusión *f* consussion
cóndilo *m* **lateral** lateral condyle
condiloma *m* **acuminado**
 condyloma acuminatum
condroblastoma *m*
 chondroblastoma
condromixofibroma *m*
 chondromyxoid fibroma
condrosarcoma *m* chondrosarcoma
conducto *m* tube (anatomical),
 duct, canal
conducto *m* **auditivo** eustachian
 tube, auditory canal
conducto *m* **espinal** spinal canal
conducto *m* **deferente** vas
 deferens
conducto *m* **mesonéfrico**
 mesonephric duct
conductos *m* **semicirculares**
 semicircular canals
condón *m* condom
congelación *f* frostbite
congestión *m* congestion
conización *f* conization
conización *f* **con cuchillo frío**
 cold knife conization
conmoción *f* concussion
conmoción *f* **cerebral** (cerebral)
 concussion
consejería *f* counseling
constipación *f* congestion
consulta *f* office
consultorio *m* office
contagio *m* contagion
contracción *f* contraction
contracción *f* **auricular**
 prematura premature atrial
 contraction (PAC)
contracción *f* **espasmódica** twitch
contracción *f* **ventricular**
 prematura premature ventricular
 contraction (PVC)
contraceptivo *m* contraceptive
contractura *f* **de flexión** flexion
 contracture

contraindicación *f*
contraindication
contrarrestar counteract
control *m* follow-up
control *m* **de**
nacimiento/natalidad birth
control
controlar monitor
convulsión *f* convulsion, seizure
convulsión *f* **epiléptica** epileptic
convulsion/seizure
coprocultivo *m* stool culture
corazón *m* heart
cordón *m* **umbilical** umbilical cord
cordotomía *f* cordotomy
córnea *f* cornea
coroides *m* choroid
corona *f* crown
corpus *m* **callosum** corpus
callosum
corriente *f* **sanguínea** bloodstream
corset *m* back brace/support
corsé *m* back brace/support
corsé *m* **lumbosacro** back brace
corsé *m* **Minerva** Minerva jacket
cortada *f* incision, laceration, cut
córtex *f***/corteza** *f* cortex
córtex *f***/corteza** *f* **cerebral**
cerebral cortex
corticoides *m* corticoids
corticosteroides *m* corticosteroids
cortisona *f* cortisone
corva *f* back of knee
costilla *f* rib
costra *f* scab
coxa *f* **vara adolescente**
adolescent coxa vara
coyuntura *f* joint
cromosoma *m* chromosome
cráneo *m* cranium, skull
creatinina *f* creatinine
cresta *f* **de la tibia** tibial crest
criocirugía *f* cryosurgery
criptococosis *f* cryptococcosis
crisis *f* **de ausencia** absence
seizure

crisis *f* **nerviosa** nervous
breakdown
crisparse to twitch
cristalino *m* crystalline lens
cúbito *m* ulna
crujido *m* **(de coyuntura)** popping
cuadril *m* hip (animal term)
cuadro *m* **de agudeza visual** eye
chart, vision chart
cuarentena *f* quarantine
cuchillada *f***/cuchillazo** *m* stab
wound
cuello *m* neck
cuello *m* **de la matriz** cervix
cuello *m* **del útero** cervix
cuello *m* **desgarrado** lacerated
cervix
cuello *m* **incompetente**
incompetent cervix
cuenca *f* **(ojo)** *m* socket
cuenta *f* bill
cuentagotas *f* eyedropper
cuerda *f* **vocal** vocal cord
cuero *m* **cabelludo** scalp
cuerpo *m* **amarillo** corpus luteum
cuidados *m* **intensivos** intensive
care
culdocentesis *f* culdocentesis
culdoscopia *f* culdoscopy
culequillas *f*, **estar en** to squat
culo *m* **de sastre** tailor's bottom
culo *m* **de tejedor** weaver's bottom
cul-de-sac *m* cul-de-sac
cumplir con la mujer to have
sexual relations
curarse heal
cureta *f* curette
curetaje *m* curettage
curita *f* bandaid
cutícula *f* cuticle
cutis *m* complexion

CH

chamorro *m* (*Mex, USA*) calf
chancro *m* chancre
chancroide *m* chancroid
chanza *f* mumps
charlatán *m* quack
chasquido *m* click
chasquido *m* **de apertura** opening snap/click
"chat" *m* (*USA*) shot (injection)
chequeo *m* checkup
chequeo *m* **dental** dental checkup
chichón *m* bump, lump
chiflido *m* wheezing, whistling (lungs)
chillar scream, shriek
chillarle el pecho wheeze
chillido *m* wheezing, whistling (lungs)
Chlamydia *f* Chlamydia
chocar bump
chochero *m* medical practitioner similar to a homeopathist
choque *m* shock (syndrome)
choque *m* **anafiláctico** anaphylactic shock
chueco crooked
chupete *m* hickey
chupón *m* hickey

D

daltónico color-blind
dar a luz give birth, deliver
dar de alta discharge, release
dar de mamar breastfeed, nurse
dar el pecho breastfeed, nurse
dar la vuelta turn (around)
darse en (la cabeza, etc.) bump
dañino harmful
daño *m* damage
de venta libre over the counter (OTC)
débil faint, frail
debilidad *f* weakness
debilitado run-down

debridación *f* debridement
dedo *m* finger
  anular/anillo ring finger
  corazón middle finger
  cordial middle finger
  de en medio middle finger
  del pie toe
  gordo del pie big toe
  gordo thumb
  índice index finger
  meñique little finger
  pequeño del pie little toe
  pulgar thumb
defecación *f* bowel movement (BM)
defecación *f* **sanguinolenta** bloody stool
defecar to have a bowel movement, defecate
déficit *m* **sensorial múltiple** multiple sensory deficit
deformado deformed
deformidad *f* **de dedos en martillo** hammertoe deformity
deglución *f* **de bario** barium swallow
delirante delirious
delirar to be delirious
demencia *f* dementia
demencia *f* **por infarto** infarct dementia
demencia *f* **por infartos múltiples** multi-infarct dementia
demencia *f* **presenil** presenile dementia
demencia *f* **senil** senile dementia
demente deranged, insane
dentadura *f* **postiza** denture
dependencia dependency
deponer to throw up
depósito *m* buildup
depresión *f* depression
depresión *f* **reactiva** reactive depression
deprimido depressed, despondent
derecho right-handed
derivación *f* bypass
derrame *m* discharge, effusion

derrame *m* **cerebral** stroke
desangramiento *m* bleeding, hemorrhage
desangramiento *m* **en las narices** bloody nose, nosebleed
desanimado despondent
desarrollo *m* **del feto** fetal development
desbridamiento *m* debridement
descansar rest
descongestivo *m* decongestant
desesperación *f* anxiety
desfibrilador *m* defibrillator
desfibrilar defibrillate
desgarrar cough up
desgarrar(se) un ligamento tear a ligament
desgarrar(se) un músculo pull/strain a muscle
desgarro *m* **de(l) menisco** meniscus tear
desgarro *m* **ligamentoso** torn ligament
desgarro *m* **muscular** muscle tear
desguanzar to weaken, tire
deshidratación *f* dehydration
deslizamiento *m* slippage
desmayarse black out, faint, pass out
desmayo *m* fainting, fainting spell
desmineralización *f* demineralization
desnucamiento *m* whiplash
desnutrición *f* malnutrition
desprendimiento *m* **prematuro de la placenta** premature separation of the placenta
desviación *f* bypass
detección *f* screening
detener la respiración hold one's breath
devolver to throw up
diabetes *f* diabetes
diafisectomía *f* diaphysectomy
diáfisis *f* diaphysis
diafragma *m* diaphragm
diagnosis *f* diagnosis

diagnóstico *m* diagnosis
diálisis *f* **renal** kidney dialysis
diarrea *f* diarrhea
diástole *f* diastole
diastólico diastolic
diente *m* tooth (incisor)
diente *m* **podrido** cavity (dental)
dientes *m* **salidos** buck teeth
dieta *f* diet
dieta *f* **de mucha fibra** high-fiber diet
dieta *f***, estar a** to be on a diet
dietilestilbestrol *m* diethylstilbestrol (DES)
difteria *f* diphtheria
difunto deceased
digital *f***, digitalis** *f* digitalis
dilatación *f* dilation
dilatación *f* **y evacuación** *f* dilation and evacuation (D&E)
dilatación *f* **y raspado** *m* dilation and curettage (D&C)
dilatado dilated
dióxido de carbono carbon dioxide
disartria *f* dysarthria
discinesia *f* dyskinesia
discinesia *f* **tardía** tardive dyskinesia
disco *m* **desplazado** slipped disk
disco *m* **herniado** herniated disk
disco *m* **intervertebral** intervertebral disk
disco *m* **roto** ruptured disk
disco *m* **zafado** slipped disk
diseminar(se) spread
disentería *f* dysentery
disfunción *f* **sexual** sexual dysfunction
disgenesis *f***/disgenesia** *f* **ovárica** ovarian dysgenesis
dislocación *f* dislocation, sprain
dislocación *f* **atlantoaxoidea** atlantoaxial dislocation
dislocación *f* **esternoclavicular** sternoclavicular dislocation
dislocación *f* **mesocarpiana** midcarpal dislocation

dislocación *f* **mesotarsiana**
midtarsal dislocation
dislocación *f* **por extensión**
extension dislocation
dislocación *f* **retrosternal**
retrosternal dislocation
dislocación *f* **subcoracoidea**
subcoracoid dislocation
dislocación *f* **tarsometatarsiana**
tarsometatarsal dislocation
dislocación *f* **unilateral** unilateral
dislocation
dislocar(se) dislocate
dismenorrea *f* dysmenorrhea
disminuir cut down (on)
dispareunia *f* dyspareunia
displasia *f* dysplasia
displasia *f* **ósea** osseous dysplasia
dispositivo *m* **intrauterino**
intrauterine device (IUD)
disritmia *f* dysrhythmia
distal distal
distensión *f* **(muscular)** strain
(muscle)
distraído absent-minded
DIU (dispositivo intrauterino)
intrauterine device (IUD)
diurético *m* diuretic
doblar bend
doblarse bend, stoop, flex
doctor *m* **de planta** (*Mex, USA*)
family doctor
dolencia *f* ache
doler feo to hurt a lot

dolor *m* ache, pain
al tocar tenderness
agudo sharp or severe pain
de bazo side stitch
de cabeza headache
de costado side stitch
de estómago stomache ache
de garganta sore throat
de oído earache
de parto labor pain
del costado stitch (side)
fuerte bad/severe/sharp pain
insistente persistent pain
insoportable unbearable pain
lento dull pain
leve slight/mild pain
ligero slight/mild pain
neurogénico/neurógeno
neurogenic pain
picante stabbing/poking/jabbing
pain
psicogénico/psicógeno
psychogenic pain
punzante
throbbing/stabbing/shooting pain
que clava stabbing pain
quelante stabbing/piercing pain
recio bad/severe/sharp pain
sordo dull pain
dolor *m* **de muelas/dientes**
toothache
dolor *m* **de parto** contraction
dolor *m* **lumbar bajo** low back pain
dolorcito *m* ache
donante *m* donor
donar sangre donate blood
dopamina *f* dopamine
dorsiflexión *f* **plantar** plantar
dorsiflexion
dorso *m* **de la mano** back of the
hand
dosificación *f* dosage
dosis *f* dosage, dose
drenar(se) drain
ducha *f* douche
ducharse douche
duelo *m* grief

E

eclampsia *f* eclampsia
ecocardiografía *f*
echocardiography
ectocervical ectocervical
efecto *m* nocivo harmful effect
efecto *m* secundario/colateral
side effect
electrocardiograma (ECG) *m*
electrocardiogram (EKG/ECG)
electroconización *f*
electroconization
electrodesecación *f*
electrodesiccation
electrodo *m* electrode
electroencefalograma (EEG) *m*
electroencephalogram (EEG)
electromiografía *f*
electromyography (EMG)
electromiograma (EMG) *m*
electromyogram (EMG)
electronistagmografía *f*
electronystagmography
elefantiasis *f* vulvar vulval
elephantiasis
eliminar to eliminate
ello *m* id
embarazada pregnant
embarazo *m* pregnancy
embarazo *m* cornual cornual
pregnancy
embarazo *m* ectópico ectopic
pregnancy
embarazo *m* intrauterino
intrauterine pregnancy
embarazo *m* tubárico tubal
pregnancy
embolia *f* stroke
embolio *m* stroke, embolism
embolio *m* cerebral cerebral
embolism
embrión *m* embryo
empacho indigestion, constipation
empeine *m* groin, instep
empétigo *m* impetigo
empujar push

encefalina *f* enkephalin
encías *f* gums
encina *f* venenosa poison oak
encoger(se) curl
enconarse fester
encondroma *m* enchondroma
encorar heal, swell
enchinar tingle
endarterectomía *f* carótida
carotid endarterectomy
enderezar (el miembro) to have
an erection
enderezar(se) straighten
endocervical endocervical
endolinfa *f* endolymph
endometrio *m* endometrium
endometriosis *f* endometriosis
endorfina *f* endorphin
endotelio *m* endothelium
endovenoso intravenous
endurecimiento *m* de las arterias
hardening of the arteries
enema *f* enema
enfermedad *f* amarilla jaundice
enfermedad *f* de Alzheimer
Alzheimer's disease
enfermedad *f* de autoinmunidad
auto-immune disease
enfermedad *f* de Bowen Bowen's
disease
enfermedad *f* de Gilchrist
Gilchrist's disease
enfermedad *f* de Huntington
Huntington's disease
enfermedad *f* de la infancia/niñez
childhood illness
enfermedad *f* de Ménière
Ménière's disease
enfermedad *f* de Paget en la
vulva Paget's disease of the vulva
enfermedad *f* de Parkinson
Parkinson's disease
enfermedad *f* de Pick Pick's
disease
enfermedad *f* de transmisión
sexual sexually transmitted
disease (STD)

enfermedad *f* **del corazón** heart disease
enfermedad *f* **fibroquística** fibrocystic disease
enfermedad *f* **infecciosa** infectious disease
enfermedad *f* **inflamatoria pélvica** pelvic inflammatory disease (PIV)
enfermedad *f* **mixta de tejido conectivo** mixed connective tissue disease (MCTD)
enfermedad *f* **transmisible** communicable disease
enfermedad *f***/síndrome** *m* **de Creutzfeldt-Jakob** Creutzfeldt-Jakob disease
enfermedad *f* **vascular periférica** peripheral vascular disease
engarrotar stiffen, go numb
engordar gain weight
engrosamiento *m* thickening
enjugar wipe
enrojecimiento *m* reddening, redness
ensayo *m* **clínico** clinical trial
entablazón *m* severe constipation, obstruction
entablillar splint
enterocele *m* enterocele
entesar (coyuntura) lock
entrañas *f* bowels
entrecerrar (los ojos) squint
entrepiernas *f* crotch
entripado, estar to have indigestion from overeating
entumecido numb
entumecimiento numbness
entumido numb
envarado flatulent, bloated, stiff or numb (joints)
envenenamiento *m* poisoning
envenenamiento *m* **de sangre** blood poisoning
envoltura bandage
enyesado in a cast

enzima *f* **de conversión de angiotensina** angiotensin converting enzyme (ACE)
ependimoma *m* ependymoma
epífisis *f* epiphysis
epífisis *f* **crural/femoral** femoral epiphysis
epifisitis *f* epiphysitis
epigástrico epigastric
epilepsia *f* epilepsy
epilepsia *f* **psicomotora** psychomotor epilepsy
epiléptico epileptic
epileptiforme epileptiform
epinefrina *f* epinephrine
episiotomía *f* espisiotomy
equilibrio *m* balance
erección *f* erection
eritrocito *m* erythrocyte
eructar burp
erupción *f* rash, blotch
escafoides *m* scaphoid bone
escalofrío *m* chills
escama *f* flake
escápula *f* scapula, shoulder blade
esclerosis *f* **múltiple** multiple sclerosis
esclerosis *f* **tuberosa** tuberous sclerosis
escleroterapia *f* sclerotherapy
esclerótica *f* sclera
escocer smart
escoriación *f* abrasion
escroto *m* scrotum
esfigmomanómetro *m* blood pressure cuff, sphygmomanometer
esfuerzo *m* exertion, strenuous activity
esguince *m* sprain
esguince *m* **ligamentoso** sprained ligament
esófago esophagus
espalda *f* back, upper back
espaldera *f* back brace/support
espasmo *m* **infantil** infantile spasm
espécimen *m* specimen

espéculo *m* speculum
espéculo *m* **vaginal** vaginal speculum
espejuelos *m* eyeglasses
espina *f* **dorsal** backbone, spine
espinazo *m* backbone
espinilla *f* pimple, shin
espirar expire (breathe out)
espirómetro *m* spirometer
espiroqueta *f* spirochete
espolón *m* spur
espondilitis *f* spondylitis
espondilitis *f* **anquilosante** ankylosing spondylitis
espondilolistesis *f* spondylolisthesis
espuma *f* foam
espuma *f* **espermaticida** spermicidal foam
esputo *m* sputum
esqueleto *m* skeleton
esquince (hueso) *m* spur
estado *m* **de ánimo** state of mind, spirits, mood
estado *m* **jaquecoso** status migrainosus
estar con la mujer/el marido to have sexual relations
estenosis *f* stenosis
estenosis *f* **aórtica** aortic stenosis
estenosis *f* **cervical** cervical stenosis
estenosis *f* **mitral** mitral stenosis
estenosis *f* **tricúspide** tricuspid stenosis
estéril sterile
esteroide *m* steroid
esternón *m* sternum, breast bone
estetoscopio *m* stethoscope
estimulación *f* **eléctrica transcutánea de nervios** transcutaneous electrical nerve stimulation (TENS)
estimulación *f* **nerviosa transcutánea** transcutaneous electrical nerve stimulation (TENS)
estiramiento *m* slippage

estiramiento *m* **muscular** muscle strain
estirar straighten
estirar(se) stretch
estirarse un músculo pull a muscle
estoma *m* stoma
estómago *m* stomach
estómago *m* **sucio** indigestion
estómago *m* **revuelto** stomach upset
estornudar sneeze
estrangulación *f* choking
estremecimiento *m* thrill
estremecimiento *m* **arterial** arterial thrill
estreñido constipated
estreñimiento *m* constipation
estreptocinasa *f* streptokinase
estrés *m* stress
estría *f* stretch mark
estribo *m* stirrup
estrógeno *m* estrogen
estudio test
estudio *m* **con perfusión (miocárdica con talio)** perfusion imaging
estudio *m* **con radionúclidos** radionuclide imaging
estudio *m* **de gabinete** laboratory study/test
estudios *m* **de tubo digestivo superior** upper GI studies
etiología *f* etiology
etiqueta *f* label
evacuación *f* bowel movement (BM)
evacuar to have a bowel movement, void (bladder)
examen *m* examination
examen *m* **de detección** screen
examen *m* **de Papanicolaou** Pap test/smear
examen *m* **dental** dental checkup
examen *m* **pélvico** pelvic examination
examen *m* **ultrasónico Doppler** Doppler ultrasound test

excremento feces, stool
exocérvix *f* exocervix
expectorar cough up
expediente *m* chart, file
expediente *m* **médico** medical records
expirar expire (die)
exploración *f* scan, examination
exploración *f* **con radionúclidos** radionuclide imaging
exploración *f* **neurológica** neurological examination
expulsión *f* **del feto** delivery
extender straighten, stretch
extensión *f* extension
extirpar excise
extracción *f* **de várices** vein stripping
extraer to extract
extremidad *f* extremity, limb
   inferior lower extremity
   superior upper extremity
extremo *m* **distal** distal end
exudación *f* exudation, secretion
exudado *m* discharge
exudado *m* **por el pezón** nipple discharge
eyaculación *f* **precoz** premature ejaculation

F

factor *m* **reumatoide** rheumatoid factor
facultativo *m* **médico** medical practitioner
faja *f* back brace/support, kidney belt
falange *f* phalanx (*pl* phalanges)
fallecer expire, die, pass away
falsear buckle (knee, leg)
falseo *m* sprain
falta *f* **de aire** shortness of breath
faltarle la respiración to be short of breath
farmacéutico *m* druggist, pharmacist

farmacia *f* drugstore, pharmacy
fármaco *m* **inmunosupresor** immunosuppressive drug
farmacocinética *f* pharmacokinetics
farmacodependencia *f* drug dependency
fatiga *f* exhaustion, fatigue
fecundación *f* fertilization
fecha *f* **de claudicación/caducidad/ vencimiento** expiration date
fecha *f* **de nacimiento** birthdate
fecha *f* **estimada del parto** estimated date of confinement (EDC), due date
fémur *m* femur
fenestración *f* fenestration
fenitoína *f* phenytoin
fenobarbital *m* phenobarbital
férula *f* splint
férula *f* **de extensión posterior** posterior extension splint
férula *f* **para miembros** orthopedic brace
festinación *f* festination
feto *m* fetus
fibra *f* fiber
fibrilación *f* fibrillation
fibrilación *f* **atrial** atrial fibrillation
fibrilación *f* **ventricular** ventricular fibrillation
fibrina *f* fibrin
fibrosarcoma *m* fibrosarcoma
fibroscopio *m* **urinario** urethroscope
fibroso fibrous
fiebre *f* fever
fiebre *f* **amarilla** yellow fever
fiebre *f* **escarlatina** scarlet fever
fiebre *f* **reumática** rheumatic fever
fiebre *f* **tifoidea** typhoid fever
figura *f* build
fijar la vista (en) stare (at)
filtro *m* **solar** sunscreen
fisioterapia *f* physical therapy

fístula *f* fistula
fístula *f* **rectovaginal** rectovaginal fistula
fístula *f* **ureterovaginal** ureterovaginal fistula
fístula *f* **uretrovaginal** urethrovaginal fistula
fístula *f* **vesicovaginal** vesicovaginal fistula
fisura *f* hairline fracture
fláccido flabby, flaccid
flebitis *f* phlebitis
flema *f* mucus, phlegm, sputum
flexión *f* **lateral** lateral flexion
flexionarse flex
flojo flabby
flu *m* (*USA*) influenza, flu
fluidos *m* **corporales** bodily fluids
fluirle la nariz to have a runny nose
flujo *m* **sanguíneo renal** renal blood flow
flunitracepam *m* flunitrazepam
fluoroscopia *f* fluoroscopy
fluoroscópico fluoroscopic
foco *m* **epiléptico** epileptic focus
foco *m* **osteoarticular** osteoarticular focus
folículo *m* follicle
folículo *m* **piloso** hair follicle
fondo *m* **del útero** uterine fundus
fonoangiografía *f* **de la carótida** carotid phonoangiography
fontanela *f* fontanelle/fontanel
foramen *m* foramen
fórceps *m* forceps
fosfatasa *f* **ácida prostática** prostatic acid phosphatase (PAP)
fosfolípidos *m* phospholipids
fracción *f* **de expulsión** ejection fraction
fractura *f* fracture
fractura *f* **abierta** open/compound fracture
fractura *f* **angulada** angulated fracture

fractura *f* **avulsiva** avulsion fracture
fractura *f* **carpiana** carpal fracture
fractura *f* **cerrada** closed fracture
fractura *f* **conminuta** comminuted fracture
fractura *f* **de Colle** Colle's fracture
fractura *f* **de esfuerzo** stress fracture
fractura *f* **de Smith** Smith's fracture
fractura *f* **del cráneo** skull fracture
fractura *f* **en tallo/caña/rama verde** greenstick fracture
fractura *f* **espiral/en espiral/espiroidea** spiral fracture
fractura *f* **expuesta** open/compound fracture
fractura *f* **impactada, fractura con impacto** impacted fracture
fractura *f* **longitudinal** longitudinal fracture
fractura *f* **oblicua** oblique fracture
fractura *f* **por compresión** compression fracture
fractura *f* **patológica** pathologic fracture
fractura *f* **subtrocantérea** subtrochanteric fracture
fractura *f* **supracondílea** supracondylar fracture
fractura *f* **transversa** transverse fracture
fractura *f* **trocantérica** trochanteric fracture
fracturar fracture
frecuencia *f* **cardiaca** heart rate
frenos *m* braces (dental)
frente *f* brow, forehead
fresa *f* drill
frote *m* friction rub
frotis *m* smear
fruncir la vista squint
fuego *m* **(ampolla en los labios)** fever blister

fuego (úlcera en los labios) cold sore
fuente *f* bag of waters
función *f* **cardiaca** cardiac function
función *f* **pulmonar** lung function
función *f* **renal** renal function
furúnculo *m* boil
fusión *f* fusion

G

gafas *f* eyeglasses
gammagrama *m* **cerebral** nuclear brain scan
gammagrama *m* **de infarto agudo** acute infarct scintigraphy
ganglio *m* **linfático** lymph node
ganglios *m* **basales** basal ganglia
garganta *f* throat
garganta *f* **inflamada** sore throat
garrotillo *m* croup
gasa *f* gauze, tissue (paper)
gasto *m* **cardiaco** cardiac output
gastritis *f* gastritis
gaznate *m* windpipe
gemir moan
germen *m* germ
gingivas *f* gums
gingivitis *f* gingivitis
glande *m* **clitoridis** glans clitoridis
glándula *f* gland
glándulas *f* **mamarias** mammary glands
glándulas *f* **sudoríparas** sweat glands
glenoide *m* glenoid
glioblastoma *m* **multiforme** glioblastoma multiforme
glioma *m* glioma
globo *m* **del ojo** eyeball
glóbulo *m* **blanco, leucocito** *m* white blood cell
golpear bump
golpe *m* bump
goma *f* gumma
gonadotropina *f* gonadotropin

gonadotropina *f* **coriónica humana** human chorionic gonadotropin (HCG)
gonorrea *f* gonorrhea
gota *f* gout
goteo *m* **(intermenstrual)** spotting
gráfica *f* **de la temperatura corporal basal** basal body temperature graph
gran mal *m* grand mal
grano/granito *m* pimple
granulocitopenia *f* granulocytopenia
granulocitos *m* granulocytes
granuloma *m* **inguinal** granuloma inguinale
grapa *f* staple
grave severe
gripa *f* flu, influenza
gripe *f* flu, influenza
gritar scream
grupo *m* **sanguíneo** blood type
guardar cama stay in bed

H

hacer del cuerpo to have a bowel movement, to take a crap
hacer eructar burp (baby)
hacer esfuerzos (estreñimiento) strain (at stool)
hacer gárgaras gargle
hacer rondas to make rounds
hacer uso de la mujer to have sexual relations
haemophylus *m* **Ducrey** haemophilus ducreyi
hallazgo *m* finding
hamulus *m* hamulus
heces *f* feces
héctico/hético frail
hematíe *m* red blood cell
hematocolpos *m* hematocolpos
hematoma *m* hematoma
hematómetra *f* hematometra
hemiartroplastia *f* hemiarthroplasty

hemoblasto *m* blast cell
hemocitoblasto *m* blast cell
hemocultivo *m* blood culture
hemoglobina *f* hemoglobin
Hemophilus *m* **ducreyi**
  haemophilus ducreyi
hemorragia *f* bleeding, hemorrhage
hemorragia *f* **cerebral** cerebral
  hemorrhage
hemorragia *f* **después del coito**
  postcoital bleeding
hemorragia *f* **intermenstrual**
  intermenstrual bleeding
hemorragia *f* **interna** internal
  bleeding
hemorragia *f* **nasal** bloody nose,
  nosebleed
hemorragia *f* **subaracnoidea**
  subarachnoid hemorrhage
hemorragia *f* **uterina**
  disfuncional dysfunctional
  uterine bleeding (DUB)
hemorroides *f* hemorrhoids
hepatitis *f* hepatitis
herida *f* wound
herida *f* **cicatrizada** cicatrized
  lesion
herida *f* **de arma blanca** stab
  wound
herida *f* **de arma de fuego**
  gunshot wound
herida *f* **incisa** incised wound
herida *f* **punzante** puncture wound
herido injured
hermafroditismo *m*
  hermaphroditism
hernia *f* hernia
herniarse herniate
herpes *m* herpes
herpes *m* **genital** herpes genitalis
herpes zoster *m* shingles
herpes zoster *m* **óptico** optical
  shingles
hidradenoma *m* hidradenoma
hidratado hydrated
hidrocéfalo *m* hydrocephalus
hidrocortisona *f* hydrocortisone

hidronefrosis *f* hydronephrosis
hidrosalpinx *m* hydrosalpinx
hidroterapia *f* hydrotherapy
hidrouréter *m* hydroureter
hidroxicloroquina *f*
  hydroxchloroquine
hiedra *f* **venenosa** poison ivy
hiel *f* bile
hígado *m* liver
hilo *m* **dental** dental floss
himen *m* hymen
himen *m* **imperforado**
  imperforate hymen
himenotomía *f* hymenotomy
hinchado swollen
hinchar(se) swell (up)
hinchazón *f* abscess, bloating,
  bump, lump, swelling
hipercolesterolemia *f*
  hypercholesterolemia
hiperextensión *f* hyperextension
hiperflexión *f* hyperflexion
hipermenorrea *f* hypermenorrhea
hipermétrope farsighted
hiperplasia *f* hyperplasia
hiperplasia *f* **endometrial**
  endometrial hyperplasia
hiperplasia *f* **prostática benigna**
  benign prostatic hyperplasia
hipersensibilidad *f*
  hypersensitivity
hipertensión *f* hypertension
hipertensión *f* **esencial** essential
  hypertension
hipertensión *f* **secundaria**
  secondary hypertension
hipertrigliceridemia *f*
  hypertriglyceridemia
hipertrofia *f* **del ventrículo**
  izquierdo left ventricular
  hypertrophy
hipertrofia *f* **prostática benigna**
  benign prostatic hypertrophy (BPH)
hipertrofia *f* **uterina idiopática**
  idiopathic uterine hypertrophy
hipo *m* hiccup

hipocampo *m*, **hippocampus** *m*
hippocampus
hipotálamo *m* hypothalamus
hipotensión *f* **de esfuerzo**
exercise hypotension
hipotensión *f* **postural** postural
hypotension
hirsutismo *m* hirsutism
hisopo *m* swab
histerectomía *f* hysterectomy
histerectomía *f* **radical** radical
hysterectomy
histerografía *f* hysterography
histerosalpingografía *f*
hysterosalpingography
histocompatibilidad *f*
histocompatibility
histoplasmosis *f* histoplasmosis
historia clínica medical history
histriónico histrionic
hombro *m* shoulder
hombro *m* **congelado** frozen
shoulder
hombros *m* upper back
honda *f* sling
hongo *m* fungus
honorario *m* fee
horas *f* **de consulta** office hours
horas *f* **de visita** visiting hours
hormiguear tingle
hormigueo *m* pins and needles,
tingling
hormona *f* **liberadora de
hormona leuteinizante**
luteinizing hormone-releasing
hormone agonists (LHRH agonists)
hormonoterapia *f* hormone
therapy
hospital *m* hospital
hospital *m* **psiquiátrico** mental
hospital
hospitalizado hospitalized
hoyuelo *m* dimple
hueso *m* bone
hueso *m* **apendicular**
appendicular bone
hueso *m* **capitado** capitate bone

hueso *m* **cuboideo** cuboid bone
hueso *m* **cuneiforme** cuneiform
bone
hueso *m* **de la rodilla** kneecap
hueso *m* **del cuello** collarbone
hueso *m* **del pecho** breast bone,
sternum
hueso *m* **ganchoso/unciforme**
hamate bone
hueso *m* **semilunar** lunate bone
hueso *m* **subcondral** subchondral
bone
huesos *m* **marmóreos** marble
bones
huésped *m* host
hule *m* condom
húmero *m* humerus
humor *m* mood

I

ictericia *f* jaundice
ideas suicidas suicidal ideation
ijada *f* side stitch
ilion *m* ilium
imagen *f* **diagnóstica** scan
imágenes *f* **diagnósticas**
diagnostic imaging
imágenes *f* **diagnósticas por
radionúclidos** radionuclide
imaging
imágenes *f* **por/de resonancia
magnética** magnetic resonance
imaging (MRI)
impactado impacted
incapacidad *f* disability, handicap
incapacitado disabled
incisión *f* incision
inclinarse hacia adelante lean
forward
incompatibilidad *f* **por Rh** Rh
incompatibility
inconsciente unconscious
incontinencia *f* **de esfuerzo**
stress incontinence
incordio *m* hard lump, tumor
indigestión *f* indigestion

infarto *m* heart attack
infarto *m* **del miocardio**
  miocardial infarction
infarto *m* **óseo** bone infarction
infección *f* **metafisaria**
  metaphyseal infection
infección *f* **micótica** mycotic
  infection
infección *f* **vaginal por hongos**
  yeast infection
inflamación *f* **de los bofes**
  bronchitis, pleurisy
inflamación *f* redness, congestion
influenza *f* influenza
ingle *f* crotch, groin
ingresar admit (hospital)
ingresos *m* **(departamento del**
  hospital) admitting, admissions
ingurgitación *f* **mamaria** breast
  engorgement
inhalador *m* inhaler
inhibidores *m* **de la**
  monoaminooxidasa monoamine
  oxidase inhibitors (MAO)
inhibidores *m* **del sistema**
  nervioso simpático sympathetic
  nerve inhibitors
inhibidores *m* **extracerebrales de**
  la descarboxilasa extracerebral
  decarboxylase inhibitors
injerto *m* graft
injerto *m* **cutáneo** skin graft
injerto *m* **de derivación** bypass
injerto *m* **de derivación de la**
  arteria coronaria coronary artery
  bypass graft
injerto *m* **óseo** bone graft
inmobilización *f* immobilization,
  strapping
inmune immune
inmunización *f* immunization
inmunoglobulina *f*
  immunoglobulin
inmunoterapia *f* immunotherapy
inocuo harmless
inquietud *f* restlessness
insomnio *m* insomnia

inspirar breathe in
insuficiencia *f* **cardiaca**
  congestiva congestive heart failure
insuficiencia *f* **hepática grave**
  severe liver failure, severe hepatic
  insufficiency
insuficiencia *f* **(órgano)** failure
insuficiencia *f* **respiratoria**
  respiratory failure
insuflación *f* **uterotubario/**
  uterotubárico uterotubal
  insufflation
insulina *f* insulin
intento *m* **de suicidio** suicide
  attempt
interacción *f* interaction
interacción *f* **de fármacos** drug
  interaction
interfalángico interphalangeal
interferón *m* interferon
internación *f* admissions
internado hospitalized
internar admit (hospital)
intestino *m* **delgado/pequeño**
  small intestine
intestino *m* **grueso/mayor** large
  intestine
intestinos *m* bowels, intestines
intravenoso intravenous
involucro *m* involucrum
inyección *f* injection, shot
inyección *f* **de refuerzo** booster
  shot
inyección *f* **intraarticular**
  intra-articular injection
iris *m* iris
irradiación *f* irradiation
islotes *m* **de Langerhans** islets of
  Langerhans
isótopo *m* **radi(o)activo**
  radioactive isotope
isquemia *f* ischemia
isquemia *f* **miocárdica** myocardial
  ischemia
isquemia *f* **subclínica** silent
  ischemia
isquion *m* ischium

J

jadear pant
jalar pull
jalea *f* **espermaticida** spermicidal jelly
jalón *m* jarring movement
jaqueca *f* migraine headache
jaqueca *f* **de la arteria basilar** basilar artery migraine
jaqueca *f* **hemipléjica** hemiplegic migraine
jaqueca *f* **oftalmopléjica** ophthalmoplegic migraine
jeringa *f* syringe
jeringa *f* **de un solo uso** disposable syringe
jeringa *f* **hipodérmica** hypodermic syringe
joroba *f* gibbus
juanete *m* bunion

L

laberintectomía *f* labyrinthectomy
laberinto *m* labyrinth
laberinto *m* **vestibular** vestibular labyrinth
labio *m* lip
labio *m* **cucho** cleft palate, harelip
labio *m* **inferior** lower lip
labio *m* **leporino** cleft palate, harelip
labio *m* **superior** upper lip
labios *m* **agrietados** chapped lips
labios *m* **(de la vagina)** labia
    mayores labia majora
    menores labia minora
labios *m* **partidos** chapped lips
laceración *f* laceration
LAD (lipoproteína *f* **de alta densidad)** HDL (high-density lipoprotein)
lámina *f* lamina
lámina *f* **epifisaria** epiphyseal plate
laminectomía *f* laminectomy

laminografía *f* laminagraphy
laparoscopia *f* laparoscopy
laparotomía *f* laparotomy
laringe *f* larynx
larva *f* larva
lastimado injured
lastimadura *f* injury
lastimar(se) injure (oneself)
latido *m* beat (heart), throbbing
latido *m* **rápido del corazón** palpitation
lavada *f* douche
lavado *m* lavage
lavativa *f* enema
laxante *m* laxative
LBD (lipoproteína *f* **de baja densidad)** LDL (low-density lipoprotein)
legrado *m* curettage
legrado *m* **por fracciones** fractional curettage
legrado *m* **por succión** suction curettage
leiomioma *m* leiomyoma
leiomioma *m* **del útero** uterine leiomyoma
leiomiosarcoma *m* leiomyosarcoma
lengua *f* tongue
lentes *m* eyeglasses
lentes *m* **de contacto** contact lenses
lentes *m* **protectores** goggles
lepra *f* leprosy
lesión *f* injury
lesión *f* **de latigazo** whiplash
lesión *f* **de trabajo** industrial injury
lesión *f* **osteoarticular** osteoarticular lesion
lesión *f* **relacionada con el trabajo** work-related injury
lesionado injured
lesionar(se) injure (oneself)
leucemia *f* leukemia
leucemia *f* **granulocítica** granulocytic leukemia

leucemia *f* **granulocítica crónica** chronic granulocytic leukemia (CGL)

leucemia *f* **linfoblástica aguda** acute lymphoblast leukemia (ALL)

leucemia *f* **linfocítica** lymphocytic leukemia

leucemia *f* **linfocítica crónica** chronic lymphocytic leukemia (CLL)

leucemia *f* **mieloblástica aguda** acute myeloblast leukemia (AML)

leucemia *f* **mielocítica** myelocytic leukemia

leucemia *f* **mielógena** myelogenous leukemia

leucemia *f* **mielomonoblástica aguda** acute myelomonoblast leukemia (AMMOL)

leucemia *f* **monoblástica aguda** acute monoblast leukemia (AMOL)

leucocitos *m* leukocytes

leucorrea *f* leukorrhea

levantar lift, raise

levodopa *f* levodopa

libido *f* libido, sex drive

ligadura *f* **de trompas** tubal ligation

ligamento *m* ligament

ligamento *m* **peroneoastragalino** talofibular ligament

ligamentos *m* **uterorrectosacros** uterorectosacral ligaments

limpiar con hilo dental to floss

limpiarse wipe oneself

limpiarse la nariz con el dedo to pick one's nose

línea *f* **epifisaria** epiphyseal plate

linfa *f* lymph

linfangiograma *m* lymphangiogram

linfedema *m* lymphedema

linfocitos *m* lymphocytes

linfogranuloma *m* **venéreo/inguinal** lymphogranuloma venereum (LGV)

linfoma *m* lymphoma

lipoproteína *f* lipoprotein

lipoproteína *f* **de alta densidad (LAD)** high-density lipoprotein (HDL)

lipoproteína *f* **de baja densidad (LBD)** low-density lipoprotein (LDL)

lipoproteína *f* **de densidad elevada** high-density lipoprotein (HDL)

lipoproteína *f* **de media densidad** intermediate-density lipoprotein (IDL)

lipoproteína *f* **de muy baja densidad (LMBD)** very-low-density lipoprotein (VLDL)

líquido fluid

líquido *m* **amniótico** amniotic fluid

líquido *m* **cerebrospinal** cerebrospinal fluid

líquido *m* **sinovial** synovial fluid

lisiado crippled

litio *m* lithium

lobulillo *m* lobule

lóbulo *m* lobe

lóbulo de la oreja earlobe

lóbulo *m* **frontal** frontal lobe

lóbulo *m* **occipital** occipital lobe

lóbulo *m* **parietal** parietal lobe

lóbulo *m* **temporal** temporal lobe

loco insane

lomo *m* back (animal term)

loquios *m* lochia

lugar *m* **de nacimiento** birthplace

lumbar lumbar

lumbosacro lumbosacral

lumen *m* lumen

lumpectomía *f* lumpectomy

lunar *m* mole

lupus *m* **eritematoso discoide** discoid lupus erythematosus

lupus *m* **eritematoso sistémico** systemic lupus erythematosus

luxación *f* luxation

L-dopa *f* L-dopa

LL

llaga *f* sore
llevar a término carry to term

M

machucar crush
magulladura *f* bruise
mal *m* disease (e.g., mal de la vesícula—gallbladder disease)
mal parto *m* (spontaneous) abortion, miscarriage
malaria *f* malaria
maléolo *m* **interno** medial malleolus
maléolo *m* **lateral** lateral malleolus
malestar *m* complaint, discomfort, symptom
maligno malignant
malparto *m* miscarriage
mamadera *f* baby bottle
mamograma *m* mammogram
mancha *f* blotch
manchado *m* spotting
manco one-armed, one-handed
mandar (con un especialista) refer
mandíbula *f* mandible, jaw
manguera *f* tube (of an instrument)
manguito *m* **de esfigmomanómetro** sphygmomanometer cuff
manía *f* mania
maníaco-depresivo manic-depressive
manicomio *m* mental hospital
mano *f* hand; arm (*Mex, USA*)
marañas *f* **neurofibrilares** neurofibrillary tangles
marcapaso(s) *m* pacemaker
marcapaso(s) *m* **de demanda** standby pacemaker
mareado lightheaded
mareo *m* lightneadedness
mareos *m* dizziness, nausea

marsupialización *f* marsupialization
martillo *m* hammer
martillo *m* **de reflejos** percussor (reflex hammer)
masa *f* **anexial** adnexal mass
masa *f* **quística paravaginal** paravaginal cystic mass
masaje *m* massage
masaje *m,* **dar** massage
mastalgia *f* breast tenderness
mastectomía *f* mastectomy
masticar chew
masticable chewable
matasanos *m* quack
material *m* **de contraste** contrast medium
materia *f* pus
matriz *f* uterus, womb
meclicina *f* meclizine
meconio *m* meconium
mediastinoscopia *f* mediastinoscopy
mediastinotomía *f* mediastinotomy
medicamento *m* medication
medicamento *m* **que no requiere receta/sin receta/de venta libre** over-the-counter medication
medicastro *m* quack
medicina *f* **familiar** family practice
medición *f* **de las respuestas evocadas auditivas del tallo cerebral** brainstem auditory evoked response test
médico *m* physician
médico *m* **adscrito** attending physician
médico *m* **de cabecera** family doctor
médico *m* **general** general practitioner
médico *m* **que atiende/trata (al paciente)** treating physician
medicucho *m* quack
medida *f* dose
medio medial

medio *m* **de contraste** liquid contrast

medio sordo hard of hearing

mediquillo *m* quack

médula *f* medulla

médula espinal spinal cord

médula ósea bone marrow

meduloblastoma *m* medulloblastoma

mejilla *f* cheek

melancolía *f* melancholy

melanocitos *m* melanocytes

melanoma *m* melanoma

membrana *f* membrane

membrana *f* **mucosa** mucous membrane

membrana *f* **sinovial** synovial membrane

menarca *f* menarche

menarquía *f* menarche

meninges *f* meninges

meningioma *m* meningioma

meningitis *f* meningitis

menisco *m* **interno** medial meniscus

menopausia *f* menopause

menstruación *f* menstruation

menstruo *m* menses

mentón *m* chin

mesa *f* **de exploración/reconocimiento** examining table

mesa *f* **de operaciones** operating table

mesa *f* **quirúrgica** operating table

metabolizar metabolize

metacarpo *m* metacarpus

metafisitis *f* metaphysitis

metástasis *f* metastasis

metastatizar metastasize

metatarsiano metatarsal

metatarso *m* metatarsus

meterse el dedo en la nariz to pick one's nose

metildopa *f* methyldopa

metilfenidato *m* methylphenidate

metotrexato *m* methotrexate

mezquino *m*. wart

micción *f* micturition

micelio *m* mycelium

micosis *f* **vaginal** yeast infection

microbio *m* germ

mielografía *f* myelography

mielograma *m* myelogram

mieloma *m* **de célula plasmática** plasma cell myeloma

mielosis *f* myelosis

mielotomografía *f* myelotomography

miembro *m* limb, member (penis)

migraña *f* migraine headache

minusvalía *f* physical handicap

miocardio *m* myocardium

miocarditis *f* myocarditis

mioclonía *f* myoclonic seizure

mioma *m*, **fibromioma** *m* fibroid

miomectomía *f* myomectomy

miometrio *m* myometrium

miope nearsighted

miosis *f* **endolinfática del estroma** endolymphatic stromal myosis

mirar entrecerrado squint

mixoma *m* myxoma

mocos *m* mucus (nasal)

modorra *f* drowsiness

mola *f* mole (mass in the uterus)

mola *f* **hidatitiforme** hydatidiform mole

molestia *f* discomfort

mollera *f* fontanelle/fontanel

moniliasis *f* moniliasis

monitor *m* monitor

monitor *m* **cardiaco** cardiac monitor

monitor *m* **(cardiaco) fetal** fetal monitor

monitor *m* **(de) Holter** Holter monitor

monóxido *m* **de carbono** carbon monoxide

morado black and blue

mordedura *f* bite

mordedura *f* **de insecto** insect bite

mordida *f* bite
moretón *m* bruise, hematoma
mortal lethal
movimiento *m* **brusco** jarring movement
movimiento *m* **espasmódico** twitch
movimiento *m* **rotativo/giratorio** rotational movement
mucoso mucous
muela *f* molar, tooth
muela *f* **del juicio** wisdom tooth
muerte *f* **cardiaca repentina** sudden cardiac death (SCD)
muestra *f* specimen, sample
muleta crutch
multípara *f* multipara
multípara multiparous
muñeca *f* wrist
músculo muscle
muslo *m* thigh

N

nacido muerto stillborn
nacimiento *m* birth
nacimiento *m* **prematuro** preterm birth
nalgas *f* bottom, breech, buttocks
narices *f* nostrils
nariz *f* nose
nariz *f* **tapada/tupida** runny nose, stuffy nose
navicular navicular
nebulizador *m* nebulizer
necrosis *f* necrosis
nefrectomía *f* nephrectomy
nefrotomografía *f* nephrotomography
negligencia *f* **médica** malpractice
nervio *m* nerve
nervio *m* **atrapado/aplastado/oprimido** pinched nerve
nervio *m* **mediano** median nerve
nervio *m* **óptico** optic nerve
nerviosidad *f* nervousness

nerviosismo *m* nervousness
neumonectomía *f* pneumonectomy
neuralgia *f* **posherpética** postherpetic neuralgia
neuralgia *f* **trigémina** trigeminal neuralgia
neuritis *f* neuritis
neurocirujano *m* neurosurgeon
neurología *f* neurology
neurólogo *m* neurologist
neuroma *m* **acústico** acoustic neuroma
neurona *f* neuron
neuronitis *f* **vestibular** vestibular neuronitis
neuropatía *f* **periférica** peripheral neuropathy
neuroquímico neurochemical
neurotomía *f* **del nervio periférico** peripheral nerve neurotomy
neurotransmisor *m* neurotransmitter
neutrófilos *m* neutrophils
niña *f* **del ojo** pupil (of the eye)
nistagmo *m* nystagmus
nitroglicerina *f* nitroglycerin
nitrosourea *f* nitrosourea
nociceptor *m* nociceptor
nocivo harmful, noxious
nuca *f* nape (of neck)
núcleo *m* **pulposo** nucleus pulposis
nudillo *m* knuckle
nudo *m* **atrioventricular** atrioventricular node
nudo *m* **sinoauricular** sinoatrial node (SA node)
nuez *f* **de Adán** Adam's apple
nuligravida *f* nulligravid
nulípara nulliparous
náusea *f* nausea
náuseas *f* **del embarazo** morning sickness
nódulo *m* **reumatoide** rheumatoid nodule
núcleo *m* **pulposo** nucleus pulposus

O

obesidad *f* obesity
obrar to have a bowel movement
observación *f* **(en)** under
  observation
obstrucción *f* blockage
obstétrico obstetric
obturar (diente) fill
oclusión *f* **coronaria** coronary
  occlusion
oftalmoscopio *m* eye scope,
  ophthalmoscope
oído ear (inner); hearing
  externo external ear
  interno internal ear
  medio middle ear
ojo *m* eye
ojo *m* **morado** black eye
olécranon *m*,
 olécrano *m* olecranon
olvidadizo absent-minded
ombligo *m* belly button, navel
omóplato *m* scapula, shoulder blade
oreja *f* ear (external)
organismo *m* organism
orgasmo *m* climax, orgasm
orificio *m* **de entrada** entry wound
orificio *m* **de salida** exit wound
orina *f* urine
orina *f* **turbia** cloudy urine
orines *m* urine
orquiectomía *f* orchiectomy
ortesis *f* orthosis
ortodoncia *f* orthodontic work
ortopedia *f* orthopedics
orzuelo *m* sty (eye)
os *m* os
osteítis *f* **sifilítica** syphilitic osteitis
osteoartritis *f* **degenerativa**
  degenerative osteoarthritis
osteoartritis *f* **glenohumeral**
  glenohumeral osteoarthritis
osteoartrosis *f* osteoarthrosis
osteoclastoma *m* osteoclastoma
osteocondroma *m* osteochondroma
osteófitos *m* osteophytes

osteografía *f* osteography
osteólisis *f* osteolysis
osteoma *m* **osteoide** osteoid
  osteoma
osteomielitis *f* **hematógena aguda**
  acute hematogenous osteomyelitis
osteomielitis *f* **hematógena**
  hematogenous osteomyelitis
osteomielitis *f* **piógena** pyogenic
  osteomyelitis
osteomielitis *f* **primaria** primary
  osteomyelitis
osteomielitis *f* **provocada por**
  Brucella Brucella osteomyelitis
osteomielitis *f* **provocada por**
  Salmonella Salmonella
  osteomyelitis
osteomielitis *f* **secundaria**
  secondary osteomyelitis
osteomielitis *f* osteomyelitis
osteonecrosis *f* osteonecrosis
osteoperiostitis *f* osteoperiostitis
osteoporosis *f* osteoporosis
osteosarcoma *m* osteogenic
  sarcoma
osteosclerosis *f* osteosclerosis
osteotomía *f* osteotomy
otoconia *f* otoconia
otoneurólogo *m* otoneurologist
otoscopio *m* otoscope, ear scope
ovario *m* ovary
ovario *m* **poliquístico** polycystic
  ovary
ovisaco *m* ovisac
ovotestis *m* ovotestis
ovulación *f* ovulation
óvulo *m* suppository (vaginal)

P

paciente *m* **ambulatorio/externo**
  outpatient
padecimiento *m* symptom
padecimiento *m* **cardiovascular**
  cardiovascular disorder/problem
padrastro *m* hangnail
paladar *m* palate

palpación *f* palpation
palpitación *f* palpitation
palpitar throb
paludismo *m* malaria
páncreas *f* pancreas
pano *m* chloasma (blotches on the skin)
pantalla *f* screen, monitor (oscilloscope, computer)
pantorrilla *f* calf
panza *f* belly, paunch
paperas *f* mumps
parasítico parasitic
parálisis *f* palsy
parálisis *f* **cerebral** cerebral palsy
parar (el miembro) to have an erection
parche *m* compress
paresia *f* **facial** facial paresis
parótidas *f* mumps
parpadear blink
párpado *m* eyelid
parte *f* **baja de la espalda** low back
partera *f* midwife
partido (piel) cracked
parto *m* birth, childbirth, labor, delivery
parto *m* **prematuro** premature labor
pasado de peso overweight
pasar gas to pass gas
pasar visita to make rounds
pasar to wear off
pasatiempo *m* hobby
pasivo-dependiente passive-dependent
pasmo *m* rash and swelling, pain and rigidity of muscles
pasmo *m* **seco** lock-jaw
pasta *f* **dental/dentífrica** toothpaste
pastilla *f* pill
pata *f* foot (animal term)
patizambo *m* bow-legged
patogénico/patógeno pathogenic
patólogo *m* pathologist

pecho *m* chest, breast
pellizcar to pinch
pelo *m* hair
pelvis *f* pelvis
pene *m* penis
penicilamina *f* penicillamine
perder el conocimiento to lose consciousness
pérdida *f* **de peso** weight loss
pericarditis *f* pericarditis
periodo *m* **(menstrual)** menstrual period
periostio *m* periosteum
periostitis *f* periostitis
peritonitis *f* **pélvica** pelvic peritonitis
perlesía *f* palsy
peroné *m* fibula
pescuezo *m* neck (animal term)
peso *m* **de corredera** sliding-weight scale
pestaña *f* eyelash
peste *f* **bubónica** bubonic plague
petit mal *m* petit mal
pezón *m* nipple (of a breast)
picadura *f* bite (insect), cavity (dental)
picar to jab
picar to smart, to sting, to prick
picazón *f* itch
piedra *f* stone
piedras *f* **renales** kidney stones
piel *f* **amarilla** jaundice
piel *f* **de gallina** goose bumps/pimples
pielograma *m* **intravenoso** intravenous pyelogram (IVP)
pie *m* foot; leg (*Mex, USA*)
pierna *f* leg
pies *m* **cavos** cavus feet
píldora *f* pill
píldora *f* **anticonceptiva** birth control pill
pinchar to prick
pinchazo *m* prick
pinza(s) *f* clamp
pinzas *f* tweezers, forceps

piocha *f* chin
piojos *m* lice
pipeta *f* pipette
pipí, hacer to go peepee
piquete *m* bite (insect), prick
piquete *m* **de insecto** insect bite
pisar en falso to take a misstep
pisar mal to take a misstep
pituitario *m* pituitary
placa *f* plaque
placa *f* **ateromatosa** atheromatous plaque
placa *f* **de la dentadura postiza** partial plate
placa *f* **senil** senile plaque
placenta *f* placenta, afterbirth
placenta *f* **previa** placenta previa
planificación *f* **familiar** family planning, birth control
plano *m* **sagital** sagittal plane
planta *f* sole
plantilla *f* insole
plaqueta *f* platelet
plasma *f* plasma
plasmacito *m* plasmacyte
plataforma *f* **del peso** weighing platform
pletismografía *f* **ocular** ocular plethysmography (OPG)
pleuresía/pleuritis *f* pleurisy
poliartralgia *f* polyarthralgia
polimenorrea *f* polymenorrhea
pólipo *m* polyp
pólipos *m* **endometriales** endometrial polyps
pomada *f* ointment
pómulo *m* cheek bone
ponerse en cuclillas squat
pons *m* pons
ponzoña *f* poison (natural)
por vía bucal orally
portio *m* **vaginalis** portio vaginalis
poscoito postcoital
posfecha *f* postdatism
posmadurez *f* postmaturity
posmenopáusico postmenopausal
posología *f* dosage

post partum, posparto post partum
postilla *f* scab
postrado en cama bedridden
predisposición *f* **genética** genetic predisposition
preeclampsia *f* preeclampsia
premenopáusico premenopausal
prensión *f* grasp, grip
prepubescente prepubescent
présbite farsighted
presentación *f* **de nalgas** breech presentation
presentación *f* **franca de nalgas** frank breech presentation
presentación *f* **podálica** footling presentation
preservativo *m* condom
presión *f* **alta** high blood pressure, hypertension
presión *f* **arterial** blood pressure
presión *f* **diastólica** diastolic pressure
presión *f* **pulmonar en cuña** wedged pulmonary pressure
presión *f* **sanguínea** blood pressure
presión *f* **sistólica** systolic pressure
primeros auxilios *m* first aid
primípara *f* primipara
primípara primiparous
principio *m* onset
procedimiento *m* procedure
producir bring on, cause, produce
productos *m* **de limpieza** household cleansers
progesterona *f* progesterone
progestina *f* progestin
programa *m* **de tratamiento de narcomanía/farmacodependencia** drug treatment program
prolapso *m* **de la vagina** prolapsed vagina
prolapso *m* **del útero** prolapsed uterus
prominencia *f* bulge
prono prone
pronóstico *m* prognosis

propagar(se) spread
propranolol *m* propranolol
prostaglandina *f* prostaglandin
próstata prostate
prostatectomía *f* **retropúbica** retropubic prostatectomy
protector *m* **solar** sunscreen
proteínas *f* **de Bence-Jones** Bence-Jones proteins
prótesis *f* prosthesis
provocar bring on, cause, produce
proximal proximal
prueba *f* test
prueba *f* **de embarazo** pregnancy test
prueba *f* **de Papanicolaou** Pap test/smear
prueba *f* **de perfusión (del miocardio con talio)** perfusion imaging
prueba *f* **de receptor de estrógeno** estrogen receptor test
prueba *f* **de receptor de progesterona** progesteron receptor test
prueba *f* **de Schiller** Schiller test
prueba *f* **del ejercicio/esfuerzo** stress test
pruebas *f* **de sangre** blood work
prurito *m* pruritis
psicométrico psychometric
psicosomático pyschosomatic
psicoterapia pyschotherapy, psychological counseling, counseling
pubertad *f* puberty
pubis *m* pubis
puente *m* bridge of the nose, bridge (dental)
puesto *m* **de enfermeras/enfermería** nursing station
pujar bear down, push (childbirth), strain (at stool)
pulmón *m* lung
pulmonía *f* pneumonia
pulpejo *m* earlobe
pulpejo *m* fleshy part of the hand

pulsar throb
pulso *m* pulse
punción *f* **lumbar** spinal tap
punta *f* **de la nariz** tip of the nose
puntadas *f* sutures, stitches
punto *m* **de sutura** suture, stitch
punto *m* **desencadenante del dolor** trigger point of pain
puntura *f* puncture
punzada *f* pang, twinge
punzada *f* puncture
punzante jabbing
punzón *m* punch
pupila *f* pupil (of the eye)
pupilentes *m* contact lenses
purgación *f* gonorrhea
purgante *m* laxative
purga *f* laxative
pus *m* pus
puño *m* fist

Q

quebradura *f* fracture
queja *f* complaint
quejarse complain
quemadura *f* burn
quemar(se) burn
queratosis *f* **actínica** actinic keratosis
quijada *f* jaw
quilomicrón *m* chylomicron
quimioprofilaxia *f* chemoprevention
quimioterapia *f* chemotherapy
quimioterapia *f* **tópica** topical chemotherapy
quirófano *m* operating room (OR)
quirófano *m* **de pacientes externos** outpatient surgical suite
quiropráctico *m* chiropractor
quiste *m* cyst
quiste *m* **de Bartholin** Bartholin cyst
quiste *m* **del conducto de Gartner** Gartner duct cyst
quiste *m* **ovárico** ovarian cyst

quiste *m* **ovárico torcido** twisted ovarian cyst
quistes *m* **sebáceos** sebaceous cysts
quitarse (dolor) go away

R

rabia *f* rabies
rabioso rabid
radiación *f* **ultravioleta**
  ultraviolet radiation (UV)
radio *m* radius
radiografía *f* X-ray
radiólogo *m* radiologist
radioterapia *f* radiation therapy, radiotherapy
radioterapia *f* **intersticial**
  interstitial radiation therapy
rasguñar scratch
rasguño *m* scratch
raspado *m* curettage
raspado *m* **por fracciones**
  fractional curettage
raspador *m* scoop (curette)
raspadura *f* abrasion
rayos *m* **X** X-rays
reacción *f* **secundaria** side effect
reanimación *f* **cardiopulmonar**
  (RCP) cardiopulmonary
  resuscitation (CPR)
rebaba *f* **(hueso)** spur
rebelde recalcitrant
recaída *f* relapse
receta *f* prescription
recetar prescribe
recién nacido newborn
recomendación *f* **(de un**
  especialista) referral (to a
  specialist)
reconocimiento *m* **médico**
  physical (exam)
recto *m* rectum
rectocele *m* rectocele
rectoscopio *m* rectoscope
recuento *m* **sanguíneo** blood count
recuperarse recover
recuperación *f* recovery

rechinar grate (noise made by
  joint), grit (teeth)
rechinido *m* **(de coyuntura)**
  grating
reducción *f* **abierta** open reduction
reflejo *m* reflex
reflejo *m* **del chorro de leche**
  let-down reflex
régimen *m* diet
régimen *m* **de comida no picante**
  bland diet
régimen *m* **de mucho residuo**
  high-fiber diet
región *f* **cervical** cervical region
región *f* **escapular** scapular region
regla *f* menstrual period
regüeldo *m* belch
relaciones *f* **íntimas/sexuales**
  sexual relations
relaciones *f* **sin riesgo** safe sex
relajante *m* **muscular** muscle
  relaxant
remisión *f* remission
renal kidney (*adj*)
renguear/renquear limp
repentino sudden
reposo *m* rest, bed rest
resbalarse slip
resbalón *m* slip
resección *f* **del intestino** bowel
  resection
resección *f* **en cuña** wedge
  resection
resección *f* **segmentaria**
  segmental resection
resección *f* **transuretral**
  transurethral resection (TUR)
resfrío *m* cold
residuo *m* fiber
resollar pant
resolverse clear up
resonancia *f* **magnética nuclear**
  magnetic resonance imaging (MRI)
respiración *f* breathing
respiración *f* **artificial** artificial
  respiration
respirar breathe

respirar profundo to breathe deeply
restablecerse recover
restablecimiento *m* recovery
restañar stanch
restricción *f* **postural** postural restriction
resucitación *f* **artificial** artificial resuscitation
resucitación *f* **cardiopulmonar (RCP)** cardiopulmonary resuscitation (CPR)
resuello *m* breathing
retachar throb
retardo *m* **psicomotor** psychomotor retardation
retináculo *m* **rotuliano/patelar** patellar retinaculum
retorcijón *m*/**retortijón** *m* stomach cramp, abdominal cramp
retracción *f* **del pezón** nipple inversion
retroflexión *f* **del útero** uterine retroflexion
retropulsión *f* retropulsion
reumatología *f* rheumatology
revacunación *f* booster shot
reventada (piel) cracked
reventar(se) burst
revestimiento *m* lining
revisión *f* examination
revisión *f* **clínica radiográfica** clinical radiographic examination
revuelto (estómago) upset
rigidez *f* stiffness
rigidez *f* **matutina** morning stiffness
rígido stiff
riñón *m* kidney
rizotomía *f* **de la raíz dorsal** dorsal root rhizotomy
roble *m* **venenoso** poison oak
rodilla *f* knee
rodilla *f* **de fregona** housemaid's knee
ronchas *f* hives
ronco hoarse

ronquera *f* croup, hoarseness
rotador *m* **del hombro** rotator cuff
rótula *f* patella, kneecap
rotura *f* hernia
rozamiento *m* grinding
rubéola *f* German measles, rubella
rubor *m* redness
ruborizado (cara) flushed
ruborizarse to become flushed
ruido *m* bruit
ruido *m* **raspante** grating

S

sacar to extract
sacar sangre draw blood
saco *m* **amniótico** amniotic sac
saco *m* **capsular** capsular sac
sacro *m* sacrum
sacroiliaco *m* sacroiliac
sacudida *f* jarring movement
sacudir jar
sáculo *m* saccule
sala *f* ward
sala *f* **de cuneros** newborn nursery
sala *f* **de emergencia/de urgencias** emergency room (ER)
sala *f* **de espera** waiting room
sala *f* **de operaciones** operating room (OR)
salazosulfapiridina *f* sulfasalazine
sales *f* **aromáticas** smelling salts
sales *f* **de oro** gold salts
saliva *f* saliva
salpingitis *f* salpingitis
salpingitis *f* **tuberculosa** tuberculous salpingitis
salpingooforectomía *f* salpingo-oophorectomy
salpingooforitis *f* salpingo-oophoritis
salpingostomía *f* salpingostomy
salpingólisis *f* salpingolysis
salpullido *m* rash
sanar heal
sanarse recover
sangrado *m* bleeding

sangrado *m* **ligero** spotting
sangramiento *m* **por la nariz**
  nosebleed
sangrar por la nariz to have a
  bloody nose/nosebleed
sangrar bleed
sangre *f* blood
sangría *f* bleeding
santos óleos *m* extreme unction,
  last rites
sarampión *m* measles
sarampión *m* **alemán** German
  measles, rubella
sarcoma *m* **de Ewing** Ewing's
  sarcoma
sarcoma *m* **osteógeno** osteogenic
  sarcoma
sarpullido *m* rash
sarro *m* tartar, plaque (dental)
sauna *f* itch
Schwannoma *m* Schwannoma
sección *f* **cesárea** cesarean section
sección *f* **del nervio vestibular**
  vestibular nerve section
secreción *f* discharge, secretion
secreciones *f* **por la nariz** runny
  nose
secuestrectomía *f* sequestrectomy
secuestro *m* sequestrum
sedación *f* sedation
sedante *m* sedative
seguimiento *m* follow-up
seguro *m* insurance
seguro *m* **médico** health insurance
semen *m* semen
senilidad *f* senility
seno *m* breast
seno *m* sinus
sensación *f* **de ahogo** shortness of
  breath
sensible sensitive, tender
sentir náusea(s) gag
seña *f* symptom
serotonina *f* serotonin
servicios *m* **de consulta externa**
  outpatient services
servicios *m* **médicos** health care

sesamoide sesamoid
sesos *m* brains
seudoartrosis *f* pseudoarthrosis
seudodemencia *f* pseudodementia
seudogota *f* pseudogout
seudopólipo *m* pseudopolyp
sexo *m* sex
shock *m* shock (syndrome)
SIDA (síndrome *m* **de
  inmunodeficiencia adquirida)**
  AIDS (acquired immunodeficiency
  syndrome)
sien *f* temple
sífilis *f* syphilis
sífilis *f* **latente** latent syphilis
sífilis *f* **primaria** primary syphilis
sífilis *f* **secundaria** secondary
  syphilis
sigmoidoscopia *f* sigmoidoscopy
sigmoidoscopio *m* sigmoidoscope
signo *m* **(de enfermedad)** sign
signos *m* **vitales** vital signs
silbarle el pecho wheeze
silibancia *f* wheeze
silla *f* **de ruedas** wheelchair
sin receta over-the-counter (OTC)
síndrome *m* syndrome
síndrome *m* **de feminización
testicular** testicular feminization
  syndrome
síndrome *m* **de
inmunodeficiencia adquirida
(SIDA)** acquired immune
  deficiency syndrome (AIDS)
síndrome *m* **de superposición**
  overlap syndrome
síndrome *m* **del túnel carpiano**
  carpal tunnel syndrome
sínfisis *f* **del pubis** pubic
  symphysis
sínfisis *f* **púbica** symphysis pubica
sinovectomía *f* synovectomy
sinovia *f* synovia
sinovitis *f* synovitis
sinovitis *f* **transitoria** transient
  synovitis
síntoma *m* symptom

sinus *m* **urogenital** urogenital sinus
sistema *m* **inmunológico** immune system
sistema *m* **límbico** limbic system
sistema *m* **linfático** lymphatic system
sistema *m* **nervioso** nervous system
sistema *m* **nervioso autónomo** autonomic nervous system
sístole *f* systole
sistólico systolic
sobaco *m* armpit
sobaquera *f* crutch
sobar massage
sobresalto *m* shock (fright)
sofocarse choke
solitaria *f* tapeworm
solución *f* **glucosa** glucose solution
somático somatic
somnolencia *f* drowsiness
somnoliento drowsy
sonarse la nariz blow one's nose
sonda *f* catheter, tube
sonograma *m* sonogram
sonrojarse to become flushed
soñoliento drowsy
soplar blow
soplo *m* **asintomático de la carótida** asymptomatic carotid bruit
soplo *m* **cardiaco** heart murmur
soporte *m* orthopedic brace/support
sorbo *m* sip
sordera *f* deafness
sordo deaf
sordo (dolor) dull
sordomudo *m* deaf-mute
sostén *m* **ortopédico** orthopedic support
subinvolución *f* **del útero** subinvolution of the uterus
súbito sudden
subluxación *f* subluxation
subluxación *f* **unilateral** unilateral subluxation

substancia *f* **tóxica** toxic substance
substantia *f* **nigra** substantia nigra
sudar sweat, perspire
sudor *m* sweat, perspiration
sudoración *f* sweating
sudores *m* **nocturnos** night sweats
sufrir un tirón pull a muscle
sulfato *m* **de bario** barium sulfate
supino supine
supositorio *m* suppository
surcos *m* sulci
surtir (receta) fill
suspensorio *m* athletic supporter
sustentaculum *m* sustentaculum
sustitución *f* **protésica de la articulación** joint replacement
susto *m* shock (fright)
suturas *f* sutures, stitches

T

taba *f* ankle bone
tabique *m* **interauricular** interauricular septum
tabique *m* **interventricular** interventricular septum
tabique *m* **rectovaginal** rectovaginal septum
tabique *m* **vaginal transverso** transverse septum of the vagina
tabique *m* septum
tableta *f* tablet
tablilla *f* splint
TAC (exploración *f* **de tomografía axial computada/computarizada)** CAT scan (computerized axial tomography)
tacto *m* **rectal** rectal examination
tajo *m* gash
tálamo *m* thalamus
talla *f* height gauge (on a medical scale)
talón *m* heel
talus *m* talus
talle *m* build
tallo *m* **cerebral** brainstem

tamoxifén *m* tamoxifen
taquicardia *f* tachycardia
taquicardia *f* **ventricular**
ventricular tachycardia
tarantas *f* dizziness
tarso *m* tarsus
tartamudeo *m* stuttering
tartrato *m* **de ergotamina**
ergotamine tartrate
TC (exploración *f* **de tomografía**
computada/computarizada) CT
scan (computed tomography)
técnica *f* **de Moh** Moh's technique
técnica *f* **de Whipple** Whipple
procedure
tejido *m* tissue (flesh)
tejido *m* **blando** soft tissue
tejido *m* **canceroso** cancerous
tissue
tejido *m* **cicatrizal** scar tissue
tejido *m* **conectivo** connective
tissue
tejido *m* **fino** tissue (paper)
temblar shake
temblor *m* tremor, shaking
tendón *m* tendon
tendón *m* **de la corva** hamstring
tendón *m* **del hueso poplíteo**
hamstring
tenonitis *f* tendonitis
tensiómetro *m* sphygmomanometer
tensión *m* stress
tensión *m* **arterial (TA)** blood
pressure (BP)
tensión *m* **emocional** emotional
stress
tensión *m* **premenstrual**
premenstrual tension
tensiómetro *m* blood pressure cuff
TEP (tomografía *f* **por/de**
emisión de positrones) PET
(positron emission tomography)
terapia *f* **adyuvante** adjuvant
therapy
terapia *f* **biológica** biological
therapy

terapia *f* **electroconvulsiva** shock
therapy, shock treatment
terapia *f* **hormonal** hormone
therapy
terapia *f* **intensiva** intensive care
terapia *f* **quiropráctica**
chiropractic therapy
terapia *f* **sistémica** systemic
therapy
terapéutica *f* **substitutiva de**
estrógenos estrogen replacement
therapy
termocoagulación *f*
thermocoagulation
termografía *f* thermography
termómetro *m* thermometer
testículos *m* testicles
teta *f* baby bottle, nipple (of a bottle)
tétanos *m* tetanus
tetilla *f* nipple (of a bottle or of a
man)
tez *f* complexion
tibia *f* tibia, shin
tibia *f* **en sable** saber shin
tic *m* **doloroso** tic douloureux
tieso stiff
tijeras *f* scissors
timo *m* thymus
tímpano eardrum, tympanic
membrane
tinción *f* **de Papanicolaou** Pap
test/smear
tiña *f* ringworm
tipo *m* build
tirantez *f* tightness
tirar pull
tirarse gases to pass gas
tiricia *f* jaundice, debilitating
disease, separation sorrow
tiro *m* gunshot
tiroides *f* thyroid
tirón *m* muscle pull
tisis *f* tuberculosis
tobillo *m* ankle
tofo *m* tophus
tomar aire breathe in

tomar la temperatura to take
one's temperature
**tomar precauciones durante el
coito** to have safe sex
tomografía *f* **axial
computada/computarizada
(TAC)** CAT scan (computerized
axial tomography)
tomografía *f*
**computada/computarizada por
emisión de fotón único** single
photon emission computed
tomography (SPECT)
tomografía *f*
computada/computarizada
computed tomography (CT)
tomografía *f*
computarizada/computada
computed tomography (CT)
tomografía *f* **por/de emisión de
positrones (TEP)** positron
emission tomography (PET)
topar bump
topetazo *m* bump
torácico thoracic
tórax *m* thorax, chest
torcedura *f* sprain
torcer(se) twist, sprain
torcido crooked
torniquete *m* tourniquet
torrente *m* **sanguíneo** bloodstream
torsión *f* torsion
tortícolis *f* crick in the neck
torulosis *f* torulosis
torunda *f* cotton ball
tos *f* cough
    ferina whooping cough
    fuerte hacking cough
    persistente persistent cough
    rebelde persistent cough
    seca dry cough
toxemia *f* toxemia
toxina *f* toxin
trabajo *m* **de parto** labor
trabar (coyuntura) lock
tracción *f* traction
tracto *m* tract

tranquilizante *m* tranquilizer
transfusión *f* transfusion
transpiración *f* perspiration
transpirar perspire
transverso transverse
tráquea *f* trachea
traquelorrafia *f* trachelorrhaphy
trasero *m* breech, buttocks
trasplante *m* **del corazón,
trasplante cardiaco** heart
transplant
trastornado deranged, upset
trastorno *m* disorder
trastorno *m* **central del aparato
vestibular** central vestibular
disorder
trastorno *m* **de dolor
somatiforme** somatoform pain
disorder
trastorno *m* **de personalidad
dependiente** dependent
personality disorder
trastorno *m* **del tracto urinario**
urinary tract disorder
trastorno *m* **periférico del
aparato vestibular** peripheral
vestibular disorder
trastorno *m* **vascular periférico**
peripheral vascular disease
trastorno *m* **vasomotor**
vasomotor disorder
tratamiento *m* **antiedema
cerebral** treatment for cerebral
edema
tratamiento *m* **con cobalto** cobalt
treatment
traumatología *f* traumatology
Trichomonas *f* **vaginalis**
Trichomonas vaginalis
triglicérido *m* triglyceride
trihexifenidil *m* trihexyphenidyl
trimestre *m* trimester
tripa *f* **ida** locked intestine due to
fright
tripas *f* bowels, guts, intestines
triquetro *m* triquetrum
trismo *m* lock-jaw

tristeza *f* **posparto** postpartum blues

trocánter *m* trochanter

trocánter *m* **mayor** greater trochanter

trocánter *m* **menor** lesser trochanter

trofoblasto *m* trophoblast

trombo *m* thrombus

trombólisis *f* thrombolysis

trombosis *f* **cerebral** cerebral thrombosis

trombosis *f* **coronaria** coronary thrombosis

trombosis *f* **medular** marrow thrombosis

trompa *f* tube (anatomical)

trompa *f* **de Falopio** fallopian tube

tronar (coyuntura) crack

tronco *m* **braquiocefálico** brachiocephalic trunk

trueno *m* **(de coyuntura)** popping, clicking, crack

tuberculosis *f* tuberculosis

tuberculosis *f* **genital** genital tuberculosis

tuberculosis *f* **osteoarticular** osteoarticular tuberculosis

tuberosidad *f* **mayor** greater tuberosity

tuberosidad *f* **menor** lesser tuberosity

tubo *m* tube (anatomical)

tubérculo *m* tubercle

tuerto one-eyed

tullido crippled

tumor *m* tumor

tumor *m* **cerebral primario** primary brain tumor

tumor *m* **cerebral secundario** secondary brain tumor

tumor *m* **de célula gigante** giant cell tumor

tumor *m* **papilar** papillary tumor

tumor *m* **óseo** bone tumor

turnio cross-eyed

U

úlcera *f* ulcer

ulcerado ulcerated

ultrasonido *m* ultrasound

ultrasonido *m* **transrectal** transrectal ultrasound

ultrasonografía *f* **Doppler** Doppler ultrasound test

ungüento *m* ointment, salve

unidad *f* **de cuidados intensivos** intensive care unit (ICU)

unión *f* **toracolumbar** thoracolumbar junction

uña *f* fingernail, toenail

uña *f* **encarnada** ingrown nail

uña *f* **enterrada** ingrown nail

uñero hangnail

uréter *m* ureter

ureteroneocistostomía *f* ureteroneocystostomy

ureteroureterostomía *f* ureteroureterostomy

uretra *f* urethra

urocinasa *f* urokinase

urocultivo *m* urine culture

urograma *m* **excretorio** intravenous pyelogram (IVP)

útero *m* uterus

útero *m* **bicórneo** bicornuate uterus

urticaria *f* hives

utrículo *m* utricle

V

vaciar void (bladder), evacuate (bowels)

vacuna *f*/**vacunación** *f* vaccination, immunization

vacunar vaccinate

vagina *f* vagina

vagina *f* **hipoplástica** hypoplastic vagina

vaginectomía *f* vaginectomy

vaginitis *f* vaginitis

vaina *f* **de mielina** myelin sheath

vaina *f* **tendinosa** tendon sheath
válvula *f* **aórtica** aortic valve
válvula *f* **mitral** mitral valve
válvula *f* **pulmonar** pulmonary valve
válvula *f* **tricúspide** tricuspid valve
varicela *f* chicken pox
várices *f* varicose veins
vasectomía *f* vasectomy
vaso *m* **sanguíneo** blood vessel
vasodilatador *m* vasodilator
vasodilatador *m* **coronario** coronary vasodilator
vector *m* vector
vejiga *f* bladder; blister
vello *m* body hair
velocidad *f* **de sedimentación globular** erythrocyte sedimentation rate (sed rate)
vena *f* vein
vena *f* **cava** vena cava
vena *f* **safena** saphenous vein
vena *f* **varicosa** varicose vein
vena *f* **yugular** jugular vein
venas *f* **pulmonares** pulmonary veins
vencer (receta) expire
vendaje *m* bandage, dressing
venda *f* bandage, dressing
veneno *m* poison (man-made), venom
venéreo venereal
venta libre, de over-the-counter (OTC)
ventana *f* **de la nariz** nostril
ventanilla *f* nostril
ventilación *f* ventilation
ventral ventral
ventrículo *m* ventricle
ventrículo *m* **cerebral** cerebral ventricle
ventrículo *m* **izquierdo hipertrofiado** left ventricular hypertrophy
vénula *f* venule
verijas *f* pubic region

verruga *f* wart
verrugas *f* **genitales** genital warts
vértebra *f* vertebra
    cervical cervical vertebra
    dorsal dorsal vertebra
    lumbar lumbar vertebra
    sacra sacral vertebra
vértigo *m* vertigo, dizziness
vértigo *m* **de Ménière** Ménière's disease
vértigo *m* **de posición** positional vertigo
vestíbulo *m* vestibule
vesícula *f* **biliar** gallbladder
vía *f* tract
vía *f* **digestiva** digestive tract
vía *f* **respiratoria** airway
vientre *m* belly, womb
vigilancia *f* **(bajo)** under observation
vigilancia *f* **intensiva** intensive care
vigilar monitor
viral viral
vírico viral
viruela *f* smallpox
viruela *f* **de gallina** chicken pox
viruela *f* **loca** chicken pox
viruela *f* **negra** smallpox
virus *m* virus
virus *m* **de inmunodeficiencia humana (VIH)** human immunodeficiency virus (HIV)
viscoso clammy
visión *f* **doble** double vision
visita *f* **de vigilancia** follow-up visit
vista *f* vision
vista *f* **borrosa** blurred vision
vista *f* **doble** double vision
vista *f* **empañada** blurred vision
vista *f* **nublada** cloudy vision
vitaminoterapia *f* **en escopetazo** shotgun vitamin therapy
volar volar
voltear(se) turn (around)

volver en sí come to, regain
  consciousness
vomitar to throw up
vulva *f* vulva
vulvectomía *f* vulvectomy
vulvitis *f* vulvitis

Y

yema *f* **del dedo** fingertip
yeso *m* cast
yeso *m* **troncal** body cast
yodo *m* iodine
yunque *m* anvil

Z

zafado dislocated, slipped
zafar(se) dislocate, slip
zambo bow-legged
zaratanes lumps in the breast
zona *f* herpes, shingles
zoster *m* shingles, zoster
zumaque *m* **venenoso** poison
  sumac
zumbido *m* buzzing, ringing (ears)
zurdo left-handed